Pride &
Politics

The Tale of a Big Story in a Small Town

Pride & Politics

The Tale of a Big Story in a Small Town

ERIN QUINN

Cover design: Hudson House Publishing
Interior design: Hudson House Publishing

Cover and author photo: Susan Zimet

ISBN 1-58776-833-X

Library of Congress Catalog Card Number: 2005931793

Manufactured in the United States of America

0 1 2 3 4 5 6 7 8 9 10 NetPub 0 9 8 7 6 5

675 Dutchess Turnpike,
Poughkeepsie, NY 12603
www.hudsonhousepub.com
(800) 724-1100

PO Box 444
New Paltz, NY 12561
www.mixmultimedia.com

DEDICATION

This book is dedicated to New Paltz—

A place like no other,

And one I'm proud to call home.

Table of Contents

FOREWORD

As one half of the first same-sex couple to be married on the east coast last year, I was thrilled when Erin told me that she was writing a book about the weddings and the media madness surrounding them. February 27, 2004, stands as one of the most exhilarating days in my life, a true accomplishment. Never in my wildest imagination did I think that my seven-year commitment with Billiam van Roestenberg would become part of history that enflamed the national debate. Who would have thought that Jason West, our young housepainter and mayor, would marry us in a ceremony so filled with controversy that 100 million people all over the world would be watching?! Talk about wedding jitters! Over a year later, it's still hard to believe.

I have often thought that being in New Paltz during that winter was like walking down the red carpet at the Oscars: everywhere we turned, reporters with cameras and microphones were looking to capture our every move, our every word. It was fabulous, of course, but that kind of attention was also scary. One minute New Paltz was just like any other small town dotting the landscape—albeit a shade more bohemian because of the university—and then the next, it became for the country the tip of a very sharp spear plunged ruthlessly into the heart of the conservative agenda and religious Right ideology. Depending on where folks sat on the political fence, New Paltz was either held up as an example of American democracy at work, or reviled as a result of what happens when you let "those people" have any power at all. Either way, the same-sex marriages outlined a complex moral and political dilemma for all to see clearly.

Erin's book, *Pride and Politics: The Tale of a Big Story in a Small Town*, is the story of that dilemma and it is a story that needs to be told. It is real, often hilariously so, and also deadly serious. I believe *Pride and Politics* will become the "gold standard" in the years to come when we look back on this tumultuous time in the history of civil rights in the United States.

I first met Erin the night before the weddings took place, which is when the media began its relentless dance with New Paltz. It was a brief encounter, and because I was frightened by the enormity of it all, I was not really focused on who I was speaking to. Erin seemed very idealistic and sweet but, frankly, I was just trying not to say anything too stupid to our local journalist, whose paper, the *New Paltz Times*, is a staple in almost every home of our community.

On the wedding day itself, when the story broke nationwide, Erin and I spoke again. With reporters swarming like unruly locusts, jamming microphones and recorders in my face and talking over one another, Erin was unique because she simply waited patiently until there was a break in the action to speak with me. While many of the big-name reporters from CNN, FOX or any of the other networks seemed somewhat jaded, like junkies who hadn't yet gotten a big enough hit of their drug of choice—the human drama—Erin's demeanor quickly convinced me that she actually cared about the weddings and the people involved as though she were one of them, and that she would be thoughtful in her reporting.

It was obvious from the minute I met her that she was intelligent and capable. Tall and trim, her eyes twinkled as she spoke, as if there were leprechauns dancing behind her eyes, creating a field of warmth around her. I felt comfortable right away, which helped me to quickly go beyond just spitting out a sound bite. As we talked, her quick wit and sense of humor kept me laughing and reminded me of the irony of the situation—all we wanted to do was get married, just like everyone else. And I loved the fact that she was from New Paltz.

As Erin and I talked over the course of the next several weeks for various articles she was writing, I began to look forward to her calls. I was smitten just like everybody else who spends even a few moments with her. Erin brings out the best in people; we just feel good after being with her. Now, one year after the weddings, we have become good friends and I cherish every minute we spend together. There is no one better suited or qualified to tell the story of the weddings that rocked a nation.

Pride and Politics is an important book for several reasons. First, no one knows all the players better or longer than Erin. Her access to the colorful cast of characters gives the book a depth that many other authors would struggle to achieve over a long period of time with no guarantee of success.

Second, Erin represents the American Dream as it is classically defined. She lives in a small town, is a devoted mother and journalist, and is an active part of her community. Who better to comment on family and what it means? Her sensitivity and understanding of what occurred on that chilly February day is a source of inspiration and hope to all who have a vision of an America that is inclusive in every sense of the word. In short, if that vision is ever to become a reality, it will be folks like Erin who will be the deciding factor in making it happen. She is a sterling reminder that most people—when given both sides of the story—are fair-minded and live on the side of tolerance and kindness.

The battle over same-sex marriage continues to rage in the courts. Not a week goes by that pundits don't bring up the subject on their shows or in their columns. Sadly, the thousands of couples in New York who desperately wanted the legal protection afforded by marriage are consigned to a limbo outside the law, until the matter can be resolved in the courts.

Whatever happens, Erin of course will be there, notepad in hand, rushed as usual trying to keep her family fed and the laundry done, but completely attentive. The story will be told—she will see to it. And for that, we should all be grateful.

—Jeffrey McGowan, author of
Major Conflict: One Gay Man's Life in the Don't-Ask-Don't-Tell Military
(Broadway Books, 2005)

Cast of Characters

Jason West

The Mayor of the Village of New Paltz, New York. At twenty-seven years old, West becomes the first elected Green Party mayor in New York State. After only eight months in office, he marries same-sex couples on February 27, 2004, an act that would create a windfall of international media attention and result in twenty-four criminal counts against him.

Don Williams

Ulster County District Attorney who levels criminal charges against Mayor West, as well as two Unitarian ministers, for performing same-sex marriages. Although the case was thrown out of the New Paltz courts on constitutional grounds, Williams appealed this decision and won.

Bob Hebel

A veteran New Paltz Village Trustee who brings a civil suit against West asking that the courts place a restraining order barring West and others from marrying any more same-sex couples. To mount his court battle, Hebel utilizes the pro bono services of Liberty Counsel, a Christian Right law firm from Orlando, Florida.

Andrew Kossover

A local attorney, co-partner with his wife, Vicki Kossover, and Mayor West's New Paltz–based attorney.

Joshua Rosenkranz

A civil rights attorney from the New York City–based firm Heller, Erhman, White & McAuliffe, representing Mayor West on both the criminal and civil charges leveled against him.

Spencer McLaughlin

New Paltz Village attorney, hired by the Green Party Village Board majority after their surprise election sweep in May 2003.

Judge Jonathan Katz

New Paltz Town Justice who dismissed all twenty-four criminal counts against Mayor West on June 10, 2004, on constitutional grounds.

Judge Michael Kavanagh

New York State Supreme Court Judge and former Ulster County District Attorney. Judge Kavanagh ruled to place a permanent injunction on Mayor West barring him from marrying any same-sex couple.

Judge Vincent Bradley

An Ulster County Supreme Court Judge who upheld New Paltz Village Trustee Bob Hebel's request to place a temporary injunction on Mayor Jason West on March 5, 2004, following Mayor West's decision to marry twenty-five same-sex couples on February 27, 2004.

Billiam van Roestenberg and Jeffrey McGowan

The first couple to be married by Mayor West on February 27, 2004. Billiam van Roestenberg is a political activist turned Democratic candidate running for a seat on the Ulster County Legislature. Jeffrey McGowan, a retired Major in the Army 82nd Airborne Division is a decorated war hero whose memoir, *Major Conflict: One Gay Man's Life in the Don't-Ask-Don't-Tell Military*, was published in spring 2005.

Susan Zimet

Former two-term Supervisor of the town of New Paltz, now a Democratic Ulster County Legislator, who is also a professional photographer and co-founder of the Hudson Valley Media Arts Center.

Rachel Lagodka

Aka "Deep Love." Local Green Party recruiter, political activist, and college English teacher. Married to Ryszard Lagodka, a Polish native and active New Paltz Green Party member.

Kay Greenleaf and Dawn Sangrey

Two Unitarian ministers who agreed to marry same-sex couples in New Paltz after Mayor West was barred by the court. A permanent restraining order was placed on the two clergywomen barring them from continuing to marry same-sex couples. Both were charged with thirteen misdemeanor criminal counts for violating the Domestic Relations Law. This case was thrown out by the New Paltz town court.

Rebecca Rotzler

New Paltz Village Deputy Mayor and active Green Party member who, like her political comrade, Jason West, solemnized a gay marriage in June 2004. This caused Village Trustee Bob Hebel to file a civil suit against the entire village board barring all of them from performing same-sex marriages.

Julia Walsh

New Paltz Village Trustee who was elected, along with Jason West and Rebecca Rotzler, in May 2003 to one of three available village board seats. Walsh, like Rotzler and West, also went on to perform several marriages before she was enjoined by the courts from continuing to do so.

John Shields

The openly gay Mayor of Nyack, New York, and political ally of Mayor West on the issue of same-sex marriage rights.

Ray Zappone

The Chief of the New Paltz Police Department, who, in conjunction with the Ulster County District Attorney's office, delivered a criminal summons upon Mayor West charging him with twenty-four counts of violating the New York State Domestic Relations Law. These charges could result in Mayor West having to pay up to $500 for each offense or serve a maximum of twenty-four years in jail.

Deb Alexsa

The news editor for the *New Paltz Times*.

Brian Hollander

The news editor for the the *Woodstock Times*.

Marian Cappillino

The three-term Democratic Town Clerk of New Paltz who refused, based on her instruction from the New York State Department of Health, to grant marriage licenses to same-sex couples.

Jonathon Wright

An active New Paltz Green Party member, as well as friend and confidant to Mayor Jason West.

Jeremiah Horrigan

A veteran reporter for the *Times Herald-Record*, a daily newspaper based in Middletown, New York.

Jim Gordon

A New Paltz Green Party member, as well as a Peace Activist trainer and long-time journalist for Ulster Publishing.

Chapter 1
Wedding Jitters

I always resented breaking news, especially after I had kids. Reporters are, in a sense, like emergency service providers: even when they're home celebrating their child's birthday, fighting with their spouse, mowing the lawn, absorbed in a good book, shaving their legs, or having a nasty allergy attack—they can get called to work at the drop of a hat. The fire siren sounds, their beepers start vibrating, their cell phones ring, their e-mail flares up. There are just too many ways to contact someone these days.

Thankfully, I didn't have to walk into a blazing fire or administer CPR, but in February 2004, I did have to drop everything. This was to be one of those stories.

I had interviewed Jason the Sunday prior to the weddings. We probably talked about the sewer problems in the village, something we talked about often. With twenty inches of rain above the annual average, the century-old sewer system made of clay pipes had sprung another major leak. Raw sewage was flowing down village streets and entering into the Wallkill River, which eventually leads to the Hudson River, a national landmark. It was also flooding apartments.

Students of State University of New York at New Paltz and their landlords were pleading for help from the village board, particularly from their mayor, Jason West, a twenty-six-year-old SUNY alumnus, who had led a Green Party sweep at the polls nine months earlier, in May 2003, shocking the small village and becoming that party's first candidate ever to be elected mayor in New York State. Not only was Jason able to defeat veteran mayor Tom Nyquist, who had held the reigns of the village for sixteen years, but his two Green running mates, Rebecca Rotzler and Julia Walsh, were also elected to the five-member board that governed the village, ousting seasoned civic volunteers and causing quite a stir in the community.

"What else have you got for me," I asked Jason. "Any sex scandals?"

He laughed. "Well, I'm considering performing same-sex marriages. But I have to work out some details first."

"Same-sex marriages? That will definitely land you on the cover of *The New York Times*," I said naïvely, not realizing how fast and how far this story would take us all. "When will you be ready to go on the record with this story?"

"I'll let you know as soon as I can. Like I said, I have to work out some details first, like legal representation."

"Let me know when you're ready and I'll write it," I said.

"Don't worry, I will."

Four days later, on Thursday, February 26, the story broke in the *Times Herald-Record*, a regional daily newspaper based in Middletown, New York, and a competitor to my paper, the *New Paltz Times*. "New Paltz Mayor to Perform Same-Sex Marriages This Friday," read the headline. The day that article appeared was also my fifth wedding anniversary. My husband, Kazik, and I had been given a gift certificate to The Locust Tree Ristorante, an elegant Italian restaurant located in an old stone and wood-framed house overlooking a public golf course and the Shawangunk Mountain Ridge. The restaurant was just off Huguenot Street, America's oldest incorporated street, with its original, circa 1600s stone houses intact and preserved. Although the food was delicious and the service sublime, I was anxious to leave.

"Why hurry, Erin?" Kazik asked, after ordering a double-espresso. "When we leave here, we leave Europe and enter New Paltz again."

Kazik and I had met six years before in a jazz bar in the Latin Quarter of Paris. I did not speak a word of French, and he, not a bit of English. After we married abruptly and decided to move to New Paltz, my hometown, we quickly churned out three towheaded kids who all looked like him. With work, young kids, a Kafkaesque immigration process, and the financial constraints of a young family, we could only make the sojourn to Europe to visit his relatives once every two years at best. So finding these little pockets of European-flavored ambiance, where wine was savored, the baguettes were fresh, and the walls decorated with faux finishes, his métier back in Paris, was a balm to his old world soul.

While I empathized with his desire to linger a bit longer in the lush dining room, I felt a compulsion to return home. I was becoming increasingly more curious to talk with our boy mayor and find out why he hadn't given me the story-and to get the scoop on the impending weddings scheduled for noon the following day.

Earlier that day, my editor at the paper, Deb Alexsa, had been very irritated. "Jason already gave the story to the *Record*," she said. Deb did not embrace Jason as I did. She was skeptical of him as she was skeptical of all politicians—just waiting for them to make a mistake, go back on their word, or do something foolish. I was the eternal optimist, a real advocacy journalist, while she in essence was from the muck-raking school. Where I saw good intentions, she smelled foul play. Where I imagined people to be motivated by the best and most sincere intentions, she concluded that they were up to no good. I guess, in a way, we helped to balance each other.

"We went to The Bistro for lunch and saw Jason there eating all alone," she said. The Bistro, located on Main Street in downtown New Paltz, just a stone's throw from the *New Paltz Times* office, was Jason's second home or, more accurately, his second kitchen, as he could be seen eating lunch there on a daily basis. It was a favorite haunt for crunchy types and college students, offering tofu scrambles, veggie burgers, homemade granola, and bran muffins, while also catering to the average greasy-spoon lover, who wanted nothing more than a well-done cheeseburger with a side of coleslaw and french fries. "We went to say goodbye to him but he 'hushed' us because he was on a cell phone call," she continued. "I bet you he was talking to Jeremiah." Jeremiah Horrigan was a seasoned reporter for the the *Times Herald-Record.*

That's what you get for being a nice reporter, I thought to myself. "He told me about this days ago," I admitted to Deb. "But did I press him? No. Did I talk about it to anyone? No. I was patiently waiting for him to get all of his ducks in a row and trusted that he would tell me first, when the time came," I explained.

"Did he have to go public with it the day after we went to press?" she retorted, now vindicated that Jason wasn't as honest as I portrayed him to be. Deb had a desire to break every New Paltz–based story, despite the fact that we were a weekly newspaper and our competitors were all dailies who have far more staff and funding than our modest operation. But her drive to do so was valiant, I thought. I was inherently a much lazier journalist, wanting the news to come to me, believing that if I was fair to everyone and portrayed them in a certain home-spun light that they would naturally come to me first. And more often than not, they did.

"I don't know why he did that," I said honestly, switching my baby girl, Zofia, from arm to arm while I talked. "We've been good to him. Who else even gave the Green Party the time of day before the elections?"

"We did," she said. It was true. There had been four different slates running, two of them filled with well-known, civically minded individuals who were respected in the community. And then there was Jason's slate, "The Innovation Party" as they called themselves, since village elections are required to be non-partisan. Of course, Jason and his two running mates were Green, and everyone knew it. Most of the dailies had marginalized them to such a degree that they were either absent from any pre-election stories, or at best had a one-line description, like an afterthought. We interviewed and

4

profiled all the candidates, giving them equal space and opportunity to express their platforms to the reading public, regardless of who they were.

"Go yell at him," she said, dead serious.

"Easy, easy," I said. "Let me find out what happened."

After Kazik finished his espresso, which he admitted wasn't half bad, we paid the bill, drove to my mother's where we gathered the kids, then headed home for our nightly routine. I read to our boys, Seamus, four, and Tadeusz, two, put them to bed, then nursed our baby girl Zofia to sleep. At 10:30 p.m., I finally headed downstairs to reclaim my ad hoc journalistic life.

"Hi, Ryszard," I said, calling Kazik's Polish friend who lived directly across from the Village Hall and was in the mayor's inner circle. "What's going on?"

"It's quite a scene," he said, with that melodious Polish accent. "There are satellite trucks and television reporters all lined up in front of Village Hall. You should come down here. It's a media circus."

"Where's Jason?" I asked.

"He's inside Village Hall. He keeps coming out to give interviews and then goes back in."

I was tired. It was my anniversary. The kids were sleeping and I was in the middle of a good book. But I was angry as hell with Jason and I had to talk to him. "I have to walk down to Village Hall," I told Kazik.

"Why?" he asked.

"It's easier to do it this way than to have to play catch-up with all of the news tomorrow," I explained.

"Hurry back, I'll try to wait up," he said, giving me a quick kiss, as he worked on a portrait he was painting of Seamus. Because we had so little space in our house, he was forced to paint in the kitchen, leaning his canvases against the baby's high chair and spreading out his paint tubes on our kitchen table. I didn't want to leave. I loved reading on the couch in the silence while he painted, peeking in every once in a while to check on his progress. But after hearing Ryszard's description of the "media circus," I began to feel territorial. It was one thing to be scooped by Jeremiah, but the idea of being scooped on my own turf by the New York City papers finally pushed me out the door, notebook in hand and Kazik's leather jacket draped around me.

It was a crisp February night. The last time I had been called out of the house at odd hours was in the early summer of 2001. That was when a young New Paltz High School graduate, Jared Bozydaj, went on a downtown shooting spree that kept the entire village hostage from 2 a.m. to 9 a.m. It was only after he had emptied more than sixty rounds from his various semi-automatic weapons into the offices, restaurants, and apartments in the small village, nearly missing two New Paltz police officers and wounding a county sheriff, that Bobby Knoth, another New Paltz High School graduate and now the village's canine police officer, was able to convince him to surrender.

This time, the air had a different taste to it, not threatening but oddly hopeful. While the village slept peacefully, the old red-brick Village Hall building, just south of Main Street, which also housed the town justice courts and police headquarters, had been completely transformed. As I approached, I couldn't believe my eyes.

All the major New York networks were there. The light from the satellite trucks and cameras cast an unnatural glow into the late winter night. The Village Hall parking lot looked like the chosen landing site for a fleet of extraterrestrial visitors. It was almost 11 p.m. on a Thursday night and the television news reporters were lining up for their live reports, ready to announce that the very next day, February 27, 2004, a small-town mayor would begin marrying gay couples.

"You know, when I heard on NPR that a mayor in a small New York village was planning to marry gay couples, I said to myself, 'That can only be New Paltz,'" said my brother-in-law, a northern

Vermonter who had been brought into the funk-town fold by marriage himself.

New Paltz has a population of approximately 12,000 people, with another 6,000 added to the mix when SUNY New Paltz is in session. Like many old communities in the Hudson Valley, New Paltz comprises a village, the more urbanized part, within a township that includes the outlying rural area as well as the village. The village and town have their own separate governments. Jason was now in charge of the village, the small yet dynamic inner sanctum with a population of 6,000, many of whom were students.

New Paltz had collected both the artistic and dissipated residue of Woodstock overflow in the 1960s and 1970s. At that time, Main Street had as many head shops and bars as drop-in counseling centers and county drug rehabilitation programs. Beneath its arty exterior lie the lynchpins of its magnetism. Founded by Dutch and French religious refugees in the 1600s, European influence is etched into New Paltz's agriculture, education, and architecture, in the many stone foundations that still anchor its village streets.

Just an hour and a half drive from Manhattan, New Paltz has become a weekend home or a getaway for New York City's rich and famous, or not so famous but still rich. It is an amusement park for those who live to play. Rock climbers, canoers, bird watchers, hikers, mountain bikers, cross-country skiers and nature enthusiasts are quickly drawn to New Paltz's 6,000-acre Mohonk Preserve—home to lakes, waterfalls, and the Trapps, a rock face of the Shwangunk Mountains famous for its technical climbing routes.

Because New Paltz is also a college town, it is infused with student exuberance, intellectualism, art and funk. It has evolved to include an intriguing enclave of rank and file IBM and new media techies and SUNY New Paltz alumni, who after graduating get sucked into the rural vacuum. As New York City grows ever closer, modern transport, technology, and increased development continue to economically nourish our provincial dwellers. Yet our town is anchored by the born and bred, the ones who till the land season after season, year after year—the multigenerational Italian apple and corn farmers and Irish working-class families. Added all together, it's a place that is seductive, complex, and often explosive.

I walked into Village Hall, which always smelled of stale cigarette smoke from the volunteer fire department's downstairs meeting room—even though the former village board banned all smoking in the building more than three years ago. Instead of encountering Jean Gallucci, the fashionable yet shy village clerk, and her various assistants, I was greeted by members of the Radical Cheerleaders—a SUNY New Paltz group that conducted subversive feminist cheers at rallies, elections, in front of the public library, or just when the mood struck them. Decked out in black fishnet stockings, combat boots, short skirts and various body piercings, the cheerleaders were "manning" the village phones, along with friends of the mayor, politically minded residents, and Green Party members.

This was the place where you went to pay your water bill or to attend a village board meeting to ask the trustees if they might consider putting in a "Drive Carefully–Children at Play" sign to slow traffic on your street. It was where you complained about a parking ticket or asked the building inspector for a permit to construct a fence around your property. It was the center of village bureaucracy, the thing that tied us all to the same water and sewer grid, collected our taxes, organized spring clean-up, and sent out letters warning us that our toilets and bathtubs might have brown water for a given day when they flushed the lines in an attempt to wash rust out of the old pipes. Yet, in only a few hours, just enough time for the story in the *Times Herald-Record* to catch the attention of the New York City TV stations and papers, our Village Hall had been converted into a same-sex marriage planning headquarters, and the last buffer between the village's young controversial mayor and the swarming media. I leaned against a municipal bulletin board advertising a diabetes clinic and rabies shots for pets, to get my bearings.

"Where's Jason?" I asked.

"He's doing an interview with CNN," said Chris White. "I

8

just popped my head in here to see if Jason needed any help and I've been here ever since." He was moving around the room in a flurry, carrying a clipboard with a list of news agencies and reporters vying to get a quote from the mayor. Chris worked for U.S. Congressman Maurice Hinchey, a Democrat from Saugerties, New York, who was about as far left as any congressman in the House, without having turned Green himself. Chris had been on his way back from the gym when he heard of the impending weddings. A slight shade of embarrassment crept over him as he looked down at his sweatpants and sneakers, since he normally wore ties and slacks at the congressman's headquarters. "I haven't even taken a shower!" he said.

"I just want to ask him a few questions," I said to Chris.

"I'll let you speak with him when he's done with this interview."

While I waited for the mayor to emerge from the village clerk's office, I decided to get some fresh quotes from the impromptu staff that had assembled. I began with Wazina Zondon, the head of the Radical Cheerleaders, which I had just featured in the local paper a few months earlier. She said that in the last several hours the mayor's office had already received hundreds of calls. "They've almost all been positive," she said, tucking her shiny black hair behind her ears.

But they had also been receiving a few calls, mostly from locals I guessed, with questions like "Why doesn't the mayor worry about fixing all of our potholes instead of marrying gays?" I wanted to know more about what all of these people who were suddenly calling Village Hall were saying. "Oh," she said with a smile. "There was this one guy from Long Island who called and said that Jason West is the best thing to happen since Cher was nominated for an Oscar."

"I think I'm going to make that into a t-shirt," said the mayor, as he walked out of his makeshift office into the room. "I'm the best thing to happen since Cher was nominated for an Oscar."

All heads turned towards him and for a moment the room was silent. I had never seen Jason wear anything more formal than a chamois shirt, a pair of jeans, and his paint-splattered Carhart jacket.

9

Even stranger than seeing Village Hall being run by radical cheerleaders was seeing Jason dressed in an ill-fitting, navy blue suit with a Village of New Paltz pin on his jacket lapel. I almost started laughing. It was like he was playing dress up and had just stepped out of his father's closet, not realizing that there were other people in the room.

"I've never seen you in a suit," I said, looking him over. I noticed that his shoe laces were untied.

"Well, I was going to be on TV. I had to dress up. This was all I had," he explained. "Let's go talk in here," he said, gesturing towards the village clerk's small private office off to the side.

"Before I start interviewing you, can I just say that I'm so mad at you?"

"Why?"

"Because you gave the story to the *Times Herald-Record* the very next day after our paper came out. Now I'm a week behind and you decide to go national the day before I'm supposed to go to Vermont for the weekend."

"I didn't give it to Jeremiah," he pleaded. "After the President made his announcement the other day"—proposing an amendment to the U.S. Constitution to prohibit same-sex couples from legally marrying—"Jeremiah must have begun calling local town clerks to ask if they had any gay couples applying for marriage licenses. The New Paltz town clerk must have said yes and implied that I was planning to solemnize the marriages. Jeremiah called me and asked me flat out. I told him that I promised you the story, but he said he already knew I was going to do it and asked if I would just confirm it."

I was studying his face. He looked tired, a little jumpy, and eager for me to forgive him, not because my forgiveness was essential in any way to his mental health, but because, as the local reporter, I was the one person who covered the ins and outs of his more mundane mayoral activities, and he certainly didn't want to alienate me or have me think he was a snake.

"What can I do to make this up to you?" he asked, flashing me that boyish grin.

"Let's start talking."

And so we did. I slumped against the wood-paneled wall of the clerk's office and Jason leaned forward in the swivel chair, in an attempt to concentrate but also, I imagined, to try to calm his thoughts and prepare himself for the camera lenses that were poised outside, aimed in his direction.

"First of all, the New York State Domestics Relations law is gender-neutral.

Second of all, the New York State Constitution requires that all citizens be treated equally regardless of race, ethnicity or sex. I took an oath of office. That oath obligates me to uphold the law and the New York State Constitution. If I refused to marry these couples then I would be in violation of the law and the constitution. It is my legal obligation and my moral obligation."

I was always impressed with Jason's ability to answer questions. Obviously he'd thought this one out, researched it, and knew what he wanted to say and what he would be saying ad nauseam for at least the next ninety days to prosecutors, judges, the public, and the local, national, and international media. He looked polished and sounded articulate, even if the suit didn't fit him too well. (He had bulked up since he took office.) When I first began writing about Jason West, he was just a sinewy college student, a civil and environmental rights advocate, and one of the usual suspects at town and village board meetings, generally there to oppose something. Whether it was the Starbucks application for a new location in downtown New Paltz, or the pepper-ball spray gun the police had purchased without town board approval, Jason was there putting in his two cents. He was remarkably astute and informed for someone his age.

He grew up in the town of Latham, just outside of Albany, New York. He was from a long line of proud blue-collar workers. Apparently his political consciousness began at a very young age when he learned that styrofoam could never be broken down. He convinced his parents to shun McDonald's, and the little activist was born.

"The only college I ever wanted to go to was Hampshire College," he admitted to me one time. "I applied and was accepted and

11

just imagined that's where I was going. It wasn't until much later that I actually looked at what the annual tuition was. There was no way in hell I could afford it. So I came to SUNY New Paltz instead."

He rode his bike almost everywhere. Not only because it was a more environmentally friendly mode of transportation than a car, but his beat-up old Ford Taurus station wagon with rust spots the size of bullet holes pock-marking the blue frame could not be trusted to deliver the mayor safely to any destination farther than the Village Hall. The village building inspector, Alison Murray, a large-framed woman with a militant interpretation of the village codes, had informed me one day that I should "follow up on a *real* environmental violation."

"Our new Green Party mayor's car is unregistered and is leaking radiator fluid all over the Village Hall parking lot!" she said. "Why don't you reporters investigate that?"

Murray, whose delicate, almost pretty facial features were in direct contrast to her personality, was a controversial local character in her own right. The previous year she had been charged with verbal assault when she got into a sparring match with a plumber at Murphy's, the local Irish watering hole. "He called me the *c- word*," she stated in her own defense. "And there are only so many times I can have men call me the c- word before I say something back. I'm one of only a few women in this line of work and a lot of times, the men I deal with don't want me telling them what's up to code and what's not."

Mayor Nyquist had chastised her for the reported display of vulgarity, but had not fired her or reprimanded her in any formal manner. "Let's just say that Alison is not a real 'people person,'" said the mayor as diplomatically as he could. "But she is a very good and very passionate building inspector." Passionate she was, but she was also someone—especially if you were applying for a building permit—that you didn't want on your bad side.

While she admitted that she thought the former mayor's political tenure, after having served four terms, had come to its natural end, she was no great fan of her new boss. "How can he come to a board meeting dressed like that?" she whispered to me during one of the newly elected board's first public meetings. "It's shameful!" Jason wore a flannel shirt, drooping jeans and a baseball hat, which I noted, in his defense, he did take off while reciting the Pledge of Allegiance.

"This is New Paltz," I whispered to her, trying to get her to see Jason with a little more compassion, since we were all going to have to work together, in some form or another. "He's twenty-six and a housepainter. Did you think he would go out and buy a new wardrobe of double-breasted suits once he was elected? He makes only $8,000 a year."

"All you reporters just romanticize him," she said with a grunt. "He just gets by on his good looks and charm. But soon you'll find out who he *really* is."

"Did you meet Billiam van Roestenberg and his partner, Major Jeffrey McGowan of the 82nd Airborne Division in the First Gulf War?" asked Jason as his two good friends, also the first couple scheduled to be wed by him the next day, entered the cramped office where I was interviewing him. "I just love saying that," Jason said with a laugh. "Major Jeffrey McGowan of the 82nd Airborne Division, First Gulf War."

"I met Billiam but not Jeffrey," I said, looking at this handsome major and wondering how in the hell he made it so high up in the Don't-Ask-Don't-Tell army without anyone knowing or alerting the military authorities to the fact that this beautiful man, with his sparkling blue eyes, was not what the army wanted to believe he was. Jeffrey extended his hand and gave me a firm grasp, very military-like, but I noticed that for a man with such large hands, the skin was soft, as if he did everything, even shooting a gun, wearing gloves.

I had snatched Billiam aside after he finished talking with the television news cameras, before I went in to look for Jason. Billiam was very tall and spindly and almost had to bend in half while he spoke to me. If you could combine the straw man from *The Wizard of Oz* with Dorothy Parker and dress it up like a Versace model,

13

you'd approximate something close to Billiam. "I love your paper," he said, a bow tie affixed neatly to his neck; everything about him was immaculate, inviting, and kind. "Thank you," I said. "Is it okay if I ask you a few questions?" "Go ahead," said Billiam. "I'm just still a little blinded from all of those lights. Why don't we talk inside?"

The two men had been together for six years and lived in Clintondale, a small town just southeast of New Paltz, in an old white farmhouse with bright red shutters, where they raised farm animals and grew organic produce. Billiam sold real estate and Jeffrey, now retired from the army, worked for a pharmaceutical sales company in Westchester. Billiam was quick to point out that he and Jeffrey were not getting married to make a political statement.

"We're doing this because we love each other. We are both very active in our community. We contribute to society, we love this country, and my fiancé is a decorated war hero," he said proudly, but in a pleading sort of way that made me sad. Why couldn't they just get married without having to defend their reasons? "We're not asking for anything special," he said. "We just want to be made equal under the law and have the right to get married like everyone else in this country."

Unlike Jeffrey, who would come out of the closet the next day, for the first time, on national TV, Billiam had been navigating the world as a gay man since he was young. He told me of a revelatory moment he had at age eighteen while walking out of an army recruiting office, after signing up for the draft: He realized that although he was ready and willing to put his life on the line to defend his country, that same country, at least by law, could not accept him for who he was. Since Jeffrey, who served overseas, had to abandon his career as a military officer for fear of being revealed as a gay man, Billiam became even more incensed when President George W. Bush announced that he wanted to prohibit gay couples from being married. Jeffrey proposed to Billiam on Christmas Eve. They planned to have a ceremony in the spring, while their apple trees were in bloom. "You know," said Billiam dramatically. "Put a rent-a-tent in our yard, invite friends and family."

When the mayor of San Francisco, Gavin Newsom, began marrying gay couples, making headline news and raising the level of the gay marriage debate nationally, Billiam and Jeffrey asked Jason if he would consider marrying them once he was elected mayor. Jason, true to his belief in civil rights for all Americans, said that he would— but none of them knew just how soon that wedding would take place, or how far from their apple-blossom-backyard vision it would stray.

"I first met Jason four years ago when I attended a 'Meet the Candidates' night at the SUNY New Paltz campus," explained Billiam. This was when Jason, then twenty-two, was running for the second time, on the Green Party ticket for a seat in the State Assembly. He was running against local Republican county legislator Fawn Tantillo and Democratic incumbent Kevin Cahill.

"I remember coming home that night and telling Jeffrey about this amazing young man named Jason West. I was so impressed with him. He sounded like a polished politician who was in his forties, yet he was a young gentleman still in college. He was smart, wise and concise and I liked his politics." The three men became friends, and Billiam and Jeffrey, shortly after Jason became mayor, hired him to paint their house.

While Jason scraped paint and applied primer to the couple's old farmhouse, the issue of gay marriage, which had exploded onto the national scene during the previous months, as judges and local officials from all over the country aggressively attempted to redefine marriage, reached a fevered pitch. At least thirty-four states had already enacted "defense of marriage laws," with the New York State Legislature considering a similar bill. Amid the furor, the president announced that he would back a constitutional amendment banning gay marriages. This announcement created a groundswell of gay marriage activity, most notably in San Francisco, where 3,400 gay couples were married, including talk show diva Rosie O'Donnell, one week before Jason stood up to the plate and took center stage in the national debate. The events in San Francisco coincided auspiciously with Jason's painting job at Billiam and Jeffrey's. While Jason was up on the ladder, Billiam watched and listened to all of the gay-marriage news, and he succeeded in convincing the young, house painting mayor to jump on the gay-marriage bandwagon and carve out their own same-sex nuptial trail on the East Coast.

While Jeffrey asked Jason his opinions on various wedding reception details, Chris White rapped at the door. "Jason, they want to interview you live for the early morning news round."

"What time would I have to be here?"

"I think by 5 a.m."

"Do I have to?"

"It's up to you. You have the right to say no to them. You have a big day tomorrow. But at the same time, the morning news has the highest ratings. You'll get a large audience."

"Okay. What was I saying?" Jason asked me, rubbing his eyes.

"You were about to eviscerate the president," I noted.

"Oh, yeah.... I'm appalled that for the first time in U.S. history a president has tried to amend the Constitution to *restrict* freedoms for Americans rather than expand them," he said. "Any more questions, Erin?"

"How are you holding up?"

"I'm exhausted. I haven't slept in forty-eight hours."

"You look good."

"Thanks."

"You look, well, mayoral."

He laughed. I gave him a kiss on the cheek and told him to knock 'em dead.

"Hang in there, Jason. You're doing great."

"Thank you, I needed that."

With that I said goodbye to the volunteers who were still answering phones and providing callers with the Village of New Paltz e-mail address. Then I walked back to what would soon be referred to locally as ground zero: the village parking lot and Peace Park, a small wedge of Japanese-style landscaping with sculptures from the village's sister city, Osa Town in Japan.

I stood back and chatted with Ryszard, who was watching the scene with a bemused look on his face. His wife, Rachel Lagodka, who taught freshman composition at SUNY New Paltz, was the local Green Party recruiter, and was arguably the person who almost single-handedly got Jason and his running mates elected. I gave him

16

a hug goodbye, but as I walked away he shouted after me. "I told you this was going to be big," he said, with a knowing grin spreading across his face. "And this is just the beginning. You wait."

Their Green Party golden boy was on his way, peddling their left-of-center ideologies and carrying the banner for what Jason himself refers to as the "flowering of the greatest civil rights movement this country has seen in a generation." The mayor walked out of Village Hall, as if he were walking out of his house to pick up the morning paper. Only the papers had come to him.

"Those who would attempt to deny these people their civil and constitutional rights are the same people that would have told Rosa Parks to sit at the back of the bus. And that will not happen in New Paltz. I will not let it happen," I heard him say to the television reporters.

By the time I got home, the mayor's sound bites had already flashed across all of the nightly news programs. "I just saw Jason on TV," Kazik said laughing. "He was wearing a suit!"

Chapter 2
Pride and Politics

"Take time to deliberate; but when the time for action arrives, stop thinking and go in."—Andrew Jackson

W hile I expected there to be one hell of a wedding on February 27, and that I would be required to cover the nuptial events slated for the Village Hall parking lot, it was also the first day of Kazik's new job renovating an old colonial home in Rhinebeck, New York. Normally, weddings are planned months in advance and we could have avoided this conflict in our schedules. But fortunately or unfortunately, these weddings—all twenty-five of them—had less than twenty-four hours notice, and so everyone involved had to do the best they could with the little notice they had. That included me.

I'm not sure what sort of lives other reporters lead, whether they forgo having children to pursue their journalistic passions, or, if they do have children, employ nannies, day care, househusbands or housewives. But during the day I have complete charge of my three children, passing the torch to Kazik at night to attend board meetings, conduct interviews and write, more often than not late into the night, when the brood is fast asleep.

So on this historic day, instead of invoking thoughts of *Brown v. Board of Education* or *Loving v. Virginia* (the 1966 landmark civil rights case in which the U.S. Supreme Court ruled that laws denying interracial couples marriage licenses were unconstitutional), I was contemplating who in the heck I could solicit to take care of my children while I attended the multiple gay wedding ceremonies two blocks away.

My father, a local State Farm Insurance agent with a very child-friendly staff, agreed to do his best. "I have an appointment in Stone Ridge, but the girls said they're willing to watch the kids if I'm a little late."

Great. The weddings had been scheduled for noon. I was busy changing diapers, pulling off crusty sweaters and replacing them with clean ones when the phone rang. It was 11:15 a.m.

"Erin, where are you?" pleaded Deb on my answering machine. "The weddings are supposed to start any minute."

I picked up the phone. "I thought they were supposed to start at noon," I said.

"No, it's been changed," she said anxiously. "They start at 11:30!"

Later I would realize that Jason bumped up the schedule to throw the district attorney off guard. Having been warned by the Ulster County District Attorney, Don Williams, that if he were to go forward with solemnizing the gay marriages he would be "knowingly and consciously breaking the law," Jason decided to act and act fast.

"I didn't tell anyone I was planning on doing this because I wanted to make sure that I was able to marry at least one couple before I was hauled off to jail," Jason would explain to me weeks later.

"Where are you?" I asked Deb.

"We're here," she said. "At Village Hall." I knew this had to be big, if it actually enticed Deb out of the office. She was like Charlie, that authoritative yet mysterious voice on the other end of the phone on *Charlie's Angels*. She was heard, but rarely seen. And I was one of her Angels, minus the Farrah Fawcett body and the feathered hair.

She told me that a reporter from ABC had just tried to interview her, along with Mala Hoffman, a feature writer for our paper.

"Why were they interviewing you?" I asked, confused, as I felt around the inside of the dryer trying to find something decent to wear that wasn't wrinkled beyond recognition.

"They thought we were one of the couples about to be married," she said, sounding almost giddy.

"What's the crowd like?" I asked.

"Very big," she said. "You better hurry!"

Struggling to get everyone buckled into their car seats, I used my cell phone to call my father's office to let them know I was on my way.

I parked the car one block up and began sprinting down Center Street towards Village Hall. It was 11:35 a.m. Our local county legislator and former two-term town supervisor Susan Zimet called after me. "Wait for me," she said as she ran down the hill, various cameras swinging over her chest. Besides being a legislator, Susan also wrote a book on condoms and safe-sex practices during the first rash of the AIDS epidemic. Add to that her Hudson Valley Film consulting business, two children, wayward dogs, and budding photography career, and it was amazing that she could get anything done at all. But she did.

"I can stick close to you and just say, 'I'm with the press,'" she said, wrapping her arm around me. Susan, in her late forties, had wavy hair, and more energy than most people I knew combined. She was tall, attractive, and gregarious, and was dressed that morning in her usual sophisticated garb, tinged slightly with hippie-style accessories, like a shawl and large, beaded earrings. Unlike Susan, I favored black, tailored clothes, turtleneck sweaters, and men's style shoes with high, chunky heels. The two of us careened towards the impending ceremonies, careful not to go flying on a piece of ice or stray rock.

New Paltz Police Chief Ray Zappone was there, wearing a large, cowboy-shaped police hat. He nodded at both of us with a smile and said, "C'mon in ladies," as he moved aside one of many wooden horses positioned all around the Village Hall parking lot to block traffic and keep protestors cordoned off from the stage where the weddings would take place.

21

I was stunned by what I saw. While I had visited Peace Park and Village Hall less than twelve hours earlier, it was now an entirely different place. It looked like the scene of a big-budget film that had just rolled into town to shoot for the day. The south side of the parking lot was jammed with satellite trucks. There was a large police presence, with local, state, and campus security circling Village Hall and Peace Park. And the crowd just continued to swell with every minute that clicked by.

Susan quickly flipped the cap off her camera and began focusing in on the wide variety of pre-marital subjects. Some of them were more easily identified, elegantly dressed in suits, tuxedos, and colorful dresses. I couldn't stop staring at one female couple that Susan was photographing. They both had long, straight dark hair and wore sunglasses. They had on chic pantsuits with white blouses and mid-length silk trench coats. Their daughter, who looked about seven years old, was dressed in a white, frilly dress, and had her hair pinned up and encircled by a wreath of white roses and baby's breath. She carried a small satin pillow with her parents' wedding rings placed on top. I wondered which of the women had carried the child, because they all looked alike, with chiseled features, large brown eyes, and light olive skin. They were beautiful.

There were other couples clustered by the Village Hall door who were dressed informally, donning blue jeans and bomber jackets, sweater sets and corduroys. There was another striking lesbian couple smiling and holding hands, being interviewed by a reporter. One had bright red, curly hair that cascaded down her pink blouse. She looked so happy that I imagined she didn't even feel the cold, dressed as lightly as she was. Her partner also had on a pink sweater, with a knit scarf wrapped around her neck. They couldn't have been more than twenty-three or twenty-four years old, and here they were, starting out their life together, ready to exchange vows amidst throngs of strangers, news cameras and controversy. I wanted to hug them all and tell them how proud and happy I was for them. I felt choked up, the way weddings often make me feel, only this time, the emotion was tinged with something different, pride, perhaps, and a bit of fear for them.

I turned away from the couples to take in the rest of the scene. The crowd was varied and enthusiastic, many people holding hand-held camcorders or disposable cameras they must have just purchased on the way. Some, like Susan, carried more sophisticated equipment, knowing that they had a rare opportunity to photograph history in the making.

I began to notice that these marriages had a certain gravity to them. Whether you were a local politician, gay newlywed, police officer, village resident, college student, journalist, cameraman, or someone just out walking a dog, the gay marriages had a magnetic pull. How they were perceived, I imagine, depended upon the individual observer. For some, attending the weddings was an act of voyeurism, for others an act of support, and then there were those people just drawn to a spectacle, regardless of its content, sucked in by spotlight and side-show appeal.

Placards jutted out from above the heads all along the Peace Park hillside, which was still covered in places by snow. Some of them read, "I'm Straight But Not Narrow," "Equal Rights 4 All!" or my particular favorite, "Bush, Stay Out of My Bedroom. We Support Our Mayor!" I recognized many of the people: They were my friends, neighbors, colleagues, SUNY professors, local activists, library board members, Village Hall employees, business owners, clergy members, civic volunteers, parents and political leaders.

Besides the townsfolk, media and wedding parties, there were also numerous gay-rights activists, as well as a dozen or so anti-gay protestors, most of whom were kept behind a wooden horse, in a special section all their own, in an effort, Chief Zappone told me later, to lessen the chance of an altercation between the pro- and anti-gay factions.

I saw Michael Zierler standing next to the stage where the couples would say "I do" for the whole world to witness. He was dressed up in a suit and looking surprisingly official. Although he always looked neat and well-groomed, he was a Levi's and flannel shirt type of guy. Michael was one of my favorite people in the village. He was a very soft-spoken, diligent volunteer on the town's environmental commission and the recently established the Open

Space Commission. He was a biologist and consultant, married to Andrea Russo, a veterinarian, who, along with their ten-year-old year old son Sam, lived on Huguenot Street and had offered to step in as transition team coordinator for Jason, Rebecca, and Julia when they secured office in the spring of 2003. Normally you wouldn't think that a transition team coordinator was needed for newly elected officials that governed only 6,000 people. It was the type of position I imagined being crucial to a newly elected President of the United States and his hand-picked administration. But, because the three of them were so young, new to village government, and had all but been abandoned by the old guard they toppled in the elections, they needed someone to ease them into their new seats and help them negotiate some uncharted territory.

"Michael, what are you doing all dressed up?" I asked.

"It's a wedding," he said.

"It's not just *one* wedding," I added. "How many is he planning on performing?"

"Twenty-four is the last count I heard. I just asked him if he needed my help and he said yes, so here I am." He was put in charge of music and scheduling.

"Scheduling I can handle," he said to me with a smile. "But music?" Like me, and probably Jason and half a dozen other people involved in the real infrastructure of the unfolding story, Michael was just doing his best. We were all sort of making up our roles as we went along, trying to hit our right stride and find just that right note, without tripping and without singing too far off-key.

When Michael decided to run for village office only a month later, a seat he easily won, he admitted to me that he hadn't really given gay marriage all that much thought until he showed up at the weddings. After volunteering to help Jason that day, he, like many of us, said that it had an enormous impact on him. "I didn't expect to be so affected by the ceremonies, so moved by these couples," he said. "Many of them had been together for so long and they finally got the opportunity to become married, and I really began to understand that this was an important civil rights issue."

24

I was amazed by how quickly Jason and his ad hoc group of volunteers had organized these weddings. While most weddings take months to plan, this one took all of two days. A pianist and a cellist were playing wedding-appropriate classical melodies on a stage. Several rows of folding chairs were set up in front of the podium for the immediate family and friends of the couples scheduled to be married. The press was stationed on either side of the wedding guests. Massive amounts of cable lead from the microphones to the video cameras and television trucks, looking like a den of snakes poised to attack their unsuspecting prey.

There were at least a dozen more satellite trucks, cameramen, television reporters and journalists than there had been the night before. We were all on top of each other, most of the print journalists kneeling down, trying to allow the cameramen a direct line of vision towards the stage. When I looked up, past the crowd of journalists, all I could see were the large white satellites attached to the tops of the network trucks. It looked like dozens of giant, white Frisbees being thrown into the air. Yesterday had been the pre-game festivities, I thought. But this was the show.

The mayor walked out of Village Hall surrounded by Chris White, Jonathon Wright, his good friend and fellow Green, and a handful of police officers. Everyone in the crowd turned towards him. For a moment he looked lost, not sure if this was the right party, if he was really supposed to be the Master of Ceremonies or if he was just another guest. But when a rush of journalists began to swarm him, I saw him take an inward breath, move forward, and begin to make his way towards the stage. There was no turning back now, and if he had any second guesses, any moment of weakness, prior to this moment, there was no trace of doubt now. Our mayor was determined to see justice served, at least for this day, regardless of the consequences.

Within twenty-four hours, Jason had become a celebrity. The cameramen flocked around him as did the TV reporters, vying for the best shot and quotes this side of San Francisco. "Hi, Mayor West, I'm Tom Crampton from *The New York Times*," I heard one journalist say as he chased after Jason. It was odd to me that Jason had always been here, doing what Jason did, but that this one action, marrying people who already lived together, and many who had children together, could cause leading journalists and cable news reporters to plead for a quote from him. But when you put cameras in front of someone, I thought, and that person had some innate, as of yet unearthed, inner-glow, a star could be created within an instant. This was the right person, in the right place, at the right time, who decided to do the right thing.

"The mayor will be making a statement to the press and will then take some brief questions," Chris White told the media, as if he said this kind of thing everyday. "Please let him through. He has a lot of weddings to conduct today." White pushed forward, trying to carve a path between the reporters and the stage. The newlyweds looked on, anxious, hoping their minister would get to the ceremony on time.

Deputy Mayor Rotzler made a few comments before introducing Jason. She urged people, particularly the dozens of journalists and cameramen, to leave the folding chairs open for members of the wedding parties.

While innately confident, Jason, at 6'1", big-boned and boyishly awkward, had a tendency towards physical bloopers. This day was no exception. After a booming round of applause, he attempted to step up to the podium and tripped. His sagging socks were visible beneath his ill-fitting pants and worn vinyl shoes.

"That is precisely why we have deputy mayors," he joked to the assembled crowd. What separated Jason from the rest, I recalled thinking at that moment and many times later, was his wit and ability to laugh at himself.

While there was an overriding celebratory air to the weddings, I couldn't help but turn to look at the various law enforcement personnel to see if they were going to make a move to arrest Jason before any of the couples could say "I do." I had spoken with the DA that morning. He told me that he had given Jason two warnings, one through the New Paltz Police Chief and then again, through himself. These warnings, at least in the DA's prosecutorial mind, were clear. If Jason went ahead with the weddings, the DA would consider him to be in direct violation of the New York State Domestic Relations Law, provisions 13 and 17, which prohibit marriages from being sanctioned by a marriage officiate without a valid marriage license. Marriage licenses can be provided only by town and city clerks. The State's marriage licensing policy is administered by the State Department of Health, which has given town and city clerks specific instructions not to provide same-sex couples with marriage licenses, claiming that the law only allows for one woman and one man to be eligible for a marriage license application.

When I had called New Paltz Town Clerk Marian Cappillino that Friday morning, she had received dozens of requests for marriage licenses from same-sex partners, but she said she did not have the legal authority to grant them. "We're not allowed to do it," she said, sounding irritated, like she wanted to get off the phone. Although she was usually chatty with me, I could tell that she felt under a lot of strain. Town clerks, to my knowledge, did not usually have to deal with many press calls, particularly from CNN. They dealt with dog licenses, records, board minutes, tax bills and tax collection, none of which were easy tasks, but the granting of marriage licenses, or the denial of a marriage license, had never caused this kind of stir.

She said she could only give me a prepared statement which she had given all the other reporters who had been calling her. "Based on legal advice from the division of legal affairs of the New York State Health Department, no provision in the Domestic Relations Law allows for town or city clerks to issue marriage licenses to applicants of the same sex."

I paused, letting the silence draw her out a bit.

"Even if I were to grant them, they would not be legal and I wouldn't want to embarrass those people," she finally said. "I don't know why Jason is doing this when he knows it's not legal."

I liked Marian. She was an unmarried, multi-generational Italian native to the area, who, on her off-hours, could be seen taking her power-walks all around the village. She was shy in front of crowds yet very opinionated one-on-one. While I could understand her legal argument—that she was under direct orders from the New York

27

State Department of Health *not* to provide same-sex applicants with marriage licenses—I still wished she had taken a different stance, become an activist, and joined in solidarity with Jason. But this did not happen.

Jason was undaunted by the DA's warnings.

"The District Attorney will do as he sees fit," he said to the crowd, who cheered loudly after each statement he made. "I'm here to solemnize these marriages between loving, committed adults. It's my moral obligation to uphold the New York State Constitution which promises equal protection under the law for all New Yorkers."

"We love you Jason," cried people from the crowd.

"For those one or two reporters who paid attention when I ran for the State Legislature four years ago, I was pro-gay marriage at that time as well," said Jason. "Originally we were hoping to do this when the weather was a little nicer, but after the recent events in San Francisco and Massachusetts and New Mexico—and I've heard rumors about Austin, Texas—we were inspired to move up our timeline and join the chorus for equal rights for all Americans regardless of race or gender."

The crowd responded with booming applause, so much so that Jason had to wait until they calmed down before he could begin again. Shortly after his speech, he introduced his pro bono attorney to the crowd, Joshua Rosenkranz, a lawyer with the New York City–based law firm, Heller, Ehrman, White & McAuliffe.

Rosenkranz was a small, fit man, smartly dressed, with a warm, intelligent face. It was obvious that he came from Manhattan, more specifically the upper-echelons of Manhattan, by the way he carried himself. He was both graceful and aloof, like a bred-in-captivity gazelle that had just been returned to the open plains of Africa after a lifelong stint at the Bronx Zoo.

Although Jason dwarfed him in size, Rosenkranz had a certain presence, a power born less of physical strength than of knowledge. He calmed the throng, like a warm-up act, knowing that the crowd was growing impatient for the main act. What he had to say was important, not only because it laid out what would be the defense team's strategy in the months to come, but because it helped to buoy up Jason's actions to that of a noble civil rights fight, one that Rosenkranz, along with one of the nation's most powerful and recognized civil rights firms, were prepared to defend, pro bono, nonetheless.

"Mayor West is not in violation of the New York Constitution, but the New York State Department of Health is in violation of the Constitution for refusing to provide people of the same gender marriage licenses," said Rosenkranz. "It is my honor to represent the mayor of New Paltz. In a long career of litigating constitutional cases in court, this is one of the best days for the Constitution of the United States and the Constitution of New York State.... We have many lawyers in our firm and an army of people prepared to fight this battle. No great battle was ever fought without great turmoil and strife, and we are standing behind the mayor until these marriages are vindicated by everyone in this country."

The crowd went wild.

James Esseks, the Litigation Director for the Lesbian and Gay Rights Project of the American Civil Liberties Union (ACLU) also lent his support to Jason and the issue of same-sex marriage as it related to civil rights. "This is not a political act, not an act of civil disobedience; these people are getting married for the same reasons that anyone gets married—because they love each other, have committed to each other and want to share their lives together and have their relationship respected by the law," he said to the crowd. He also pointed out that without the legal rights of marriage, should a loved one die unexpectedly, partners may not be allowed into the hospital because they would not legally be considered "family." Esseks went on to say, in a convincing but less than dynamic voice, that without the same rights that heterosexuals are granted, gay couples are unable to receive the economic benefits of marriage, such as shared health insurance benefits and being legally entitled to each other's inheritance. "We should be celebrating love and commitment between two people, not desecrating it," he said.

Then, as promised, Billiam and Jeffrey became the first couple to be married by Jason.

"In the five years that I've known these men, they have demonstrated a relationship filled with such love and dedication that they should serve as role models to us all," said Jason. "It is my great honor and privilege to preside over their marriage."

"Every generation produces a great leader, someone unique and forward thinking who rises above the herd and grapples with issues in a novel way," Jeffrey had said to me in a previous interview. For Jeffrey, Jason was one of those promising leaders. He was someone who Jeffrey would describe with his military lingo as "one of these true leaders who are committed to working *with* and *for* one another, as opposed to other leaders who are trying to win a zero-sum game."

"Hold hands you two, let's be romantic," encouraged Jason. After Billiam and Jeffrey read the vows to each other that they had written, Jason said proudly, "With the powers vested in me by the State of New York, I now pronounce you legally wed!" The cheers from the crowd were deafening.

Jeffrey and Billiam kissed and hugged, then turned to Jason and embraced him. It was a powerful moment. The three of them looked so happy. They had accomplished what they set out to do. Billiam, always a ham, turned towards the cameras and threw his left arm up, with his fist clenched in victory. This was the scene that would be played and replayed on the networks for the next year, each time the issue of gay marriage was featured on the news.

"I raised my hand a few seconds after we were married and had the affidavit of marriage in our hands," recalled Billiam months later. "It was the moment when I realized that I had done something powerful, both politically and emotionally. I clenched my fist in victory, as if to say to people that ordinary people like me can do extraordinary things, if they just stand up for what they believe."

I was crouched down, just at the front of the stage, next to a reporter from the New York *Daily News*. She was young and sweet, and compared to some of the other, more famous journalists in the crowd, had a refreshingly modest air about her. In between vows, I gave her some information about the key players, the difference between the "town" of New Paltz and the "village" of New Paltz, pointed out who and where our police chief was. The wind began to pick up, stealing a bit of the unusual February warmth that we had been soaking in while watching the weddings. I saw one woman's hat blow off. It was a purple velvet hat with a yellow rose affixed to its brim. I made a move to catch it, only to have the FOX News cameraman yell at me to get down. They were certainly an aggressive bunch. I felt like pinching his leg or yanking his cable, but instead, I squatted down, my thighs aching from the unnatural position and my heart constricting, as the second couple made their way up the aisle, with friends and family proudly bringing up the rear.

Marianne Mandola and Joanna Still were a middle-aged couple who had been together for more than twenty-five years. Asked if she would love and cherish Joanne in sickness and in health, Marianne cried, "Yes! And I won't change that now!" There were young couples, old couples, local couples, and many couples who had heard the news the night before and traveled long distances just hoping to grab the chance to get married without having to fly to San Francisco.

After Jason's decision to marry gay couples was broadcast across the New York TV stations the night before, by Friday morning there were at least 300 couples who logged onto the village website to get on a waiting list to be married by the mayor. Within the next week or two, that number would grow to 1,200.

If you ignored the satellite dishes, the yellow police tape and dozens of television cameras, February 27 was actually a beautiful day for a wedding—or twenty-five weddings. For a few hours, maybe even a few days and weeks following the weddings, the village of New Paltz felt much like Provincetown, minus the salty sea air, the smell of fresh fish, and the drag shows.

I remember reading about Block Island off the coast of Rhode Island and how it is situated above a naturally high concentration of negative ions. There is a theory that negative ions charge the brain in a certain way to lend an air of calm and happiness. Now, I'm not sure if Provincetown is situated above a wealth of negative ions, but it certainly had a celebratory and accepting feel to it. In P-town, people could be whatever they wanted to be, dress however they chose to dress, act the way they wanted to act with the knowledge that they would still fit in, regardless of the overall theme of the puzzle or exactly how their particular figure and image was constructed.

While the crowds cheered, a small but noisy group of protestors heckled: "Marriage is between one man and one woman," screamed a lone man from the sidewalk above Peace Park. "This is an abomination against the Lord," cried one shrill woman. And then someone else, with a message targeted specifically for Jason, shouted, "Stop marrying gays and go back to house painting!"

One of these protestors standing behind the yellow police tape was Mike Sweeney from Kingston, who held a cardboard sign that said, "Pray For Them." Sweeney believed that Jason had intentionally planned to conduct the gay marriages on Friday when many of the SUNY students didn't have class in order to bring them out in force "and create an illusion that the majority of Americans are for gay marriage," he said, letting his placard drop while he concentrated on his interview with me.

He also believed that Jason scheduled the event in the early afternoon when God-fearing, anti-gay marriage people, like himself, were at work. "The news only broke last night and so many working people, the people I represent, can't just leave their jobs at the last minute. We don't have the luxury your mayor here has."

Although the protestors were a small posse, Sweeney believed that their representation was far greater than the pro-gay marriage supporters. "As far as the polls are concerned, I am among the sixty to seventy percent of Americans who oppose gay marriages. So they can have all the press they want, but the laws ain't going to change."

Pastor Michael Johnson of the Rockland County Evangelical Ministry was also on hand to protest the gay marriages. His reasons for showing up I found to be a bit more thoughtful, tied to his interpretation of religion and history and what he believed the Bible did and did not condone. "The recorded history of the institution of marriage between a man and a woman dates back 5,000 years," said the pastor, who was dressed in black pants and a black shirt with his white collar showing through a Woolrich winter jacket. The pastor went on to say that no major religious faiths "in the entire world" support gay marriage and that Jason was single-handedly trying to damage the sanctity of marriage.

"I'm sorry, but for the mayor to take this matter into his own hands, to try and rewrite human history for the sake of his own political expediency is not appropriate," he said, raising his right hand to adjust his collar.

Vocal Republican resident Butch Dener was on the scene as well. "As for the couples that are here today, God bless them and I wish them happiness," he said. "As for Mayor Jason West, I think he should get back to doing the work of the village—the job he was elected to do."

New Paltz Town Supervisor Don Wilen, who governed the other half of New Paltz, the "town outside the village," came to the ceremonies to show his support. He was a short man, in his early sixties and had a middle-aged paunch, with salt-and-pepper curly hair that poked out of his "New Paltz" baseball cap. I had heard that Wilen's son was a gay performance artist in New York City, and so I imagined this touched a personal chord as well as a political one. "I strongly support gay marriage," he said. "This society has changed since Stonewall—and it's quite obvious that gay people have their place and honorable role in society."

But he also said that he was afraid of potential lawsuits the town and village might be facing from the mayor's actions and that he was concerned about what would happen if Jason was hauled off to jail. The New Paltz police, State police, and Campus police patrolled the crowds, the threat of Jason's potential arrest creating an undeniable tension.

I spotted Chief Zappone standing inconspicuously a few feet from the anti-gay marriage protestors. He looked serious. While Jason continued to tell couples to hold hands and kiss their respective bride or groom, I wandered over to interview the chief and see if he would provide me with any indication of whether or not Jason would be arrested.

"The crowds have been good," he said. "The media has been respectful. There are people here protesting, which they have every right to do and others carrying banners of support...."

"Ray, are you going to arrest him?"

"At this point Mr. West is not under arrest," he said. "The final determination lies with me after consultation with the District Attorney. The DA's office and my department's interpretation is that Mayor West is acting in violation of the law. He interprets his actions differently." Like the town clerk, Ray suddenly had a very terse and serious air about him, giving me rehearsed answers, rather than just talking to me the way he normally did.

"Ray, I have to pick up my kids," I pleaded. "Can you just tell me, off the record, whether or not he will be arrested today?"

"Go get your kids," he said, finally breaking a smile.

"Are you sure?"

"Go get your kids and call me tomorrow."

Later, both the DA and Chief Zappone told me that they had agreed the morning of the weddings that they were not going to "fan the flames" and have Jason arrested while 600 gay rights supporters surrounded him. "That would have only caused an unnecessary spectacle," said the DA.

When I called the DA later he said that he would need to review the police report and request an opinion from Eliot Spitzer, the New York State Attorney General.

"Once I have all of that information and have a chance to look it over carefully, I will make a determination as to whether or not my office will be charging Mayor West with any criminal violations," he said, his voice, like Jason's, sounding hoarse from talking so much.

"When do you anticipate making that decision?" I asked.

"Erin, I can't say exactly. Monday I'm up in Albany on another case, so I would guess that I will be making a decision Tuesday or Wednesday."

"What issues will you consider in making that determination?" I asked, trying to keep him on the phone a little longer to get a sense of whether he really was going to arrest Jason.

"What I must resolve is whether or not Mayor West violated the law, whether or not he should be charged and if so, how aggressively he should be prosecuted," he said. "I tried to explain to him the gravity of his actions and advised him that under the law any individual, regardless of sex or gender, has to have a marriage license before he can legally marry them. Without a license, he is committing a criminal act.... The constitutional legality of same-sex marriages is not an issue to be decided by a local mayor, nor a local district attorney," he added. "It is a question for the State Attorney General, the State Legislature, or the State Courts, and I truly hope that Mayor West is not using this issue to further his own personal agenda."

While his office had told the DA that it would not give an "opinion" on whether or not to prosecute Jason, New York State Attorney General Eliot Spitzer did release a "legal analysis" on gay marriages four days after the wedding bells had already sounded in New Paltz. "The language of the New York State Domestic Relations Law—which includes references to 'bride and groom' and 'husband and wife'—does not authorize the issuance of licenses to same-sex couples in New York; therefore, the opinion recommends that local officials in New York should not issue marriage licenses to same-sex couples, and officiants should not solemnize same-sex wedding ceremonies."

Spitzer's opinion was a boon to the DA and a major blow to the West camp. After reviewing his opinion for the coming week's edition, I vowed to do more research the next time state elections rolled around to find out exactly what issues candidates stood for, and which ones, like Spitzer had just demonstrated, they would waffle on.

But the rattling of the various political chains was not within earshot on February 27. They were going on behind closed doors and far from Peace Park, where newlyweds were busy kissing and crying, thrusting their "affidavits of marriage" towards the crowd and the press, flashing their rings, hugging their children.

While the couples smooched, cried, and had bird seed thrown over their heads as they walked up the makeshift parking-lot aisle, the mayor and the Village of New Paltz were broadcast live, their moment in the February sun shining like a beacon, advocating for gay civil rights: an unexpected platform, but one that the village and town residents would take in stride. Most would embrace it, some would shun it, a few would take legal action against it.

It was an exhilarating day. Not only had the weather cooperated, but it felt like the entire community had "come out" to witness an act of history. Some would later call it heroism, others a publicity stunt and successful political maneuver for Jason, still others would focus on the overtime cost to the taxpayers for the police presence, while those who supported Jason and the issue would say that paying a few extra dollars on their tax bills was well worth the effort towards ending what they saw as the persistent discrimination of their fellow citizens' and neighbors' basic civil rights.

"I think this is one of the best things to have ever happened to New Paltz," said one SUNY New Paltz professor I ran into just as I was leaving the ceremonies to go gather my own flock and return to our nest. "Just one more reason why New Paltz is such a special place," he added—his sunglasses perched on top of his head and his leather satchel resting against his leg. New Paltz was now on the map for being the East Coast's gay Vegas and concierge to same-sex marriages. In less than one day, our identity had become completely reconfigured.

Late that night I called Jason on his cell phone.
"I spoke with the DA," I said.
"What did he say?"
"If you're going to be arrested it won't be today. He will not make any decisions until he has time to review the police reports

36

and hopefully receive an advisory opinion from Spitzer. I just wanted to let you know that you probably won't be pulled off the streets or out of bed by the police."

"That's a relief."

"How are you?"

"I'm exhausted," he said. "But this was really the best day of my life."

"Can I print that?"

"Sure."

"I'm leaving town for a few days," I said, both relieved at the thought of getting out of town and suddenly anxious that I might miss something. "I have to file the story ahead of time. So can I get some quotes?"

"You don't have enough?"

"I have plenty about the Constitution and Rosa Parks, but I need something specific to New Paltz. What do today's events say about the spirit and character of New Paltz?"

"What does it say?" he repeated to himself. I could hear him pumping gas in the background. "This is a great day for the Village of New Paltz. It reaffirms our commitment and dedication to human rights, fairness and equality under the law, and our belief and support of basic family values. How's that?"

"That's good," I said. "What about the deluge of media attention? What's your response to that, Mr. Straight Eye for the Queer Guy?"

"The deluge is irrelevant. I would do this regardless—whether or not anyone was covering it. It's the right thing to do."

"Okay, that's all. Get some sleep and don't go getting arrested until I come back."

"I'll try my best."

Chapter 3

Justice Calls

I was in constant contact with Deb the following Tuesday, four days after the mayor had conducted the first round of weddings. It was also the day we sent the *New Paltz Times* to the printer. We were awaiting word from Chief Zappone letting us know if and when Jason would be arrested.

"As of this time the mayor has not been charged with a crime," he said to me Tuesday morning, as he had Monday morning.

"Ray, you're killing me here," I pleaded. "Can you just tell me whether or not he will be arrested today or tomorrow so that we can have it in for this week's edition?"

"When is your absolute latest deadline?"

"No later than 4 p.m."

"Call me as close to 4 p.m. as you can. If something happens earlier than that I'll call you."

"When is your absolute deadline?" echoed the DA, also a good friend and regular golfing buddy of my father.

"No later than 3:00 p.m.—4:00 p.m. at the very latest."

"Erin, I will be in conference with Chief Zappone later today. Call me as close to deadline as you can."

"So he *will* be arrested?"

"I would *strongly* suggest that you call me before deadline."

"He's going to be arrested. I can't believe it," I said to Deb after hanging up with the DA. "Why would Donny Williams do that? He's going to be buried alive in paperwork from Jason's pro bono attorneys."

"Because he broke the law," she said soberly, sounding much like the DA. "Like it or not, he broke the law."

My cell phone rang at around 3:30 p.m. "Hey, Erin, it's Ray Zappone."

Unfortunately, I was in the doctor's office holding Zofia on my lap as she was being diagnosed with a double ear infection. The poor thing was screaming, more from fear of the doctor and her telescope than from the pain of swollen inner ears.

"Can I call you back, Ray?" I asked.

"I'm just calling to let you know that after consulting with the district attorney, I have presented Mayor West with a criminal summons for twenty-four counts of violating the New York State Domestic Relations Law by solemnizing marriages without a valid marriage license. He is to appear in court before Justice Jonathan Katz at 6 p.m. tomorrow to be arraigned."

"What kind of penalties is he facing?" I asked, scrawling notes on the back of a parenting magazine, the only piece of paper, albeit waxy, in my immediate reach. I stroked my daughter's hair with my other arm, trying to soothe her as best as I could while trying to catch the chief's exact words.

"Each count can carry a maximum of $500 in fines or up to one year in jail."

"Can you fax a copy of the summons to the office?" I pleaded.

"Anything for you, my dear," he said.

"Thanks, Ray, you're the best."

I walked around the tiny cubicle in the doctor's office, holding Zofia close to my chest. "You're going to be okay baby," I cooed. "The worst is over."

On the way back from the doctor's we swung by the office so I could pick up the fax. It read:

"People of the State of New York vs. Jason M. West; dob 03/26/1977"
Case no: 04030054
CRIMINAL SUMMONS
Original Charges: DOM 017 Marriage w/o license
Arraignment Date: 03/03/2004
Accusatory instruments filed with this court charge you with the charges shown above. Therefore you are ordered to appear in person before this court for arraignment. Failure to appear on the arraignment date shown will result in a warrant for your arrest.
Signed Jonathan D. Katz, Justice

While waiting outside Dedrick's Pharmacy in New Paltz for Zofia's prescription to be filled, I called both Deb and my *Woodstock Times* editor, Brian Hollander.

"You're doing great, Erin," said Brian. "Call me when you get the DA's response. I'm going to keep the story open until after the court arraignment."

While I would be able to get the news of the criminal charges against Jason in the *New Paltz Times*, I would not be able to include the arraignment in the story. Because our sister paper, *The Woodstock Times*, went to press a day later than we did, I would be able to cover the night's events at the courthouse for it.

I explained to Brian that I'd have to call the news in to him as I would have to go directly from the arraignment to the regularly scheduled village board meeting. While there was a good half an hour between the two, I also knew that I'd want to run home and check on Zofia and nurse her before I went back to Village Hall.

"That's fine. Call in the plea and the mayor's statements and I'll do my best to make it work. There's a lot of copy here, but it's all good."

By Wednesday at noon, the satellite trucks had descended again. The story, only four days old, was becoming bigger by the day. With the advent of the 24-hour news programs, today's news cycles seemed to spin faster and faster, but part of me still didn't believe that gay weddings in a small upstate New York village could cause this much controversy and national press coverage. Obviously, I was wrong. The Associated Press, CNN, all of the regional and metropolitan stations, and New York City newspapers were there.

I knew very little about the criminal process. But what I did understand was that the chief, with the support of the DA, had given Jason a "criminal summons," as opposed to snapping the handcuffs on him and placing him in the back of a squad car. Their reasoning for this was twofold: one, they did not want to "further fan the flames of the circus atmosphere in the village by arresting the mayor," as the DA explained to me, and two, they believed that he would show up at the arraignment without skipping town.

To get a better handle on what would happen the following evening at the arraignment, I called a friend, Chet Mirsky, a Columbia University criminal law professor who had offered his services on a pro bono basis over the past decade for local grassroots environmental watchdog groups. These organizations, made up of residents, environmentalists, biologists, and downtown business owners, were collectively responsible for kicking Wal-Mart out of town and chasing the Marriott Hotel off the Shawangunk Mountain Ridge, while at the same time convincing New York State to purchase the land with its two pristine lakes and turn it into a public park.

I asked Chet what he thought about Jason's legal chances. "There are a lot of ways this could go, but I have to say that I wish he would have called me first," he said with a worried sigh.

"This case, I hate to say, is pretty clear-cut. The DA has a solid argument. The Domestic Relations Law states clearly that a marriage license is required before a union can be legally solemnized. But don't print that. I don't want to say anything that could harm Jason. He's doing a great thing."

The next afternoon, I was pacing the room, waiting for Kazik to get home from work so that I could head down to the courthouse to cover Jason's arraignment. The local Green Party secretary, Steve Greenfield, had been busy organizing a rally to support Jason outside the building.

I called Rachel. I had begun to refer to her as "Deep Throat" which she, in typical Green Party activist style, took too seriously. "Erin, I am *not* Deep Throat. Deep Throat helped expose the corruption in the Nixon administration. I'm not exposing any corruption!"

"I'll call you 'Deep Love' then," I said. "You're exposing the *love* in the West administration."

I told her that I was nervous about getting into the courtroom during the arraignment and asked her whether or not the press would be allowed in.

"I don't know. But you can certainly go into the Village Hall. There's a sign on the door that says "No Press Beyond This Point," but just ignore that and tell whoever is at the door that you are allowed in."

"Are you sure?"

"Of course I'm sure. If you want, I'll walk over there right now and tell them that you're on your way."

"Thanks, Rachel."

"No problem."

"I agree," said Brian. "If they'll let you into Village Hall, then just stick as close to Jason as you can and follow him into the courtroom."

Kazik was late. Zofia didn't want to let me go. My just-laundered pink oxford-cloth shirt was wet and crusty on the shoulders from her cereal-streaked drool. "Just keep your jacket on," Kazik counseled me, when he finally arrived. "No one will notice the stains."

By the time I was able to leave the house and walk downtown, the adrenaline surging from the Village Hall parking lot was exhilarating. I could hear voices cheering, even from a block away. There were police cars on every corner. All movement seemed to be heading downtown and turning a sharp left onto Plattekill Avenue, pausing only to grab a cup of coffee at Jack's Deli before joining the pre-arraignment masses. There were hundreds of Jason supporters gathered outside the courthouse and Village Hall. There was a brass band playing Battle Hymn of the Republic. There was a vast array of flashy signs: "If we can go to war why can't we go to the altar?" and "All great leaders have been tried"—with pictures of Nelson Mandela, Martin Luther King Jr. and Mayor Jason West.

Ryszard was manning the door to Village Hall. "Come on in," he said and gallantly opened the door. I felt like an underage drinker who had the good fortune of knowing the bouncer at the most exclusive nightclub in town. It was oddly quiet inside Village Hall. Inside the smaller conference room was Jason's lawyer, Rosenkranz. He was conferring with James Esseks of the ACLU. They were making cell phone calls and whispering to each other while flipping through papers in their briefcases all at the same time, like a pair of octopuses able to handle at least eight different tasks simultaneously.

I sat in a folding chair and wrote notes to myself, trying to look purposeful. Jason was in his office, the door shut. The stale air upstairs in the Village Hall was suddenly charged with an invisible sense of anticipation. The cheers from the assembled crowd grew louder. "We support Mayor West! We support Mayor West!" I could almost smell the sweat of the late-winter masses, cocooned inside their down jackets, chanting, their warm and jubilant breath forming small puffs of frozen air.

Both of Jason's newly ordained "assistants" were slinking in and out of doorways, up and down the stairs, whispering quietly into their vogue-style headphones. "Okay," announced Jonathon Wright, who was volunteering his services to Jason. "Jason said that only local reporters are allowed into the board meeting. That means Erin, *The Poughkeepsie Journal*, *The Kingston Daily Freeman*, *The Record* and Tom from *The New York Times*—no one else."

"What about getting into the courthouse?" I asked Jonathon.

"Good question. I don't know. Call Chief Zappone. From what I've been hearing the press isn't being allowed in."

I had never manhandled a cell phone to the degree I had these past few days, but it is a seductive little piece of machinery that can really inspire a sort of pseudo self-importance. Although I did have many occasions to use it for work or to call home and check in with my family, there were times, usually when I was out of the house and encountered someone who I didn't want to talk to, that I'd flip it open and pretend to be engaged in a very important conversation. That way I could wave to the person I was wanting to avoid, point to my cell phone and whisper, "Sorry, I have to take this call." I liked the slight weight of it in my coat pocket, letting me know that I was connected, that I was reachable, as if my life was filled with urgent tasks. Of course, most calls were from Kazik, reminding me to get dog food or diapers.

I called the police station, located ironically right around the corner from Village Hall, attached at the hip so to speak, but I was hesitant to leave, afraid that if I did I would get swept up in the crowd that continued to swell as 6 p.m. drew near, and would not be allowed back inside.

"The chief is in a conference," said the dispatcher, with a hint of annoyance, as if all callers should have known that he would not be available at this moment.

"He's busy," I said to Jonathon.

"Jason?" he said, as he craned his head into the mayor's office. "Is it okay if Erin goes in with us?"

Out of his office stepped a smaller, thinner and older version of Jason. It was his father, Ron, accompanied by his younger sister, Amanda. I remembered meeting his mother on election night, after Jason's surprise victory. She and Jason and the rest of the Greens and West supporters all went out to celebrate at Cabaloosa's, a local bar and the unofficial party site for the Greens. I briefly wondered why she wasn't there. Or was she there? Had there been a divorce in the family? This was all completely irrelevant to my story, but I was curious.

While Jason and his lawyers were sequestered in his office for a last-minute conference, Jason's sister, father, and I stood in the upstairs foyer of the Village Hall, looking out of two large windows that overlooked the crowds and cameras. We introduced ourselves.

"You two look a lot alike," I said to his father, thinking it was a corny thing to say, but true. The whole family was good looking-very all—American, small features, long eyelashes and wide smiles.

"You said you write for the *New Paltz Times*?" his father asked me.

"Yes."

"Jason's been promising me a subscription to your paper for months now and I still haven't gotten it. Every time I ask him what he has been up to he says, 'Dad, I'm just going to send you the paper so you can read about it.'"

We laughed.

"He's going to be in the papers a lot more now," I said, glancing out the windows at the swelling crowd. "Do you mind if I ask you two a few questions?"

"That's fine," he said.

"What is your reaction to Jason's decision to marry gay couples?"

"I couldn't be more proud," he said. "Really, I'm just bursting with pride. It's hard to put into words. Seeing him on TV like that, doing what he's doing for these people. I'm so proud. But if you know Jason, then this really doesn't surprise you. This is just who he is."

His father did look puffed-up with pride, the way he kept his hands in his pockets and his posture very straight. Someone told me later that his father and his sister have painstakingly clipped and saved every article written about Jason and placed them into scrapbooks, which they proudly show to anyone who shows an interest. I asked him why he had made the journey to New Paltz today to be with his son.

"To show our support," he said, looking back towards Jason's office at the end of the hallway. I could tell that, unlike his son, this was a man who was not used to being interviewed. While he did not shy away from me, and seemed generally pleased to be talking about his son, he struggled to find the words that matched what he was feeling. "I think that family can sometimes cut right through everything else you know? I want Jason to be able to look up and see us when he is in that courtroom and know that we are here for him."

I asked him whether the charges Jason faced worried him. His son could potentially spend years in jail if convicted. Although it wasn't a likely scenario, as a parent it would certainly terrify me.

"I'm not really worried," he said. "Jason's a smart boy. He's researched this very carefully and knows exactly what he's doing, why he's doing it, and what the potential consequences could be. My *daughter*, however, is a nervous wreck," he said, pointing to Amanda, who was dressed conservatively, appeared to be much younger than her brother, and looked a bit wide-eyed and jittery.

I told them that I, too, was proud of Jason, that his political views were refreshing, and that he continually surprised me with his ability to negotiate local issues while still keeping his ideals and innovative projects at the forefront.

"I have to say though, it was funny to see him dressed up in a suit," I said. "I had never seen him wear one before. Not even for his inauguration!"

"When I saw him on TV the other night I thought he looked like such a dork!" said Amanda, speaking for the first time.

"His friends went and picked out a new suit for him for tonight," his dad added. "This one really fits him well."

Soon Jonathon bounded up the stairs. "We're going in at ten of six," he announced. "This is how it's going to go: Jason and his lawyers will walk in first, followed by his family. Erin will be behind them, then the deputy mayor, and we'll bring up the back. Whatever you do, keep walking. I'll be leading the way and Ryszard will bring up the rear."

I heard his office door open and then Jason and his lawyers walked down the hallway and onto the upstairs landing with us. Jason looked out the window and waved to the crowds who spotted him.

"Stop," I said. "You'll look like Michael Jackson if you do that."

"And look, here's a white glove," he said, picking up a lady's glove that had been left draped over the back of a row of folded chairs.

"Are you nervous?" I asked.

"Not really, I feel great."

47

He did look surprisingly confident, relaxed, and happy, considering the circumstances. All of a sudden Jason reminded me of former President Bill Clinton, though Jason would certainly not appreciate the comparison. Both had large frames and a large presence when they entered a room. Jason had that jovial, affable quality that Clinton had, which could charm the masses and piss off their enemies. He also had that Clintonesque ability to make you feel, when he spoke to you, like you were the most important person in the world, and that what you had to say was fascinating, if not downright profound—at the least, a skill of a talented party host; at best, a sign of a savvy politician. There is something eternally optimistic about the two of them, some elusive quality that makes people feel good in their company. Yet that same quality also invites envy and jealousy from those who are not privy to the warmth, or who have been shunned.

I wondered if the Greens could ever elect someone to become President of the United States. I personally had voted for Ralph Nader during the past two presidential elections, but for a moment I thought that if any Green stood a chance it was the man standing before me, in his freshly purchased gray suit.

The doors to the Village Hall opened and we were thrust into a mob scene; it was a friendly mob scene, but intimidating nonetheless. I held on to the striped oxford-cloth shirt of Jason's father with one arm and the deputy mayor with the other. Ryszard held on to me, trying to keep the caboose attached to the conductor's car. "We support Mayor West!" the crowd cheered. I kept my head down. There were cameras and microphones lunging at Jason and, subsequently, at us. I could see many recognizable faces, friends of mine and village acquaintances, but there was no stopping to say hello.

We lost Jason's sister for a moment but I grabbed her arm and didn't let go, even when I couldn't see the rest of her. Rebecca and Ryszard pulled up the back like expert linebackers moving in for the sack. At one point we were roadblocked by the throngs of supporters and media. Jonathon swiftly and, I must admit, quite gracefully maneuvered us back and to the side, so that we finally made it to the village steps where the New Paltz police helped to clear our path.

This was the kind of scene played out in the news every single day: Lawyers shuffling their clients past the media, bodyguards shielding stars from the paparazzi, crime victims and their families being swarmed on their front porches by eager journalists. And although it has become normalized, like a rite of passage for anyone's ticket to their fifteen minutes of fame, when you were on the inside it was terrifying as hell.

Jason seemed to thrive on it. He stopped halfway up the court steps, turned and shot both arms up in the air with his fists clenched. The supporters went wild. As they escorted us into the courthouse, which was only about 150 feet from the Village Hall entrance but felt like several miles, I saw many of the familiar faces of our NPPD. Sergeant Karl Baker, arguably the most handsome of the lot, was smiling, seeming to enjoy the excitement as much as Jason.

"Erin, you come this way," said Sergeant Baker, who led me towards one of two entrances into the court. Jason and his entourage were led towards the opposite doorway. I figured that was it for me. I guessed that there was no admittance into the courtroom for the press after all, even for the local press. Or maybe there was some procedural thing I should have done, like contact the courthouse earlier to sign up, or call the chief. Why didn't I call the chief? Because I'm normally not in these situations, I thought. When do we have court cases that go national? In fact, I thought, when do we have court cases that we bother to cover in our local paper? Jared Bozydaj, who went on the downtown shooting spree, was one. Before that, it was when that woman in Gardiner and her cyberspace boyfriend conspired to murder her husband. Then their adopted son, who was brutally abused by them, set fire to several barns. I covered that story extensively for *Ulster Magazine*. Before my day, there was the New Paltz housewife who claimed to have suffered from years of abuse at the hands of her husband and decided to shoot him, reload and shoot him several times again, after the autopsy reports showed that he was long dead. Those were the high profile cases. Nothing glamorous, mostly grisly and disturbing. These thoughts ran through my head just as the smell of the polished wooden benches and recently washed floors filled my courtroom senses.

49

When I turned the corner, instead of being ushered out the side door, I saw a room full of local, regional, national, and international press sitting quietly in the first two rows. Jeremiah, who I had forgiven for "stealing" Jason's story, waved me over. "Here you go," he said, pointing to a chair with *New Paltz Times* written on it, right next to the chair labeled *New York Times*. I'm such an idiot, I thought to myself. Is this what people learn in journalism school? While I was busy reading Faulkner and Hemingway, Jane Austen and Jean Rhys, these other "who, what, when and where" writers were busy learning about journalistic entitlement into all chambers of newsworthy fodder.

Chief Zappone gave out some basic instructions about when and where photographs could be taken. "All recording devices should be placed here," he said, motioning to a ledge that divided the court audience from its participants. At least seventeen arms pulled miniature devices from their pockets or purses and volleyed for the best shelf position of their particular recording device. I, of course, had no such apparatus and thus flipped through my steno pad trying to look professional.

There were two tables set up before the judge's bench. At one of the tables was Assistant District Attorney Paul O'Neil, another person I knew from high school. His back was turned to everyone, and I could imagine, given the particular pro-West climate raging outside, this was probably not as exhilarating for him as it was for Jason and the defense.

"No, I won't be there tonight," DA Williams had said earlier in the day. "Our office will be represented by Paul O'Neil, who is a heck of a lot better looking than I am." Paul had been a sought-after fox in high school, and there was nothing in his appearance that night to indicate that this status or physical appeal had changed. "I like to say that I have a great face for radio," said the DA, whose self-deprecating sense of humor was oddly very similar to Jason's. They both had enticing voices. The DA's voice was low and resonant with the clarity of bottled water.

I had interviewed Don Williams when he took office after veteran DA Michael Kavanaugh left the post to take the job of State Supreme Court judge. Williams had been Kavanagh's assistant DA for many years and was the obvious choice to replace him. The first time he had to officially run for the elected post, he ran unopposed. The second time he was cross-endorsed. But with the traditionally Republican-dominated county losing seats to Democrats lobbying for open space protection, environmental safeguards, and affordable housing, the Republicans were losing their long-held ground.

"Don needs this like he needs a hole in the head," said my father, repeatedly, since his friend had been thrust into the spotlight for leveling criminal charges against the young mayor. "With the murderers and rapists and sexual abuse going on, you think he has the time or resources to deal with this?"

"My dad is a loyal friend," I said to Don during one of our now daily phone interviews. "Not only does he defend you to anyone who will listen, but he wouldn't give me your private line, no matter how many times I pleaded."

"You know I think the world of your dad," said the DA. "And I have tried to the best of my ability to give priority to local media, even though the *Kingston Freeman* has not painted a very good portrait of me. My mother called me the other day and said, 'Don, doesn't anyone in this county like you anymore? Where have all your supporters gone?'"

"This is a small office with limited resources," he continued. "I'm right in the middle of a hit-and-run case that resulted in the death of a Kingston school teacher. But this is all part of the job. Like it or not. I have a responsibility to the oath of office I took, to the people I serve and to the law which I swore to uphold."

I hoped that everyone's true and best nature would emerge from this story, including the DA who called criminal justice his "calling."

"My family likes to call it my curse," he said with a laugh.

Soon Jason and his lawyers walked towards the other table and sat down. After a minute or two, I heard the "All rise" announcement and then Justice Katz walked out of his chambers, his black robes billowing dramatically behind him, and took his seat. The judge was a handsome man, in his mid-forties, with short, whitish-gray hair, athletic looking and clean-shaven with a pedigreed quality about him.

This would have been one of those times to have a voice recorder of some sort, because what transpired during the next three and a half minutes was inaudible. "What? What did he say?" asked the AP reporter. "I can't hear a damn thing!" Katz, a very reserved, erudite man was certainly not one to shout, which he would have had to do in order to be heard over the "Go West!" chants that were growing louder outside the courtroom.

There was some talk about a motion to dismiss from the defense, then Katz set a date. Then another date was set for the DA's opposition and a third date for the defense's reply. I'm not sure if the judge was feeling the pressure from all of the media present or from the protestors outside, or maybe he just didn't have his second cup of coffee that day, but he forgot to ask Jason to enter his plea.

Later, a lawyer on another case, who happened to be present at the arraignment, told me that he had joked with Judge Katz after the arraignment about forgetting to enter a plea. "He said that it wasn't the media that had him rattled, but the fact that the lawyers and their client were sitting at *tables* in front of the bench!" Typically, the court is much looser than that, with lawyers and public defenders milling about, dashing between clients and the water cooler.

"Not guilty," Jason finally said. And it was over.

The reporters scrambled, checking their dates, the names, exactly what had transpired, and then we were all herded through the back of the courtroom, down the stairs, and out the police department's side-door exit. It was dark. It was cold. The cameramen were asking the reporters to get down. The female TV reporters were caked with make-up, hair dyed or streaked blonde, wearing smart, coordinated pantsuits, matching eye shadow and nail polish, with recorders and headsets to boot. I felt like a bus of out-of-town kids had come to play in my small private park. I could relate to the print journalists more than the TV personalities. They, like me, had a little notepad and pen. They, too, were being knocked around by the cameramen and told to move aside, move back, and squat down.

As the door opened, everyone jostled into position. But it was just Sergeant

Baker. "You guys have been waiting for me?" he said with a smile. "I'll be available afterwards to sign autographs, so don't worry."

"When's the mayor coming out?" asked one humorless guy.

"It will be just a few minutes," he said and then asked that all of the reporters and cameramen step back off the sidewalk to give the mayor and his attorneys ample room to exit the building.

I noticed that one of the cameramen was stepping on a rhododendron. I wanted to tell him to get off it, but just then my cell phone rang. It was Kazik, checking in to see how things were going. I didn't want to lose my place just outside the door, so I talked to him amidst the other journalists. Since we spoke French to one another, as well as to our kids, I always felt relatively secure that most people around me would not know what we were saying, and if they did, my accent was so terrible that they might not understand it. It felt like our own pig latin, with bits of Polish thrown in to really keep people off their guard. He told me that Zofia was better, playing with her blocks, and that the boys were driving him crazy, pleading with him to take them for ice cream even though it was freezing outside. I talked to all of them, told them to be good, blew kisses over the phone and then told Kazik that I should go, that Jason and his lawyers were about to step out any minute and give a statement to the press. I slid the cell phone into my jacket pocket and looked again towards the door.

"Are you an international reporter?" the woman next to me asked. "*Le Monde*?" she said with a certain amount of authority, as if she could spot a *Le Monde* reporter a mile, or in this case, 6,000 miles away.

"No," I said. "I don't work for *Le Monde*," and I left it at that. She stared at me for a while, trying to figure out exactly which paper I worked for. It wasn't often that I felt so mysterious or intriguing.

As we waited for Jason and his lawyers to come out into the frigid, dry air, the banter between the assembled media was not at all focused on Jason West or this particular case, but on Jayson *Williams*, the New Jersey Nets basketball star who was on trial for manslaughter, charged with murdering his limo driver. The other hot topic of the day was Martha Stewart, the multibillion-dollar home design maven who was tried and convicted on four felony accounts-the same week that the mayor performed the same-sex marriages in New Paltz—for lying to the government investigators.

"I've been running back and forth between the Williams trial and this town," said one reporter.

"I've been on the Martha case and then got sent down here. I don't know if it was a demotion or what."

"Does anyone know what the judge's name was here?" asked one reporter.

"How about the district attorney?" asked another. "Was it Don Williams?"

"No," I said. "That was Paul O'Neil. He's an assistant DA."

"O'Neil? Are you sure?"

"Yes, I'm sure. I went to high school with him."

"You're from here?" he asked with a sardonic grin.

"Yes."

"How about that?"

Yes, how about that.

Rosenkranz, Esseks, and Jason finally emerged. They told everyone that the mayor would be making a statement in the Village Hall parking lot. "There he is!" screamed a pair of supporters, a young lesbian couple with matching Yankees baseball caps. "You will go to hell, Mayor West!" screamed one lone man off in a dark recess of the parking lot.

As Jason and his small entourage moved swiftly from the police station exit around the corner to the village parking lot, cameramen from all of the stations went running after them. I kept thinking that one of them was going to trip. Some of the local volunteers who had offered their services to Jason after he decided to marry same-sex couples were helping to set up a podium and working with the media to get their lights, microphones, and cameras set up. Jason, his lawyers, and his family had made it safely inside Village Hall, which was now being guarded by four of our more well-built police officers.

I took this time to make a phone call to Brian. I leaned against the metal signpost which said "Parking Reserved for The Mayor," cupped my left ear with one hand and pressed my other ear to my cell phone so that I could better hear him above the roar of the supporters. "Well?" he asked. I rattled off the plea and the court deadlines for the motions to dismiss. I characterized the crowd, its size and texture. I talked about Jason, how cool and collected he appeared to be and about our former village mayor, Tom Nyquist.

"I hate to see this happen," Tom had said to me earlier that evening, as he walked around the Village Hall grounds prior to the arraignment. I was surprised that he had ventured back to his old stomping grounds, particularly at this moment, when he had been in reclusion ever since his election upset nine months earlier. "See *what* happen, Tom?" I asked, wanting a quote from the former mayor, but approaching him cautiously, as if he were someone still recovering from a serious illness.

"This," he said sweeping his eyes over the protestors. "Look at this spectacle. The mayor was elected to serve the people, not to become a political activist and create a circus here in the village, which will result in tremendous overtime costs for the police and the Department of Public Works." I too hated to see this. Not what Jason had sparked, but Tom's bitterness. He was still so resentful over his election loss to the twenty-six-year-old that he would not acknowledge Jason in the local butcher shop or when passing him on one of our narrow village streets.

I had enjoyed working with the former mayor over the years and liked how his sort of Midwestern modesty and conventional upbringing in Montana dovetailed curiously with his more radical, East Coast pursuits in the field of African-American studies and progressive Democratic politics. He embodied what one would imagine the mayor of a small, intellectual town to be. He wore suits to meetings, jeans and a polo shirt on the weekends. He cut ribbons and made hokey proclamations when called upon. He was always available to the local press. He stood up against Wal-Mart when they tried to move into town. He also championed zoning in the village that would prevent big-box retailers from overshadowing our small independent businesses, particularly one large pharmacy chain that would have posed a great threat to our beloved Dedrick's, a family-owned pharmacy. And he was just, well, kind and polite, a bit goofy, in fact. Towards the end of his political tenure, he began leaning towards more conventional ideologies, a pull of age or wisdom or ignorance that cost him the election in New Paltz.

Tom walked around the Village Hall grounds like a man returning to the home he had grown up in, or raised his children in, only to see it, several months later, fallen to neglect and ruin. But when I followed his gaze, I didn't see what he saw. Instead, I saw the oldest tradition in America at work. People exercising their freedom of speech, their right to protest what they believed to be unjust. And when it came right down to it, this was not about Mayor Jason West but about people who wanted to get married, raise children together, and share a life.

The crowd was throbbing with anticipation. I told Brian that I had to go and that the mayor was due to address the crowd at any moment. "I'll call you back with his quotes," I said and snapped the cell phone shut, just as the door to Village Hall opened. Jonathon Wright came out first and the police quickly shut the door behind him. He saw me standing off to the side and walked over to me. "Erin, he's going to make his statement from the podium. Do you want to walk to the podium with us so you get a good spot?" he asked. I felt flattered by his concern that I have the access I needed to the mayor and the story, but the hundreds of supporters packed tightly around the podium in the dark looked sort of foreboding and claustrophobic. I decided I had a better view from where I was.

"That's okay, Jonathon," I said. "I think I'll hang back for this one."

When Jason did come out of Village Hall with his lawyers, more than a dozen police officers surrounded them and began moving quickly towards the podium which was situated about 125 feet away. The officers kept one hand on Jason and his lawyers while their other hand created a path through the throngs of people and media, trying to get Jason and his lawyers to the stage. "Scan the crowd! Scan the crowd!" I heard Sergeant Baker order his men. Their dark blue uniforms seemed to engulf Jason as they moved him safely towards the stage.

Then it dawned on me, all at once. Jason had placed himself in danger. Suddenly, I looked out over the crowd and saw someone perched on the branch of a crab-apple tree on the village lawn. Because it was a dark winter night and the camera lights were blinding, it was hard to see who, exactly, was in the tree.

"I had already received death threats by that time," reflected Jason, almost a month later. "Do you know why all of those police officers escorted me to the podium? They were trying to keep me at arm's length from any of the demonstrators, because they wanted to make sure that I wasn't stabbed. Someone could, theoretically, just reach in and stab me and they'd have no idea who did it."

Some of his volunteers had suggested that he stand up in the back of a pickup truck to make his post-arraignment speech. When Jason mentioned the suggestion to the police they rejected it right away, claiming that he would be too easy a target standing in the back of a truck. "They told me that they wanted me down low, where they could protect me."

Later, I would find out that the person in the tree was just a rebellious supporter who felt compelled to stand above the masses. But I kept replaying, in slow motion, Jason walking towards the platform with twelve pairs of policemen's eyes trying to pierce into the crowd like radar and uncover any potential threat. It was eerie to consider the darker side of what he had done, and the instantaneous fame it had afforded him. Now his face was known, for better or for worse, as a high-profile political advocate of gay rights. While this would make him a hero to many, it could also make him a target for those who passionately, sometimes violently, attempted to squelch the advance of gay rights.

"The issue before us today is that of civil rights, human rights and basic human decency," Jason told the cheering crowd. "Our State Constitution supports these marriages. I have read the New York State Constitution and I encourage you all to read it. I also encourage the governor of New York State, the attorney general and the Ulster County district attorney to read our Constitution. Obviously they need to reread this document if they think that marrying people is against the law."

His proclamations were bold. His voice was booming. I cringed a few times, not at what he said, but the tone in which he said it. All of a sudden our white, straight, upstate New York mayor sounded like Bishop T. D. Jakes, or Reverend Al Sharpton, with a sort of black Southern Baptist—lilt to his homily. Oddly enough, Al Sharpton had called Jason that same day to lend his support.

"Why was he screaming like that?" Deb asked me later that night after watching Jason on the round of 11 p.m. news programs. "He sounded ridiculous."

"I think it's unconscious," I mused. "He's drawing on his civil rights inspirations like Martin Luther King Jr. and Malcolm X, and I don't think he's even aware of how it sounds."

I felt for him. I remember attending a Christian camp when I was younger. Most of the kids came from the inner city and were of Puerto Rican descent. By the end of my two-week stay, I had picked up a Puerto Rican accent that I couldn't shake. I think it was an unconscious attempt to relate to my newfound friends. I experienced that same sort of verbal tic years later when traveling in Ireland. After only a few weeks I began to say things like "I was talking to himself and herself" with a brogue that would not release its grip on my tongue until I was back in the States for several days.

"I don't think anyone noticed," I said hopefully.

"Maybe not at the rally, but on TV it didn't sound good," she said.

But in that moment, with Jason basking in the national spotlight and surrounded by supporters, progressive village residents and recently married gay couples, I thought that *what* he said mattered more than *how* he said it.

"I had the pleasure of watching the wedding video of my dear friends Charles and Maurice, who were legally married in Holland a few years ago," Jason continued to bellow in the darkness. "The pastor who performed their marriage said something that I had been thinking, but could not find the words for until I heard her speak. She said, 'Marriage is the act of making public what is already written in two people's hearts.'"

The young mayor went on to make a statement that the crowd and certainly the reporters had been waiting for: that regardless of the twenty-four misdemeanor counts charged against him, as well as the temporary restraining order prohibiting him from marrying any more gay couples, he would go forward with his plans to conduct a second round of same-sex marriages that following Saturday, March 6, at noon. "I intend to go forward solemnizing marriages this Saturday," he said. "I have also spoken with Mayor John Shields of Nyack who today has said that he will begin solemnizing same-sex marriages."

Within the next few days, Jason would change his mind, after receiving a personal invitation from Attorney General Eliot Spitzer to meet with him and discuss the legality of same-sex marriages. Spitzer would agree to meet with him only if he stopped conducting the marriages. Jason's attorneys advised him to obey the provisions of the restraining order. If he did not, then he would be in direct violation of the court. He decided to follow their advice, meet with Spitzer, and stop marrying people, until his lawyers had the chance to argue against the restraining order and hopefully win in a higher court.

Later I would call Bob Hebel, who had served on the Village Board with Nyquist for ten years. He was the last of the old guard who remained on the board once Jason and his running mates climbed aboard. Feldman had resigned and Michael Zierler would soon run for and win his seat. And then there was Bob who remained in the same spot, situated to the far right side of the village board conference table, looking at Jason curiously, as if he didn't trust one word that came out of his mouth.

Bob not only mistrusted Jason, but like the DA, felt that what Jason had done on February 27 was not only wrong, but criminal. He quickly scoured the phone books, trying to find a law firm that would help him take Jason down. Within days he would have a pro bono offer from none other than Liberty Counsel out of Orlando, Florida: a Christian Right law firm whose mission statement, among other things, calls for the reintegration of Church and State. Their lawyers were all over the country, leveling lawsuits in any and every court where the issue of gay marriage was being considered. They were also the Reverend Jerry Falwell's legal arm, and now Bob Hebel's legal representatives. With their help, he was able to file a petition, as any resident can do, with Ulster County Judge Vincent Bradley, requesting that a temporary restraining order be placed on Jason, banning him from performing any more same-sex marriages, until the legality of his actions could be addressed in more depth by the courts. Bob was successful in convincing Judge Bradley that Jason's actions could potentially cause "irreparable physical or mental harm."

"Some people would argue that marriage causes irreparable mental harm, but I'm not one of them," Jason would joke with the media when asked about the restraining order.

When I spoke with Bob the night of the arraignment, explaining to him that Jason claimed he would be going forward with the marriages, regardless of the restraining order, Bob wasn't laughing.

"If he continues with these marriages then he will be disobeying the court," he said. "No more slap on the wrist from the DA. He will be handcuffed and hauled off to jail." Bob also told me that he was discussing the possibility of filing another lawsuit, with the help of Liberty Counsel, at the Albany Appellate Court Division, "to try and have the mayor removed from office."

I decided to get another perspective on the night's events and walked towards Chief Zappone, who was standing back from the crowd surveying the scene with a not-so-pleased look on his face.

"How much has this cost the police in overtime?" I asked him, leaning my notepad on my knee so that I could catch the dim glow of an overhead streetlight to see what I was writing.

"The day of the marriages cost us about $1,200 in overtime," he said. "I would guess that today would run about the same, but I haven't calculated that yet."

"I'm from the International Free Press," interjected Fernando Schirripa, a local electrician and childhood friend of mine who grew up down the street from me on Cherry Hill Road in New Paltz where he lived with his Italian-born aunt and grandparents.

"What are you doing, Nando?" I asked, knowing very well that he was not there representing any news organization, but just to agitate.

"I'm a taxpayer," he said. "I have a right to ask questions. This is a free country, right?" He was pretending to scrawl notes on his to-go coffee cup.

I had to laugh. I knew Nando and loved him, and imagined that his Catholic roots were seizing hold of his vital organs and strangling the oxygen out of his brain.

"Who's going to pay for the police overtime and the DPW's overtime?" asked the incredulous Nando. The chief reiterated the costs and I said, "I have to get home to the baby Nando, why don't you speak your mind at the village board meeting? It starts in about 45 minutes."

When I was musing to my dear friend and editor of the arts section of our paper, Julie O'Connor, also a born and bred New Paltzian, about how the weddings seemed to bring out the entire community in force whether or not they agreed with gay marriage, she said to me, in her usual serious but provocative tone: "We're not an oasis, Erin. That's what people want to think about New Paltz, especially newcomers, but we're really a mongrel. We've just learned to co-exist without killing one another."

I dashed home, which was about two and a half blocks away. I paused at the Trailways bus station, where one of two buses from New York City was emptying out its commuter clientele. I leaned against a parked car and called Brian. I rattled off Jason's quotes, the estimated police overtime costs and some random commentary.

"Excellent job," he said and I had to smile to myself. Only two months earlier he had cut one of my stories to shreds. It was a review of a visit by the Nobel laureate Toni Morrison, who had recently conducted a reading in New Paltz from her latest novel, *Love*. I had been ecstatic. I was fortunate enough to have my two favorite authors come to town—William Kennedy, author of the Pulitzer Prize–winning novel *Ironweed*, and now Morrison. I wrote a preview of her visit for the arts and culture section of the various regional papers. It was succinct, academic, and full of the necessary biographical and literary information. The second story, which I solely intended to be for the *New Paltz Times*, was a review. I wanted to write about the evening, what Morrison was like to behold in person, the book itself, and the great fortune of having been in the company of such colossal talent. Because I have to write four articles every week on top of eight news briefs, it is hard to put my all into any one article. But when it came to one of my great literary heroes, I did just that.

Unbeknownst to me, my publisher wanted to use the story for the *Mid-Hudson Post/Pioneer*, *The Kingston Times*, and *The Woodstock Times*. With help from Brian my treasured story was dissected, parts amputated and ultimately reduced from its metaphoric and emotive grandeur to simply a question-and-answer period with Morrison and the public. "You were there to write about Morrison, what she had to say," Brian had said to me sternly, "not to gush about what a great talent she is or tell us what your mother thought about the night." They had the right as editor and publisher to do what they wanted with the story, but at the time it felt really crappy.

In one brief moment, the sting of that particular humiliation made me clench my teeth while leaning against a Westchester County transplant's Range Rover. I think that Brian took my silence to mean that I was unhappy that he couldn't use everything I'd given him. "I know this is *your* story and I don't want to touch it, but I don't have the room that the *New Paltz Times* has to run every-thing," he said in an oddly deferential tone. "Do the best you can," I said and walked the remaining block and a half to my house.

Chapter 4
Justice Leaves a Message

It was such a heightened time. I had never before had the sensation of being part of such a big story. It wasn't the Iraq War or the presidential election and it wasn't Watergate or the OJ trial, but it *was* our small, modern-day version of Selma, Alabama—thankfully without the police dogs or the violence. My life with three small children, a full-time job, and a late-night passion for reading had always been very scheduled, ridiculously routine. But suddenly, with this news implosion, there was an extra spark in the day, like one of those practical joke birthday candles that won't go out no matter how hard you blow. Part of me regretted having to be so busy, while the other part of me enjoyed playing with the big boys. I felt almost as if I were acting, like in that old commercial where the soap opera star said, "I'm not a doctor, but I play one on TV."

Things seemed to move at warp speed. I was on the cell phone constantly with Jason, the DA, my editors, and "Deep Love." Between covering this story and caring for my kids, I barely slept. My one-year-old daughter, in pain from her earache, woke up nearly every two hours. At one point, I became so delirious nursing her in the middle of the night that I didn't know where I began and she ended. I must have fallen back asleep with her in my arms as I rocked because my husband woke me up panicked, the baby and I having fallen to the floor. Thankfully she was fine, and all I had was a slight bruise on my forehead.

After giving the kids hugs and kisses and nursing the baby to sleep, I shoved a cold piece of pizza in my mouth and headed back downtown for the village board meeting. I know the city dwellers always tease us native New Paltzians that we distinguish between "uptown" and "downtown"—the span being less than a mile—but for us, the distinction is more than evident: they are two different worlds separated by an invisible line, just past the Ulster Savings Bank, when New Paltz starts looking homey and inviting, rather than like an aging strip mall in a lost corner of upstate New York.

After getting off the thruway at exit 18, visitors to the town are greeted by a Mobil station, then the Shop Rite supermarket plaza, then the Ames Plaza, minus the Ames, since the retailer went bankrupt in 2001 leaving New Paltz and a multitude of other northeastern towns without access to a department store. There is also the typically depressing hodgepodge of McDonald's and Burger Kings, Midas Mufflers and Dunkin' Donuts, with old residential homes now turned into hair salons or real-estate offices, squished between the fast-food facades.

Then there is the Plaza Diner, open twenty-four hours a day, seven days a week, always busy with busloads of tour groups who have come to pick their own apples at one of our many apple orchards, or to videotape their child's hunt for his or her own pumpkin. It's also popular with senior citizens' clubs that enjoy having lunch before embarking on a leaf-peeping tour of our changing autumnal landscape. The diner is home to students, passing an evening over bitter coffee and a shared plate of french fries, and to families with Cheetos-stained children and parents who look like they need a break from cooking. The diner smells of grease and bacon, no matter what time of day, and the endless chatter sounds like a Tom Waits song being played on a worn eight-track.

Past the diner, within a flash, the neon dissipates, and half a dozen old Sears and Roebuck-catalogue houses, fashioned in the early 1900s, begin to line the streets. They are adequately buffered from Main Street by large, centuries-old shade trees, guarded by the village's volunteer Shade Tree Commission. Former mayor Nyquist mentioned more than once how proud he was that New Paltz was recognized as a "Tree City," and to that end, the Village Department of Public Works, along with a local arborist and dozens of school-children plant new trees every Arbor Day in various village parks and green spaces.

After traveling past the older homes in the village, there is a slight hill, which brings motorists past the old brick public middle school on the left, banks and gas stations on the right, and the first view of the Shawangunk Mountains and the Mohonk Tower, an old stone edifice built in the nineteenth century by the Smiley brothers, a Quaker family that founded and continues to own and operate the Mohonk Mountain House. As you descend the hill, you enter into the heart of New Paltz, the village, which alternates between look-ing dingy and dilapidated one minute and then romantic and quaint the next, depending on the light, or the aesthetic filter of the ob-server. The village streets contain many old colonial and Victorian houses. There are also historic stone buildings, and beautiful Queen Anne-style homes tucked into various residential pockets. There are the old storefronts, some dressed up, some dressed down, almost all with apartments on the second floor. Wherever the sun's rays have the potential to oxidize young, nubile skin, students can be found, with a magazine and beer in hand, sunbathing on rooftops, spread out on old towels, or if the roof pitch is flat, on lawn chairs.

Jason had gotten me into major trouble several years earlier, when he vehemently opposed an application by the owners of a lo-cal bookstore to build an addition. Susan and Dean Avery had turned a former gas station into Ariel, a top-notch book lover's bookstore that was always bringing in dozens of award-winning authors to read from their latest works. The store was on the corner of Plattekill Avenue and Main Street, an intersection that included three historic buildings: a Colonial revival bank, the stone and wood-framed public library, and P&G's restaurant—an old casino-turned-bar, a family restaurant by day and watering hole by night. I spent more time in that bookstore than most Americans spend in Wal-Mart. While visiting friends in New York City, I would often stop at Barnes & Noble to peruse the books. If I found something I was interested in, I would write down the title and then order it from our local, independent bookstore.

It wasn't the addition that caused the uproar, but the planned tenant for the addition, Starbucks, which, in Jason's opinion, had infested the globe like a fungus without any natural predator. "Instead of 'Welcome to New Paltz' that critical village intersection will now say, 'Welcome to Starbucks,'" said Jason West, then an undergraduate at SUNY New Paltz, at a village planning board meeting in 1999. "The Averys are just out for money. Instead of soliciting a local, independent coffeehouse, they're bringing in a multinational chain which will negatively affect the independent character of New Paltz, not to mention the economic impact on the three other local cafes."

At the time, I quoted Jason—not all of his comments, but some of them—believing that his were well-articulated views opposing the addition. I felt a bit queasy writing the article, not only because I wanted to support my favorite bookstore but because I was a friend and high school classmate of the owners' daughter. But it was my job to write what transpired at the local meetings.

In the end, the attorneys and architects for the Averys defended their application, and the village planning board quickly pointed out that it was not its role to refuse a specific tenant, but to judge the site plan application on its merits and its ability to fit within the village code.

Unlike Jason, who had never stepped foot in, I conducted a successful, three-year boycott; but eventually my morality gave way to late-night cravings for a mocha. Deb, who proudly patronized Starbucks from the day it opened, teased me to no end, when she discovered this gaping flaw in my code of consumer ethics. "You told me that you would *never* buy coffee from Starbucks!" she said to me one day, after catching me sneaking into the side entrance for my daily iced mocha grande. "The devil comes in all kinds of disguises," I told her. "This time the pull is too strong for me, especially since I haven't had a full night's sleep in four years!"

Deep Love, too, would chastise me when she saw me darting into my den of iniquity. She was always staging protests outside Starbucks, sometimes with just her daughter Sylvie and their dog. It wasn't quite enough public pressure to get them to serve only free trade coffee as per her request, but she was successful in getting them to at least have one free trade coffee flavor for the day.

"Do you know what kind of trouble you got me into with the Averys?" I took the opportunity to tell Jason when I was interviewing him at his Village Hall office after he had met with Spitzer.

"Oh yeah," he said, chewing on the remnants of a corn muffin that had disintegrated into its plastic wrapping. "I remember the letter Susan Avery wrote to the paper asking, 'Why is Jason West making this issue personal when he doesn't even know us?'"

"They did try you know," I said, feeling compelled to explain why they felt Starbucks was their only alternative.

"Try what?" he asked.

"They told me that they tried, for eight years, to solicit a local vendor but were unsuccessful." The Averys had explained to me that to survive in the world of big-box bookstores, they were forced to hook up with a coffee vendor. "Economically there was no other choice," said Susan Avery. "Coffee goes with books, and if we didn't do it, then there would be no more 'independent' bookstore in New Paltz."

It was not only the Averys who had an allergic reaction to Jason, but one of their employees as well. I remember searching for a book in my compulsive late-night need for a good read, when the guy behind the counter struck up a conversation with me. "You write for the *New Paltz Times*, don't you?" he asked. His name was Johnny and he was a young literary type. While he tried to be of service to the store's clients, he often couldn't help acknowledging his approval of your book choice, or worse, unleashing his disapproval.

While I scanned the aisles for a book, Johnny asked me what I thought of Jason West, who at the time was only in his second or third month in office.

"I'm consistently surprised by his ability to negotiate the issues as well as articulate and offer solutions," I said carefully, not sure where this discussion was going. "What do *you* think of him?" I asked.

"I think he ran for mayor just to get laid," he said. "Have you seen the way he operates down at Bacchus?" Bacchus was a local left-leaning, rock-climbing, pool-playing, bar. "It's disgusting."

When I repeated this conversation to Rachel at a party Kazik and I were having for Seamus' fourth birthday, she scoffed. "Jason did not need to be elected mayor to get laid, okay?"

My friend, Melissa Halvorson, a SUNY graduate student who was also at the party and overheard us talking, agreed wholeheartedly with Rachel. "He's twenty-six and single!" she said, as if that was enough to justify however he chose to act at a bar. "He *should* be getting laid. And hey, power is sexy, we all know that."

Much later, after the weddings, I recounted this story to Jason as well. "That guy has always hated me and I have no idea why," he said, blushing. One of Jason's more endearing traits is his tendency to turn bright red when anyone has anything critical to say about him, particularly during a village board meeting.

"He's one of the neo-libertarians," he said throwing up his hands.

"He's probably jealous," I offered, trying to ease his embarrassment.

We returned to the topic of the interview. As we spoke, Jason's personal assistant, Brittany, was in the office with us, busy answering his e-mails and working on his daily schedule. She wore a thinly quilted powder-blue down jacket with a negligee underneath. Because she was young and attractive and had volunteered her time and talents to Jason without payment, I shamefully wondered if she had a more emotional investment in him, rather than just championing his politics. She had abandoned her job and apartment in

Washington, D.C., and returned to New Paltz, where, like Jason, she had graduated from SUNY. "I just stopped in his office one day and said, 'Do you need help?'" she told me. "And he did. So here I am. I'm completely broke. I want to go out and get drunk but I can't even afford to!" I hoped that Jason appreciated her. I felt that she was deserving of appreciation as she had almost single-handedly negotiated the press during the media deluge. She had done it with skill and grace and I kept telling her that public relations was her calling.

Jason's cell phone rang. "Hi, Jeremiah. Listen, can I call you back? Erin's here and we're just finishing up." The cell phone rang again. This time it was Tom Crampton, a reporter that *The New York Times* had sent in to cover the story. "When are you liberal media jackals going to leave me alone?" Jason said with feigned irritation. But I could tell he was loving it. "I've never been in a position to turn media away before," he confided with a smile.

Jason wasn't the only one in trouble with the DA. After he was barred by Judge Bradley from performing same-sex weddings, he received a phone call from a Unitarian minister, Kay Greenleaf, who lived in Poughkeepsie, just across the Hudson River. "She offered to help and I said "sure," Jason told me, a few days after his arraignment. "That's exactly what I wanted to see happen," he mused. "More mayors, more clerks and more clergy stepping up to the plate to marry same-sex couples." Step up to the plate they did. On March 6, Greenleaf and fellow Unitarian minister, Dawn Sangrey of Bedford Hills, New York, came to New Paltz to continue the marriages.

In an effort to keep the marriages away from Jason, lest the DA or Judge Bradley should get wind that he was up to no good again, the newly organized New Paltz Equality Initiative, a group of volunteers who rallied around the mayor after the first round of weddings, set up a new staging ground for the gay marriages at Blueberry Fields, a small parcel of land off Main Street in downtown New Paltz. In less than a week, they had these two Unitarian ministers willing to take the risk of marrying gay couples—something that they had been doing for the past two decades in the quietude of their own church. They also were able to coordinate trellises, bouquets, a white tent in case of rain, and dozens of same-sex couples eager to say "I do" in New Paltz.

The crowd at the second round of weddings was large—not as large as the one in front of Village Hall, but sizeable nonetheless. The first person to be married that day, under the tent in the pouring rain at Blueberry Fields, was Greenleaf herself, to her longtime partner. After she kissed and hugged her bride, she put her robe and collar back on, and began solemnizing weddings along with Sangrey. I noticed one of the NPPD detectives, Dave Dugatkin, undercover, in a dark suit and sunglasses, making notes and snapping photos. I figured he was there for security purposes, or to make sure that the mayor didn't show up and say "I now pronounce you...." I couldn't imagine that the DA would consider charging the ministers as well. But a few days later, I would find out how wrong I was.

On Monday, March 22, Sangrey and Greenleaf walked into the New Paltz courthouse, just as Jason had been forced to do two weeks earlier. The DA had charged them each with thirteen criminal misdemeanor counts for allegedly violating the Domestic Relations Law. These two women, both in their early sixties, with short hair and warm, generous faces, did not pack the star power that Jason did, but they certainly elicited from the crowd great empathy and respect as well as outrage that the DA had brought criminal charges against two women of the cloth. The pre- and post-arraignment rally, while similar to that of Jason's, had more of a religious flavor. As the two ministers entered pleas of "not guilty," the crowd outside, many of whom were parishioners of Greenleaf's and Sangrey's churches, sang hymns, prayed and proudly carried placards which read, "Let Our Reverend Go!" and "New Yorkers Want the Right to Marry."

"I'm here in support of the clergy," said Mayor John Shields of Nyack. "It's a disgrace that the Ulster County DA would prosecute members of the clergy for marrying two people who love one another and want their commitment to be legally recognized. They've done nothing illegal." Mayor Shields had by this time decided not to go forward marrying gay couples himself, but instead to level his own civil suit against the Westchester town clerk for refusing to provide him and his longtime partner with a marriage license. Shields and Jason posed for photographs outside of the courthouse while they waited with the crowd for the two reverends to exit and make their statements.

The two women, along with their pro bono attorney Robert Gottlieb, spoke to the crowd after they both pleaded not guilty to the charges. Greenleaf told her supporters the same thing she had told the DA a week earlier: that the marriages she and Sangrey presided over had been civil and not religious and were intended to be binding and legal. "I did not ask, nor do I know what religious background the couples have," said Greenleaf. "These were civil ceremonies and ones that we consider to be just as valid as anyone else's in the State. The constitution supports these marriages, the Domestic Relations Law supports these marriages and I maintain that I have broken no law. One year in jail or a $500 fine is nothing, nothing compared to the length of time those of us who are gay and lesbian have been waiting to get our civil rights recognized."

"It's time for justice to roll down like water," said Sangrey. "God loves us all the same—whether black or white, gay or straight, old or young. I hope that these marriages continue in every village, every city, every state where there are two people who commit their love and lives to each other." Like Jason, Sangrey, who would soon be featured in a *New York Times* "Public Lives" column, was a straight ally to the gay community. And like Jason she said that she decided to act, knowing that there could be criminal charges brought against her, because, "It was the right thing to do."

The DA had gone from prosecuting a mayor to prosecuting women of the cloth. While legally I could understand it—had he just prosecuted the mayor and not the clergy, Jason's defense could have claimed that his prosecution of the mayor was inconsistent and therefore arbitrary—I wondered how the DA would defend himself on this one. These were not elected officials; they were *ministers*. Before he even responded to my questions over the phone, I could hear him struggling, taking a deep breath before he answered.

71

"Because this decision involved members of the clergy, it was one that was very difficult and troubling for me to make," the DA told me. "I'm a man of faith myself and I have the utmost respect for those who dedicate their lives to their faith, regardless of what faith that is. But simply and exclusively being a member of the clergy does not allow one to knowingly and consciously violate the law."

The DA would decide, after prosecuting Sangrey and Greenleaf, to let the courts determine whether or not Jason or the clergy had the right to officiate marriages without valid licenses. He claimed that his office was too small, their resources too limited, to charge every single member of the clergy that would go on to marry gay couples in New Paltz for the next eight months. "I think that the two cases my office brought before the courts contain all of the pertinent issues that the judges now need to consider," the DA explained.

While we waited for the town court to consider our mayor's case and Sangrey's and Greenleaf's motions to dismiss the charges on constitutional grounds, Jason was quickly becoming a national celebrity, his face splashed across the front pages of newspapers, on the news and in magazines. The village became star-struck, suddenly looking at their mayor in a whole new light.

Chapter 5
The Cult of Jason

"Fame usually comes to those who are thinking about something else." —Oliver Wendell Holmes Jr.

Forbidden to conduct any more gay marriages without the threat of being hauled off to jail, our now-famous mayor sat holed up in his office, conducting interviews with *The New York Times Magazine* and *New York* magazine, and being filmed in his "natural habitat" at The Bakery by MTV's *Rock the Vote* film crew. It was bizarre to see someone who might otherwise appear to dwell on the margins of society—someone so diametrically opposed to mainstream politics—suddenly seized by the cameras of media conglomerates that he would normally despise.

"He made Katie blush," said Deb, during one of our routine afternoon calls. "Katie who?" I asked, trying to do the dishes while the kids napped.

"You didn't see him this morning? On the *Today* show?"

"What?" I asked, drying my hands on one of Kazik's painting rags.

"Yeah, Katie Couric asked him if he had plans to run for president and he said, 'Ask me in about ten years.' And she said,

'Why wait ten years?' and he said, 'Because that's when I'll be of eligible age to run for president!' and she blushed."

Two weeks later Jason appeared on Conan O'Brien's late-night talk show. While I didn't see this live, I did happen to catch a rerun and couldn't pull myself away from the screen. Conan hit all of the right buttons to place Jason inside his own quickly spun celebrity myth. "So you're a housepainter? And a puppeteer? And make $8,000 a year?"

"Yes," said Jason, proudly.

"What a plum job!" said O'Brien, who added sarcastically that maybe he had chosen the wrong line of work. The audience cracked up.

I found the entire show a bit daunting. I wasn't in the habit of watching late-night talk shows, nor in the habit of watching much TV at all. It was hard for me to follow. The whole thing felt frenetic and surreal. Not only were these shows a slick competition of wit, but our mayor had a habit of mumbling—not mumbling exactly—but talking so fast that his words overlapped one another to the point where you wanted to push some elusive pause button and let him catch his leftist breath. "He looked like such a geek," said Rachel later that night. "He decided to cut his own hair for the Conan show and he has these little bald tufts where he cut it too short."

When I walked into our local cooperative nursery school to drop off Seamus and Tadeusz the following morning, many of the mothers were talking about the mayor's appearance on Conan. "I thought he did pretty well," said Jill Burke, whose husband, Ed, was often at local board meetings I covered, lobbying for more ball fields for the various athletic leagues in town. "He was smart and funny, and what the hell? Who really cares who's zooming who?"

While Jason had survived on very little money for quite some time, things began to turn swiftly in his financial favor. Within a matter of weeks he would sign a six-figure book deal with Miramax for his memoirs, go across the country on a paid speaking tour, and the village board would vote to increase his part-time position to a three-quarter time job with an $18,000 annual salary. While his critics would use his media appearances as further proof that he was an opportunist and someone out to further his own agenda, I couldn't help but think how ironic it was that his fast-track entrance into our national pop-culture arena gained him more points with the town's rank and file who might have otherwise just scoffed at his election victory and radical idealism, and chalked him up as another vaudeville sideshow that's par for the course when you live in New Paltz.

"If you could just put a circus tent over New Paltz we could charge admission," said Ed while we watched our kids at the playground. Kathy, the mother of Alexis, a classmate of Seamus, agreed with Jill Burke's assessment. "What's wrong with people?" she said, looking left and right to make sure she didn't offend anyone within ear shot. "I mean, if a man wants to marry a man or a woman a woman, why not? We have no business going into people's bedrooms and telling them who they should love!"

Kathy, a manager at P&G's Restaurant and Bar, also noted the economic windfall that had blown into the small village since the mayor began his nuptials. "We've had CNN crews, the MTV crews, CBS, NBC, ABC—all of them coming in for lunch and dinner. Business is hopping!"

This purported economic windfall was an angle I decided to pursue in my coverage of the weddings, to help offset Jason's critics who cited the thousands of dollars in overtime the New Paltz Police Department incurred from having to provide security at the first few rounds of weddings, the arraignments, and post-arraignment rallies. I started banging on some local downtown business doors to see if Kathy's estimation of a post-nuptial financial injection into our economy was accurate. David Santner, owner of The Bakery in downtown, said that his numbers were up twenty percent since February 27. Abdul Julani, of Jack's Meats and Deli, located just a few doors down from P&G's in the heart of downtown, concurred with Santner.

"Every time we have a wedding we have lots of people ordering organic meats," said Julani who had married Jack's daughter and brought his brother Abraham in as a manager of the deli. The two brothers are from Jordan and while they slice up free-range chicken breasts, their mother and sisters sit at a small table, near the store's front window, chatting away like school girls, wrapped from head to toe in hajibs.

I didn't want to ask Abdul what he thought of the gay marriage issue. I imagined, based on his body language—the way he pulled himself back and looked up towards the rack of cigarettes and fine cigars above the cash register—that same-sex marriage was not something a person from his religious and cultural background would advocate or go on record as actively supporting. But at the same time, he was a businessman and was proud to report the spike in sales whenever the weddings came to town. Abdul was also one of the friendliest human beings I had ever encountered and I suspected that in his own way, he had accepted the same-sex wedding fate of our small village.

Our mayor, while barely accepted as a credible elected official, had suddenly become the town's symbol of pride or shame, depending on the person who hoisted the flag. One of his critics was Peter Fairweather, another born and bred New Paltzian and a friend of mine. He and his wife Karen lived just up the street in a well-tended Victorian home. They had two grown daughters. Peter, a tall, sturdy man, with an upright posture and a gentlemen's gait, wore sensible shoes, jogged or rode his bike and was the kind of man who adjusted to the climate. When it rained, he wore a parka and rain hat. When it was sunny he worked in the yard or repainted the trim of their house. He had a quiet, serious nature, at least on the surface. That's why it was always surprising to see him dressed up on Halloween in a goofy mask to entertain the young trick-or-treaters or to see him at an annual New Year's Day party singing classic show tunes. I liked Peter. He was kind, smart, and a well-respected municipal planner with whom I generally agreed. So I found his intense dislike of our young mayor to be something that always shocked me and caught me off guard.

"If you want to be an activist, then be an activist," he had said at the village board meeting that directly preceded the mayor's arraignment on March 3. "But you have no business being an activist on the backs of local taxpayers. We have serious problems in this village. Problems that merit attention. We need to repair our side-walks, our infrastructure, make sure that people who live and work here can continue to live here and enjoy a decent quality of life."

While I wouldn't disagree with Peter's last point, I felt that he, like many of the more established New Paltz residents, weren't giving the mayor a fair shake. In my coverage of him since he took office, Jason was working diligently to try to find solutions to the problems he inherited. He combed through the budget worksheets looking for pockets of money he could cut or reduce to help offset the taxes. He worked closely with the village Department of Public Works, often going out with them to inspect a water main break or suggest ways of improving the failing infrastructure. Unfortunately, the village was unsuccessful in receiving a $120,000 State grant they had applied for to create and install three artificial reed beds into three old greenhouses at the sewage treatment plant. Jason quickly decided to work with the head of Public Works, Bleu Terwilliger and the head of Highland, New York's Water and Sewer Depart-ment, John Jankiewicz, an expert in the field of reed bed treatment of municipal sewage, to pursue his more environmentally sound vision. Their goal was to create at least one reed bed without the grant money.

I'll never forget Jason standing with Jankiewicz's granddaugh-ter, up to his knees in sludge, the rain pouring through the dilapidated greenhouse, officially planting the last reed, in what was to become one of many symbols of alternative energy and infrastructure initiatives his administration would implement. A cigarette hanging out of his mouth, his jeans drooping, his boots covered in mud, and his smile serious and proud, Jason planted the last reed and then we watched the raw sewage come flooding in. "Who says local journalists aren't muckrakers?" joked Jeremiah, who like myself was balancing delicately on a two-by-four several feet above the sludge.

It was a photo very different from the one in *The New York Times Magazine* that showed him in a tuxedo clutching a bouquet of roses. The sludge image was, in my opinion, the real Jason. While the same-sex marriages were publicly defining him, and were certainly part of his mission, his platform was actually much broader than that. Jason's greatest passion was environmentalism. His heroes were people like Jankiewicz, or Nobel Prize–winner Wangari Maathai, who started a tree-planting initiative in Kenya to reforest her country.

With some money finally weighing down his pockets, Jason wanted to install himself permanently in the village, to put his green design ideals to use and to be able to join the ranks of his home-owning critics who painted him as just another student renter, with no greater stake in the village than that of a transient looking for a warm night's sleep. He scoured the available lots in the village, which were few and far between, and found nothing.

One evening I was covering a village planning board meeting that became painfully dull. I wandered into Jason's office to ask him about an upcoming story. Before I could ask him anything, before even saying hello, he looked up from his computer and asked, "Have you ever heard of straw-bale construction?"

"Of course. I went to college in Oregon where it was all the rage with the off-the-grid hippies."

"I want to build a straw-bale home with a living roof," he said, madly clicking away at his computer. "Do you want to see a picture?"

"Sure."

He turned the computer screen towards me. There was this sort of Hobbit-like mud hovel with grass and flowers for a roof. It was something a child would hope to discover deep in the woods.

"Who would trim the roof?" I asked.

"I would!" he said.

"You'd have to get up there with a weed-whacker."

We both laughed at the thought of that.

Afterwards, I started asking around for Jason, hoping I could help our mayor find a tuft of village land to call his own. One morning when Peter Fairweather was taking a walk past our house, I thought to ask him.

"The mayor is looking for land," I said.

"Oh, he is?" said Peter.

"Yeah. He wants to build a straw-bale home in the village."

"Are you kidding me?" he said. "It's like someone beamed a cartoon character into Village Hall!"

I decided to drop the subject. I asked another friend of mine in the village if they would consider subdividing their property and selling it to Jason. "I don't want that media circus in my backyard," she said dismissively.

Jason moved from the straw-bale house idea to a pole-barn construction concept which he said he could build for less than $20,000 and then finish himself. When no lots appeared in our real-estate frenzied village, he began to look for pre-existing homes. But they had more than doubled in price since he became mayor.

"The prices are unbelievable," he complained to me once.

"You're not helping matters," I said. "Now we're featured in the "Queer Eye For Real Estate" section of *New York* magazine." In fact, the *New York Post* had also begun running stories about us in its travel and lifestyle sections. They coined New Paltz the "Birkenstock Burbs" and mentioned our same-sex marrying Green Party mayor.

"At least they won't increase the school tax burden on residents," he said.

"And the neighborhoods will look nice," I added. "But you need to get to work on affordable housing."

"I'm trying," he said earnestly. "We have a draft law in place that will require developers to include at least twenty percent affordable housing for any large subdivision plan." He *was* trying. But the circumstances had grown beyond him. It was what one friend of mine had claimed was the "unintended law of consequences."

After the *Today* show and Conan appearances, Jason was asked to lead the Gay St. Patrick's Day Parade in Queens. the *Times Herald-Record* ran a front cover picture of him with the title, "The King of Queens." "Mayor Bloomberg was two hours late, but when he finally showed up I went to shake his hand and he recoiled from me," Jason reported the following day, shocked. But the crowds went crazy for the gay-championing, straight mayor. There were throngs of signs that said, "Jason West for Governor" and "Jason West for President." This young mayor from upstate New York had become the straight poster-boy for the Gay Rights movement on the East Coast. He was a media darling and people couldn't get enough of him.

Before his decision to marry same-sex couples cast him in the national and international spotlight, Jason had already captured the interest of DreamWorks. According to Jason, DreamWorks had approached him soon after his election victory. Being the first-ever Green Party candidate in New York to make claims on a mayoral position, and only the second Green Party mayor in the nation, did not give him anywhere near the notoriety as the gay weddings would; but just the fact of a young, radical, mayor in a small upstate town had been enough of an interesting storyline to get him in the New York City papers, and soon after, to pique the interests of the movie moguls.

Apparently, the deal went sour. I never understood all of the details, but Jason said that his attorney did not adequately represent his interests and in the end the offer was not as convincing or as lucrative as he had wanted. Billiam told me that it was he and Jeffrey who convinced Jason to withdraw from the deal. "We were having this party and Jason was there, with this beautiful brown-haired girl. He was all excited about this DreamWorks deal," Billiam recounted. "When I asked him what they were proposing, he said '$50,000 for my life story!'"

According to Billiam, he and Jeffrey sat down with Jason and explained that while $50,000 might seem like a lot when you're young and in debt, in the end it would add up to very little for him and potentially big bucks for DreamWorks. "Jeffrey basically talked him out of it. Thank God!" said Billiam. "They wanted to buy the rights to his life and he was only twenty-six years old!"

It was 9:00 p.m., and I still needed some quotes from Jason to wrap up the story I was working on. He was in his office with Jonathon Wright. If I wanted to interview him I now had to sched-

80

ule meetings with Brittany, his assistant. "How's he doing?" I asked her. "He's doing okay," she said. "We're scheduling massages for him once a day and a siesta."

"Massages?"

"Yeah, a local masseuse offered to give him massages for free."

Unbelievable, I thought.

It was quiet in the office, and dark. It looked like the scene of something completely innocent or illicit depending on how the streetlight fell through the skylights. "You're keeping some late hours these days," I joked, when I was finally given access.

"I can't leave the office," he said. "I tried to go to Cabaloosa's with an old friend and catch up but was interrupted every minute by someone wanting to thank me or give me advice on my legal strategy. I think that's why I've been smoking so much. It gives me an excuse to go outside and get away from people."

"You're not going to leave here if you don't find your wallet," said Jonathon, who like Brittany was almost always flanking one side of our mayor, whispering advice, providing moral support, and helping him with life's little annoyances.

"You lost your wallet?"

"I must have lost it during those days following the weddings," he said hopelessly. "I'm supposed to catch a flight to Texas tonight and I have no ID."

"Just bring a copy of the *New York Post* and say 'Hey, this is me!'"

He laughed.

"Or just go down to the police department and ask them to give you an official letter of some kind that says you are who you say you are and that you have reported your wallet was lost or stolen. Just bring anything and everything you can. They'll let you on," I suggested.

"That's a good idea," said Jonathon.

Jason was going to be the surprise guest speaker at the National Gay Rights Organization fundraiser. "They offered to fly me out and put me up in a hotel so I said, sure. It's just a nice excuse to get away for twenty-four hours."

"That's all the incentive they gave you?" I teased. "It's not like you have any chance of getting laid in a room full of lesbians!"

"Hey, you're right. That's not fair," he said, laughing at himself.

I asked him questions for the week's edition. There were at any given time two or three stories that required him to weigh in. He reminded me of a horse standing alone in a field with a swarm of flies buzzing around him. He had to retreat into his barn for silence. But unlike the high ceilings of a barn, the mayor's office in Village Hall was a tiny cubicle with low, angled ceilings. The only components which eased the claustrophobia were the two skylights.

"All this wasted space," he said, gesticulating towards the A-frame ceilings. "I just want to knock this damn roof down and build up."

I remembered this comment later, when the popular TV drama, *Law and Order*, came out with an episode starring Mayor Jason West. In the episode, Jason is played by an actor twice his age and who has a cathedral ceiling in his office. "Not only that, but his ears are big and he eats at a place called Al's Luncheonette—whatever the hell that is!" Jason scoffed later.

Jason did get on the plane that night, much to the chagrin of the folks at our local brewpub, the Gilded Otter. They had asked him to be on hand to tap the keg of their newly brewed "Nuptial Ale." The beer party was on my story list for the week-just a brief with a photo op. The brewpub was hopping, and the manager, Rick, was anxiously looking around for Jason.

"I don't think he's coming," I said to Rick.

"What do you mean he's not coming? He told me he'd be here."

"He's in Texas."

"What the hell's he doing in Texas?"

"A gay fundraiser. He's a special guest."

"He's supposed to be our special guest!"

Prior to his overnight celebrity status, Jason was hardly punctual. He showed up more often than not to various civic functions but when he did show up, he was late. Not five or ten minutes late, but half an hour to an hour late. He was able to get away with this, I think, because he starved people with his lack of attention. Just when they were about to give up or cancel the press conference, he would show up with a broad smile, always a bear hug for the organizers, and a brief apology. It worked every time.

To maintain his credibility as an elected official, he did show up at his board meetings on time. In fact, for someone who dressed like a shabby college student, and whose home was rumored to be less than tidy, his office was surprisingly neat. The job of mayor had made him focus and call on the better parts of himself to get the job done. No matter how late he stayed out drinking, or how many days and nights he shuttled back and forth to New York City for some function or another, his files were in order, read through, highlighted, and he was ready for business come time for his twice-monthly Wednesday night village board meetings.

"Jason's personal life is one area I won't touch," said Jonathon, months after the marriages had taken place. "He gets rabidly defensive when people suggest that he not smoke in front of Village Hall or that he not hang out at Bacchus until four a.m. 'Don't go there,' he said to me. 'My personal life or how I conduct myself outside of my responsibilities as mayor is no one's concern but my own. I have a job to do and I do it. That is the only area where people have the right to criticize me.'"

His determination to live the life of a feral twenty-seven-year-old, despite the fact that he was now a world-famous, small-town radical mayor, was sincere, self-protective and oddly admirable during the politicians-as-celebrities era. Part of me really respected him for so boldly denouncing any attempt by others to judge him based on his personal preferences, i.e., smoking, drinking, and women. Could this type of off-hours behavior not be ascribed to many other politicians, most of whom were older, purportedly wiser, and more than likely married?

Yet it was also naïve on his part to think that others would see this separation of the personal and political as clearly as he did. There was public opinion to contend with and luckily for him, most people who were out at the bars in the middle of the night were the college students that would vote for him again based solely on the fact that he was under thirty and had a taste for chocolate martinis.

"This is his power base," said Jonathon pointing to the crowds of drunken twenty-somethings, when I ran into him at Cabaloosa's one night while out with friends for a rare adult birthday celebration. The place was packed, a reggae band was playing, and there was our mayor, front and center, as usual.

"I would be embarrassed if I were him," said one of my friends. "I mean he is a public official. What the hell is he doing out every night? How does he get any work done?"

"He can sleep in," I offered. "He doesn't have kids."

A few days later, I was waiting for Jason along with some other members of an ad hoc committee. When he finally pulled in thirty-five minutes late, he walked over to us carrying a jug of spring water.

"I got desperate," he said to me, pulling up his shirt sleeve to reveal something.

"You got a tattoo?" I said.

"No! The patch." He pointed to a round nicotine patch on his bicep. He had been trying to quit smoking for several weeks. "I smoked a pack and a half the other night," he admitted, sitting down and taking a long slug from his water jug. "What happened to me? I was a social smoker for years. I would have one or two at a party and that was it. But I've been smoking a pack a day for months now. I feel like shit."

"You're under a lot of stress," I suggested.

"It was the weddings that killed me. February 27."

"Was it one in particular? Or all twenty-five?"

He laughed. But I felt sorry for him. Here was a guy who suddenly had it all—a budding political career, a real civil rights feather in his leftist cap, more money than he had ever had in his young life, the adoration of many—and yet he looked absolutely miserable.

"I'm boring. That's what I keep trying to tell people," he said to me during an interview. "I don't want this to be a Jason West human interest story. I want this to be about the movement which started long before I stepped in and will go on without me."

84

Only a month after that statement and after adamantly denying the rumor to Deb a week before, Jason appeared in the June 28 issue of *People* magazine as one of the "Top 50 Hottest Bachelors" in the country. Here was our Green Party mayor, sandwiched between pop icons like Ben Affleck and Orlando Bloom, being profiled as one of America's hottest bachelors for his role as the Justice of the Peace for twenty-five gay couples in a small village in upstate New York.

"Aspiring First Ladies of New Paltz entertaining visions of political grandeur should know that West pulls in only $8,000 a year for his duties and still rooms with three buddies in a house with a skateboarding half-pipe in the backyard," cautioned the article. "If that picture appeals, West says he is looking for someone intelligent, beautiful, funny and easy to get along with. Bigots are a big no!"

It was the talk of the small town. "Hot off the presses!" my mother exclaimed as she walked into our house wielding a copy of the magazine, after returning from a day of working in Manhattan. Deb's going to kill him, I thought. She was becoming increasingly skeptical of Jason and tended to lean towards the depiction of him as a headline grabber and opportunist. But she had told me that when she asked him, straight up, if the rumor was true, that he denied it. Not only did he deny it, but he went on and on about how humiliating that would be.

That same night was a village board meeting. I was walking into Village Hall when Jason pulled up on his bike. "So, how does it feel to be one of the country's hottest bachelors, Mr. Mayor?" I said, showing him his glamour shot in *People*.

"Oh, my god. That is *so* embarrassing," he said, grabbing the magazine from me to get a closer look. "I haven't seen this yet. That doesn't even look like me. It looks like a mask of me." In the photo, Jason was leaning out of a vintage car and stroking a handsome looking dog. He had a big horse grin and what looked to be a lot of eyeliner and mascara. "Where did you get the car and the dog?" I asked.

"The car is Rebecca's and the dog's my neighbor's. They just came one day for the photo shoot and liked these props," he said. "I didn't realize that it would look like this." He took a deep drag off his cigarette. I realized that the patch must not have done the trick. He handed the magazine back to me. "Why did you let us get scooped?" I asked. "Deb said that you denied the rumor. Not only denied it, but expounded on the reasons why you would never stoop this low."

"All I said was that it was a rumor, which it was. I didn't lie," he said. "It was part of the contractual agreement I signed that I couldn't leak it to the press until the issue hit the stand. I didn't know it was coming out this soon." Like the TV appearances and the profile in the *Times Magazine*, Jason said that he agreed to be included in *People*'s big bachelor edition to "help advance gay rights and talk about the Green Party platform." He truly seemed pained, so I let it go.

I could tell that while it might have helped to further his agenda to a massive audience, locally it didn't always sit so well, particularly with some high-minded liberals who supported him. "When my husband and I saw that we both said at the same time, 'sell-out,'" remarked one of my friends who lived in the village. "He's peddled himself as this anti-corporate, anti-consumer radical but then he does this glamour shot for *People*?"

Rachel had her own take on Jason's recent celebrity. "He is certainly someone who was not out looking for fame," she told me. "That was a complete shock to him. I'm not saying that there aren't aspects of it he's enjoying. Who wouldn't? Is he arrogant? Absolutely, but the media is coming to him. And I know for a fact that he turns down way more requests than he accepts. Besides, fame is just a distraction."

No matter where you went, someone had an opinion about Jason. They loved him, usually for his politics and radical idealism, or they hated him because they felt he was a "sell-out" or an "opportunist," but most of the dislike seemed to stem from a rootless source, just some visceral reaction to a young man having risen so high so fast, and having done so by one simple act of courage. Even our accountant, Kevin, had to put in his two bits while Kazik and I were filing our returns.

"That punk," he said to me as soon as I sat down to go over the numbers.

"Who?" I asked.

"That punk mayor you guys got over in New Paltz."

"Are you opposed to gay marriage?" I asked, assuming that was the reason for his assault on Jason.

"Not at all. But what I am opposed to is this kid claiming the status of a civil rights hero. If he truly believed in what he was doing then he would have kept on marrying those people. Instead, he gets slapped on the wrist from the judge and he stops. If you are going to stand up for something, then *stand up*. Did the civil rights activists get off the bus? Did they leave the all-white counter? Did they stop marching when they were being beaten alive?"

I tried to lighten things up. "He stopped because he felt he could do more outside of jail than inside of jail, though now he says that a year in jail might give him a chance to catch up on some rest," I told Kevin, trying to make him laugh.

I kept thinking that the world is filled with critics. No matter what Jason did, or how he did it, just the act of taking a stand for something would generate as much criticism as accolades. If he hadn't gone through with the marriages after the DA gave him a warning, then many of his supporters and certainly the gay community would have been disappointed. By deciding to go ahead, critics said that he should have pursued other legal avenues. As for the publicity, he was damned if he did and damned if he didn't. He could avoid the press, piss them off, and look like he had something to hide, or worse yet, he could have abandoned the gay rights movement altogether, leaving that camp without a powerful straight ally.

I realized how much inner strength a public official needs to have. Any attempt to affect change is second-guessed and scrutinized from every angle. You just can't win, I thought to myself.

"It's sad that people are so ready to tear someone down as soon as they start to have any success or achieve something," said my friend, Mary Marshall, whose son Nicholas was in the same preschool as Seamus. She had taken her boys to see the weddings, and we both laughed over the fact that we had to respond to questions from our four-year-olds as to whether or not men can marry men and women can marry women.

"Might as well deal with it now," I said to her. "If we normalize it, it won't seem so shocking later and you never really know which way they're going to go."

Growing up in the 1970s in a fairly traditional home, I was not introduced to gays and lesbians at a young age, certainly not at Seamus' age. In fact, the first time the concept of homosexuality was presented to me, at age 11, was when I snuck into our TV room to watch HBO illicitly while my parents were out.

The movie I watched that night was *Personal Best*, an intriguing tale of two female Olympic runners who were friends and training partners. I, being the girl jock that I was, loved a good sports story and sat in my dad's easy chair, eating a bowl of cornflakes, completely absorbed in the film. At one point, the two female athletes were running on the beach and ended up tackling each other on a sand dune. The next thing I saw was them taking off their clothes and kissing, rolling passionately around in the sand. I threw my cereal down and went running through the house, screaming in shock.

My sister came running out of her bedroom, Ted Nugent blasting from her eight-track. "What?" she said nervously, looking up and down the hallway as if for an intruder. "What happened? Why are you screaming?"

"Because there are two women kissing!" I said, breathless from the sheer horror of it.

"What are you talking about?" she said, now utterly perplexed.

"On the TV," I whispered, feeling dirty just from having seen what I saw. "They're kissing on the TV."

My sister broke it down for me in her own clumsy way. Looking back now, I think she did a pretty good job. "I know it's weird," she said. "But there are some guys who like guys and some girls who like girls. I don't know why but they do."

"Don't tell Mom and Dad," I said, still feeling ashamed.

"I won't," she said, and we sat on the bed listening to her new Styx album.

Mary started laughing when I recounted this story to her. She, having grown up in Woodstock, had a little more exposure than I had, but she agreed that we were having to tackle the subject, since it was on the front page of all the local and regional papers, a lot sooner than we might have thought.

"I think it's great that Jason did what he did and that he is getting public recognition for it," she added. "That helps the cause and also helps him. He's only twenty-seven. Of course he's going to make some mistakes along the way, but how many twenty-seven-year-olds are political activists and are out there trying to make a difference?"

My mother concurred. "There are some people who don't like the mayor for whatever reasons," she mused. "But what I remind them of is the fact that he risked going to jail. That he risked his career. And he did this not for himself, but for the gay community!"

"I think the reason that the media was so drawn to this story is because it dealt with a young, straight, Green mayor in an upstate New York village," said Susan Zimet. "People expect to see something like this in San Francisco or in Massachusetts, but not in a small upstate town. People imagine it's Hickville up here. But what they come to find is this dynamic, somewhat cosmopolitan town with gun-toting hunters, rabid environmentalists, multigenerational farmers, and now a Green Party mayor, barely out of college, who decides to marry gay couples in the village parking lot, the DA be damned. Now *that's* a story."

Chapter 6
Humble Beginnings

What had been appealing about Jason as a mayoral candidate was that he truly *lived* in the village. In fact, he lived directly above the *New Paltz Times* office on Church Street, downtown, a coincidence that became quite convenient for the paper, both before and after he was elected.

Many small towns and villages have difficulty recruiting anyone decent to run for local office. While that has never been the case in New Paltz, where there is an army of political soldiers lining up for nearly every post, the May 2003 village elections for the mayor's chair and two trustee seats created a windfall of interest.

By early March there were ten official candidates, running on four different slates—including six Democrats, three Greens, and one Independent, a janitor from P&G's bar—all vying for the three available seats. While our staff at the paper hashed out the pros and cons of each candidate, it was Deb, typically among the more conservative in the group of left-leaning writers, who oddly enough championed Jason.

"The thing about Jason is that he's on the streets of the village," she said. "He knows everyone, he talks to everyone, and I think that gives him a real good sense of what the issues are. He's a real people's candidate."

I agreed. While I admired the other two candidates for mayor—Tom Nyquist and Robert Feldman—I actually agreed with all of Jason's platform issues: sustainable infrastructure, open space preservation, open government and "in-fill development," a concept that was later echoed by our famous New York State Senator, Hillary Rodham Clinton, who would visit New Paltz a year after Jason was elected.

Before being elected mayor, Jason was nothing more, and certainly nothing less, than one of 6,000 threads in the village tapestry that kept us all bound together for better or worse. Although friendly and chatty with friends or acquaintances on the street—many of whom might be playing a bongo or a guitar, or stringing beads—he could often be found alone, strolling to and from the post office, or riding his bike through the village streets. Jason had always been a high-visibility guy. He was either eating breakfast at the Bistro, drinking with friends at Bacchus, carting home various newspapers from Jack's, or loading and unloading his paint supplies in and out of his Ford Taurus on Church Street—as he was, up until the same-sex marriage implosion, the owner and sole employee of his business, *Blue Sky House Painting*. Besides operating a house painting business, Jason's other passion was his work with the Arm of the Sea environmental puppetry group, peddling its pro-conservation ideology both locally as well as in inner-city schools in New York City.

While the events of February 27 would cast him in his role as a gay-marriage advocate extraordinaire, his notoriety had begun nine months earlier, when he shocked this small hamlet and won the four-way race for mayor, ousting sixteen-year incumbent Tom Nyquist and seven-year village trustee Robert Feldman from their well-worn seats.

The Greens had entered the race late. They were recruited, pushed and supported by Rachel. And it wasn't until Rachel, ever on the lookout for good Green Party candidates to run in local races, had successfully recruited Julia Walsh and Rebecca Rotzler that Jason even agreed to run. Julia was the key student attraction, with her work at Synthesis, a not-for-profit student activist organization that she had single-handedly founded and fostered. At twenty-three years old, Julia was often dressed in jeans and a poet's blouse, her long, straight, dirty blonde hair cascading down to her back. Some days she reminded me of a Rubens model clothed in 1960s garb. Her cheeks, like Jason's, often flushed red under criticism. She had a warmth to her, a genuine affection. She claimed she wanted to change the world—make students active in local politics, end any wars, discrimination, environmental degradation, and other unseemly ramifications of our modern, corporate, consumerist world.

Rebecca was a mother of one and an activist. She was an Alaskan Eskimo with short bangs and long, straight black hair that reached almost to her waist. Like Jason, she was a familiar face at board meetings, advocating for certain progressive policies and en-vironmental legislation or protesting what she believed to be any form of potential police brutality, like the pepper-ball gun the police had wanted to purchase. While I was confident that Jason could be effective on the board, I had little faith that Julia had what it took, and wasn't sure about Rebecca. In the end, it would be Rebecca, a forty-two-year-old single mother with a full-time day job, that worked as hard or possibly harder than anyone else, to live up to her role as a village trustee. I would learn that while Rebbeca didn't draw the spotlight as naturally as Jason did, her heart was always in the right place, and that she would work ceaselessly to make the Village of New Paltz a better, more socially and environ-mentally sound place to live.

I had been telling Rachel for years that the best way to pro-mote the Green cause was to put Jason in a leadership position. He had the skills, intelligence, humor and sociability that could prove to be successful. Candidates like Rebecca or Julia, I feared, would only appeal to special interest groups or secular voting blocks. Jason, however, with his conservative good looks, easy personality and clever mind, could appeal to many, convince some, and eventually push the Green ideology forward.

"I'm trying," she would say. "But he won't commit."

Rachel saw the value in Jason before others did, and she also saw the potential for a Green slate to win the village elections a year earlier. She even has a copy of an e-mail that she sent to Steve Greenfield, the local Green Party secretary, one year before the village race, stating that a Green candidate might finally have a chance to secure a political seat.

In the span of a year, Rachel worked unceasingly to convince Jason to run for mayor. "He would say yes, then he would say no. He would say things like, 'It would be so great if we were in power' and the next week he would say, 'I don't want to talk about village politics! I don't want to run,' and walk away from me."

"He wanted to win this one," she mused, as I sat with her and Ryszard at Bacchus one night while they regaled me of how the Greens had come to power in the village.

Jason had already been the local Green Party's sacrificial lamb twice for the position of New York State assembly, running against Democratic incumbent, Kevin Cahill. He knew that there was no great glory in running for a seat you could never win. While he had always volunteered to advance the Green platform by not allowing a candidate for a political office to go uncontested, Rachel sensed that Jason was interested in running for mayor only if he believed he had a good chance of winning. To convince him that it was possible, Rachel had to solicit strong running mates. This was not easy.

Ryszard, who remains a behind-the-scenes Green supporter, believed that Jason's ego was the driving force behind his last-minute decision to run. "Rachel said at some point that she would run a candidate whether or not it ended up being Jason," he recalled. "So she called a meeting together with all of these potential candidates. Jason happened to walk in and see this. That got him. He didn't want to run and lose, but he also didn't want someone else to run and win on the Green ticket."

"He didn't just walk in," Rachel corrected her husband as she sipped from her rum and Coke. "I had invited him but of course he showed up late. But you're right, he did look annoyed."

Rachel claims that the deciding moment for Jason came early Tuesday morning on March 3, 2003. "I was fed up with begging him," she said. With the elections less than a few weeks away, Rachel went ahead and reserved a table for 10 a.m., out in front of the college's Student Union Building to gather signatures on a petition "naming Andrew as the Green candidate for mayor," she recounted proudly. Andrew is Rachel's dog, a little rat terrier that goes everywhere with her, including her office on campus.

"You mean it was Jason or your dog for mayor?" I asked, laughing so hard I almost choked on a piece of ice.

"Yes," she said, hinting that she wouldn't have minded too much if her dog had been the first canine candidate in New Paltz. "I was tired of begging him and it was Nyquist or Feldman over my dead body!"

Only minutes before 10 a.m., Rachel received a call from Julia telling her that she and Jason and Rebecca had finally agreed to run.

"I think that Jason must have found out that I was prepared to run my dog, and that did it. Of course, I was planning on turning over all of Andrew's signatures to Jason if he changed his mind down the road."

The rest is history, but not the history that Jason, Rebecca, and Julia would recount to the press. According to their story, they were all celebrating Rebecca's birthday, the same evening that the United States began their military assault on Afghanistan and eventually Iraq. "Since we were powerless to do anything globally about the pre-emptive war in the Middle East, we decided that we *could* do something locally," Jason told me when I interviewed him for our pre-election coverage.

Only in New Paltz, I thought to myself. Not only are dogs potential candidates for mayor but later, to get out the student vote, Jason's supporters would take turns dressing up in a chicken suit on campus to catch the students' attention and direct them down to Village Hall on the day of elections.

"Did he really dress up in a chicken suit?" one friend asked me after Jason had achieved a certain amount of celebrity status and these types of errant details and rumors became intriguing. I wasn't sure, so I asked Rachel while we had a second round of drinks.

"No!" she scoffed, pulling her long brown hair behind her ears. "Jason would *never* wear a chicken suit. But we did have some other people do it. I think there were three or four in all. One was even a break-dancing chicken."

Rachel, with Ryszard and I listening intently, went on to describe the chicken suit as if it, in and of itself, were a piece of art.

"It's a fantastic chicken suit," she said. "It's very realistic with a rubbery head and a furry body. It comes with red stockings but not all of the chickens agreed to wear them. It also got really stinky so I would run to the Faculty Tower bathroom and try to wash the sweat out before the next person put it on."

As Rachel explained it, even giving us a quick imitation, the chicken would do little dances and tell the students that if they walked down to Village Hall and voted for the Green's "Innovation Campaign" that they would "make the chicken very happy," and possibly entice him to do a special dance.

Suddenly, the smile left Rachel's face and she stared down at the wooden table. "We did have one unfortunate incident where one of our chickens was harassing women, but we won't dwell on that," she said, flinging her hand back and fourth as if to chase the groping chicken image away.

"A chicken that harassed female students?" I asked, thinking that this story couldn't get any more bizarre.

She stirred her drink and looked thoughtful.

"Because the costume obscures identity, I think that this one chicken couldn't help but try and peck at females passing by."

This time, I laughed so hard that my diet Coke went up my nose. I couldn't wait to go home and translate this story to Kazik.

Village elections were always exciting to me. Not because they were sexy, but because they were small and intimate, with typically no more than 500 to 1,000 people voting in any one race. Unlike town board elections, or state or federal elections, the village race took place in the spring as opposed to November with everyone voting at the same location, downtown at the village firehouse meeting room. It was cozy. All of the players were there: the candidates, or their representatives; party organizers; local, politically minded residents; the village clerk; the elderly elections inspectors.

Rather than having to wait for the numbers to be calculated and called in from various voting locations, the village races allowed for interested parties, including the media, to be "locked-in" once the polls closed at 9 p.m. It was often hot and sweaty, the air sticky with anticipation and dread.

It took on average about twenty minutes for the inspectors and village clerk to calculate the numbers from the three voting booths. Then they would call out the results, with the candidates' reactions to their subsequent victory or defeat right there for all to see.

As the local reporter, I was secretly embarrassed to have missed what many people later saw as an obvious political maneuver by the Greens. "They saw a great opportunity and went after it," said Susan Zimet. "I said that to Jeremiah Horrigan two weeks before the election. I told him, 'Nyquist and Feldman are going to split the vote and the Greens are going to round up the college students and vote West in.' It was painfully obvious. Tom and Robert were campaigning against each other, not taking the Greens seriously enough. One of them should have just agreed to step down."

Feldman had served as Nyquist's protégé on the village board for seven years. "During the last race I expressed my interest in running for mayor but Tom said that he was not ready to retire," said Feldman. "I told him that I would support him for another term if he agreed to let me run in 2003, which he said he would."

Nyquist never admitted to this conversation, and decided to throw his veteran hat into the race after Feldman announced his decision to run in the winter of 2002–2003. Tension had already been developing between the former political allies and running mates, as Feldman had emerged a very vocal trustee, one who wanted to work closely with the town and who had formed a very close relationship with Town Supervisor Wilen.

Nyquist, on the other hand, ever suspicious of the town, had guarded village interests close to his chest in an effort to protect duplication of village taxpayer dollars. But some could argue that he also wanted to keep a tight rein on his little kingdom.

Election Day finally rolled around.

"How do you think it's going?" I asked Floyd Kniffen, one of Feldman's two running mates, who was standing outside the Village Hall waiting for the polls to close. "Not too good," he said. "I think the Green's are going to win."

"What?" I said.

"Have you been out here at all today?"

"No, I just got here."

"There have been droves of students coming in," said Floyd looking bummed.

Jeremiah said the same thing. "This is going to be a big upset," he said.

"But do you think that just Jason will win, or Julia and Rebecca as well?"

"I think it's going to be a sweep," he said confidently.

When Jean Gallucci, the village clerk, went to lock the doors at 9 p.m., Feldman and Nyquist were nowhere to be found. Apparently they too had gotten word from reliable sources, obviously much more politically savvy than I, that West and his Green Party crew were poised to win the race.

Jason was sitting in an old wooden swivel chair with his Carhart jacket on and granny glasses. He looked nervous.

"I heard you might win," I said to him.

"I hope so," he said.

There were murmurs and whispers among the spectators. Only two candidates were present besides Jason: Tom Cotton, a trustee and loyal supporter of Nyquist, and Floyd. The rest were holed up in a local bar or at home awaiting the results.

I couldn't imagine how the candidates felt during this twenty-minute vote-counting interval. But my stomach was clenched tight, already anticipating that a number of contestants would have to lose, and my sympathy for them was beginning to swell.

The chatter abruptly stopped when Jean stood up with a piece of paper in her hands.

"The votes for the candidates for mayor are as follows," she said.

"Jason West, 322, Tom Nyquist, 258, Robert Feldman, 255, Carl Heissenbuttel (the janitor), 34."

The cheers were loud. Jason's face turned bright red. We hugged. "You did it!" I said.

"I did, didn't I?" he asked, looking as shocked as many village residents would the next day when they opened their morning papers to discover that their new mayor was twenty-six, a Green, a housepainter, and a radical environmentalist.

The cheers and congratulations had to be subdued to allow Jean to call out the results from the six-way board race. Only two would win.

"The votes for trustees are as follows: 343 for Julia Walsh, 342 for Rebecca Rotzler...."

"Holy shit!" I said to Jeremiah. "It's a sweep."

Of course the media swarmed Jason as he was receiving congratulatory handshakes from Floyd and other losing candidates. He was also busy hugging and kissing his running mates, and adjusting his glasses. I stayed back for a moment or two, knowing the dailies had very little time to file their story and very little space to quote Jason at length. Two advantages of a weekly paper: time and space.

Elections, which always take place on a Tuesday night, forced us to hold the paper. Typically, it's put to bed by 4 p.m. on Tuesday afternoon, but during elections, it's not laid to rest until I finish writing the story.

"We had no idea what was going to happen today," said Jason. "We were out there knocking on doors, making phone calls, trying to get people to vote up until 9 p.m. Obviously our message was well-received. We attempted to unite the college campus and the village. It wasn't a college vs. village race—it was about uniting the entire community."

Jason talked about his two previous bids for a State assembly seat. "I think all of that work in the past five years has culminated today," he said. "Those other races weren't about me; they were an effort to garner support and awareness, and help educate the public on Green Party issues." Jason went on to reiterate his platform which called for sustainable, renewable energy sources and infrastructure.

In the span of a twelve-hour voting day, the village of New Paltz had witnessed a radical changing of the guards. Seeing Jason's beat-up vehicle parked outside Village Hall or hearing Rebecca speak at fundraisers for the volunteer fire department would later become commonplace: on May 6, 2003, it was a shock.

"What do people think is going to happen?" asked Rebecca, in response to fears some of the resident homeowners were airing in the local press. "They're going to wake up tomorrow and everything is still going to look the same, maybe a little *greener*," she said with a laugh. "But we all live in the village, care about the village and want to work to make it the best place it can be. Is there something so terribly dangerous about that?"

While it is always enjoyable to talk with the winner, whose excitement and relief is intoxicating on some level, it is equally unenjoyable, if not downright painful, to talk to the loser, or in this case, the losers. I knew it would be especially tough talking to Nyquist, who had served at the helm for so long, only to be ousted by someone less than half his age. Although it was only a block away, it felt like a long walk from the Village Hall to McGillicuddy's Bar and Restaurant on the corner of Plattekill and Main, where Nyquist and his running mates were headquartered with their small, very somber entourage.

Obviously, Nyquist, like Zimet and Jeremiah and almost everyone else I spoke with that night, had some previous knowledge and understanding that Jason and his "Innovation Campaign" were going to be victorious.

"I have prepared something and it will speak for itself," said Nyquist, who, anchored by his wife and running mates, was seated in a corner of the dark bar, the neon glare of the Budweiser sign casting a mournful glow on his face. He handed me a press statement that he must have written only an hour or two earlier. Besides noting that he was a fortunate man to have such a supportive family and group of friends, his statement went on to take the newly elected "Innovation Campaign" to task.

"Obviously, I don't like to lose, particularly having devoted as many years as I have to our community.... But I am sorry to see the

Green Party elected. They were the spoilers in the presidential election, and now they have used the students, most of whom are ill-informed on New Paltz community issues, to get themselves elected. They have set a precedent of students determining who will provide the leadership of our community. Further, they have introduced for the first time a national party into village elections, which have until now been non-partisan."

"I'm sorry, Tom," I said, as gently as I could. "You did a great job as mayor."

He nodded and turned away, both of us embarrassed by his loss.

When I left McGillicuddy's, I all but ran to *The New Paltz Times* office, just half a block down the road. The editorial posse was standing outside waiting for the news.

I felt like a doctor or nurse coming out of the hospital room to announce, "It's a girl!" or "It's a boy!" Their eyes scrutinized me trying to determine what I would say just seconds before I could say it.

"Green sweep!" I shouted.

"No!" said Mala.

"Oh, my god," said Deb.

Julie took a deep drag off her cigarette. "Wow!" she exhaled.

"Nyquist wrote a real bitter statement," I reported. "He wouldn't even talk to me. He looked so angry and defeated."

"He should have stepped down," said Mala.

"That's what everyone is saying, but it's too late now," I said.

"Do you need for me to call Feldman?" I asked Deb. "I talked to Floyd, Jason and Rebecca, and I have Nyquist's statement."

"Just write," she said and gestured towards her computer.

And so I wrote.

There was always a real sense of camaraderie on election night in the village. The editorial staff gossiped outside the office door, letting anyone and everyone know the news, while I wrote furiously, feeling the weight of the entire production team in Kingston who were waiting for me and me alone to file the story so that they could put the paper to bed and get some shut-eye themselves.

I had asked my mother to stay at our house with Seamus and Tadeusz until we could get home. Kazik had to walk around the village with Zofia, who was at the time only three months old, in one of those Swedish Baby Bjorns in an effort to keep her close to me in case she needed to nurse. I thought, "Is this how other people work?"

"What do you think of this picture?" asked Deb, showing me a file photo of Jason when he had one of those trendy goatees.

"He looks more like a revolutionary poet than he does a future mayor, but it works."

"I'm going to use it," she said and joined the others on the office stoop.

"It's done!" I announced.

"Is she sleeping?" I called out the door to Kazik who was walking up and down Church Street with the baby, talking on his cell phone.

He nodded yes.

"What does this mean?" I said to no one in particular.

"I think it's exciting," said Julie.

"It's certainly going to shake things up," said Deb.

"Will we all be driving electric cars and living in solar energy homes and composting our own waste by the end of his four-year term?" I joked.

"I won't be!" said Deb. "I live in the town."

"I think Jason is extremely capable," I added. "The others, I'm not so sure about." I asked Kazik if he was ready to head home.

"Ryszard called me and they're all celebrating at Cabaloosa's. Do you want to go in for one drink?" he asked.

"You want to take the baby into Grab-a-Loser?" I asked incredulously. "She's sleeping, it's going to be packed in there—and don't forget my mother is waiting for us so she can go home."

"Just one drink?" he pleaded. "You're a Green too, you should celebrate!"

It was hard for me to say no to him when it came to his Polish friends. Having been born in a small village in southeast Poland during the Communist era, Kazik was forced to leave his native land, along with five of his seven brothers and sisters, and go to France in hopes of seeking better economic opportunity and personal liberty.

When we married and began our family, he left both cultures behind to come to New Paltz. Within a few years, he had established a small circle of Polish friends as well as a dozen or more French friends. But it was the relationship with his Polish comrades that really nourished and energized him. Ironically, many of these friends were Green Party enthusiasts. Worlds kept colliding.

"Okay," I said. "One drink."

The music was pouring out onto the streets from the small bar, located on Main Street, just kitty-corner from the *New Paltz Times* office. They were charging a $5 cover, capitalizing on the Green victory and the knowledge that hundreds of students, activists and Green Party members would be lining up shots of tequila and singing "Hail to the Chief."

Jason was there, front and center, when we walked in after getting one of those annoying plastic bands secured around our wrists. He looked ecstatic. He hugged me and swung me around. He gave Kazik a hearty handshake. Then he introduced me to his mother. "You must be so proud," I said.

"What?" she said, the music drowning out any chance of verbal communication.

"YOU MUST BE VERY PROUD!" I repeated louder.

She nodded her head yes and looked at her son who had two shots of tequila in hand. Kazik immediately found Ryszard who offered to buy us all shots. I passed on the shot but said a glass of merlot would hit the spot. It was a wild scene. People were dancing and shouting and hugging. Rachel was crying.

"I'm so happy," she said, and one thing Rachel never attested to was happiness; there were always too many injustices being committed and too many battles to fight.

A year later, when the same-sex marriage implosion began reverberating through the village, Ryszard boasted proudly to me

103

about the role his wife had in Jason's election. "Without Rachel, there would be no Green Party majority on the village board, there would be no Mayor West, and without Mayor West there would be no same-sex marriages in New Paltz, or the entire avalanche effect," said Ryszard. "That's the truth." I loved how fiercely proud he was of his wife's achievements.

"I don't even talk directly to Jason anymore," said Rachel months later. "If I need to communicate with him I talk to Jonathon, who then talks to him. It's a weird relationship. It has some mother-son overtones—but my dog irritates him, my kids irritate him and his ego irritates me. But I'm a supporter, not a critic. Even if he is a dick sometimes, he's *our* dick, and you can't cut off your own dick, now can you?"

Regardless of any interpersonal chafing between the two, Rachel would do anything to defend Jason and help ensure his success.

"Why did I want Jason to be mayor so badly?" she mused. "Because I trusted him to do the right thing for the environment and for social justice. And I still do."

The two first met six years earlier when Jason was still an undergraduate at SUNY New Paltz and very active in the student Green Party, an organization that has since folded. The Lagodkas had recently moved back to town after Rachel completed her under-graduate degree in Washington, D.C. They purchased an old Victorian home that, thanks to Kazik's handy work, is now painted bright purple with eggplant trim—a conscious pro-gay color choice that was executed two years prior to the same-sex ceremonies which would take place, unbeknownst to them or anyone, directly across the street from their house at the Village Hall parking lot.

"I was looking for allies to help me fight McDonald's," she explained to me that night at Bacchus, when I asked her how she had become involved with Jason and the local Greens. According to Rachel, while she was busy raising two young girls and struggling to make ends meet, she had stumbled upon some studies that convinced her that McDonald's was the leading perpetrator of all social and environmental ills in the world. In her activist mind, she also believed it might be the easiest to stop.

According to Rachel and most Greens worldwide, the McDonald's fast-food chain is the largest corporate polluter. They purchase the largest amounts of industrial farm and slaughterhouse meat, and their food is high-fat and high-salt—two qualities with a direct link to obesity and high blood pressure. "What makes me crazy is that their number-one target is kids!" she said. "Not only kids, but specifically kids in low-income areas."

At the time, Rachel believed naïvely that if she could just convince people to stop eating at the fast-food chain that she could help save the world. She decided to go to the campus Green Party, which was very strong at the time, to help garner support for her anti-McDonald's campaign. That was where she first encountered a young, long-haired, undergraduate activist named Jason West.

"He was totally receptive to my thoughts and ideas," she remembered. "And I could always count on him to show up for a protest. I really liked him. Sure, he was good-looking, intelligent and charismatic, but he was also a dedicated Green Party activist."

Although the Greens in New Paltz and in the rest of New York enjoyed a brief glory of ballot status in New York when Grandpa Munster ran for Governor, after that it was an uphill battle, at least until May 6, 2003. For that one night, inside Cabaloosa's, Rachel and Ryszard drank and danced and kissed. It had all come together for her, for them, for Jason and most importantly, for the local Green Party.

Hungover or not, Jason showed up the next morning at The Bakery to get his usual bagel and coffee.

"Say hello to your new mayor," he said to the girls who worked behind the counter.

It wouldn't be an easy first few months for the young house-painting mayor. The former administration shunned him and his trustees, completely leaving them out on their own trying to make sense of the village, the budget, and the policies they were inheriting. Those who had supported Feldman or Nyquist continuously showed up at village board meetings criticizing everything the new board attempted to do.

Many of the dailies would run sarcastic if not downright condescending articles about the new administration. One of the worst, according to Jason, was a front-page article in The *Times Herald-Record* with a full-page picture of Jason walking his bicycle on Church Street and a headline that read: "Dude—Where's My Office?"

February 27, 2004

The Weddings

Photos courtesy of Susan Zimet

New Paltz same-sex marriages caused a media frenzy.

Mayor Jason West, assisted by Deputy Mayor Rebecca Rotzler, presided over twenty-four same-sex marriages amidst crowds of supporters and protestors.

Major Jeffrey McGowan and Billiam van Roestenberg,
the first couple to be married by West.

New Paltz and Mayor West in the glare of the spotlight.

March 3, 2004

The Arraignment

*New Paltz Town
Justice Jonathan Katz*

*Ulster County District
Attorney Don Williams*

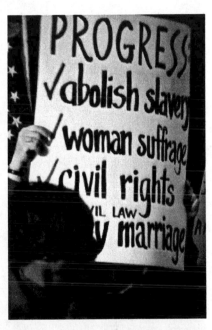

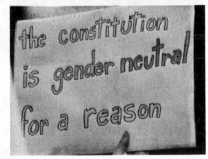

March 6, 2004

More Weddings

*Unitarian ministers Kay Greenleaf and Dawn Sangrey
conducted more same-sex marriages.*

Palm Sunday, 2004

The Protest

The Phelps family of the Westboro Baptist Church descended upon New Paltz to preach their message.

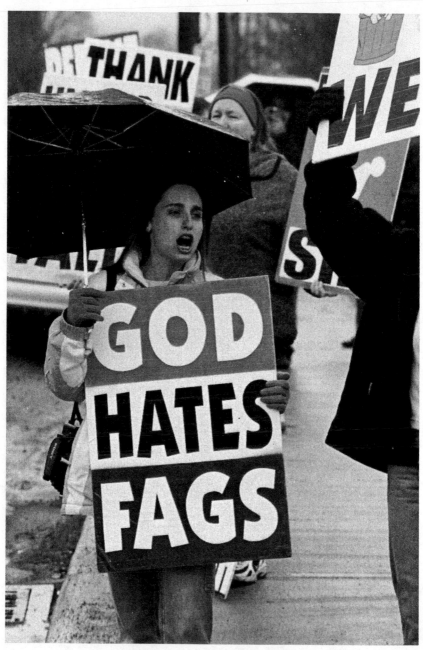

*Sarah Phelps, granddaughter of Westboro
Baptist leader Fred Phelps.*

Palm Sunday, 2004

The Counter-protest

The community, along with local churches and businesses respond to WBC.

The Times Herald Record *reporter Jeremiah Horrigan pictured with animal activist Marion Dubois.*

Author Erin Quinn interviewed Mayor John Shields of Nyack, New York.

Detective Lucchesi of the New Paltz Police Department with fellow officer.

Rachel Lagodka, aka Deep Love.

Fall 2004 / Winter 2005

The New Paltz
Social Society

U.S. Congressman Maurice Hinchey with Susan Zimet at fundraiser hosted by New Paltz Social Society.

County Legislator Susan Zimet, Mayor Jason West, Attorney Andrew Kossover, and Billiam van Roestenberg with the Out on a Limb awards.

Chapter 7
Dream Team

Rumors began to fly the moment the "Innovation Campaign" candidates were elected. "I heard that at their organizational meeting they decided that they would no longer recite the Pledge of Allegiance at board meetings," said one former village official.

"I didn't know that they even had a re-organizational meeting yet," I responded. Immediately I was on the horn with Jason, who was up on a ladder painting the trim of an old house. "You had a re-organizational meeting?"

"Oh yeah, it was no big deal, Julia couldn't even be there," said our new mayor.

"Jason, it *is* a big deal. One of your main platforms during the campaign was 'open government,' yet there was no press release announcing the meeting. How were we supposed to know?"

"I'm sorry," he said sincerely. "I thought someone was supposed to call you."

I asked him if there was any interesting news to report. At first he couldn't think of anything. "Oh yeah," he said, asking me to hold on while he switched his cell phone from one hand to the other so that he could reach the trim on the other side of the ladder.

"We hired a new village attorney. His name is Spencer McLaughlin, and get this—he's a Republican!"

"So not only did you young radicals oust a lawyer who has safeguarded village interests for more than thirty years, but you decided to replace him with a Republican? No wonder you didn't let the press know about your meeting," I joked.

"Yeah, but what you didn't know is that he also has a degree in seventeenth-century English literature."

I started laughing, imagining a Republican lawyer trying to corral a bunch of young Greens by quoting lines from Shakespeare to them.

"People are saying that you're not going to recite the Pledge at the meetings," I added, trying to get a sense of where things were really headed with this new board.

"What? Where did they get that from?" he said, shocked by the rumor.

I didn't tell him the rest of the rumors that were flying, because I didn't want to give him a heart attack or cause him to fall off the ladder before he was even inaugurated. One nasty rumor was that Jason's money came not from house painting but from drug dealing. Another was that Julia Walsh had slept in and missed their first meeting. Yet another was that the newly elected board had plans to clean house and fire everyone in the Village Hall only to replace them with their friends from the Green Party and NORML (National Organization for the Reform of Marijuana Law). These were only a few. But none of them, to my knowledge, had any basis in reality.

The newly elected board's first decision together was a significant one, and involved who they would hire to replace Jack Zand, the village attorney for more than thirty years. In fact, Jack was really the only village employee that the new administration decided to replace. Everyone else stayed, and almost all of them would get substantial raises in the next year—except for the building inspector, Alison Murray, which only encouraged her to hate Jason even more.

Spencer McLaughlin was one of ten lawyers who were interviewed for the post, and he became the board's top choice. The veteran lawyer and Republican Orange County Legislator, located about 30 miles closer to New York City than Ulster County, described himself as "a child of my times."

"As a young man I was absolutely, unalterably opposed to the Vietnam War and did what I could to help the movement. You have to remember that we were raised as young kids in the 1950s to believe that if you were truly right, you would prevail. And we did not see anything 'right' about the Vietnam War. So our parents really got what they raised—a bunch of revolutionaries."

At first glance, sixty-year-old Spencer McLaughlin might not have appeared to be the logical choice for the radical Green Party majority village board. He had your standard good ol' boy look—adorned always in a tailored suit with a leather brief case, neatly trimmed salt-and-pepper hair and a low, reasoned authoritative voice. But like almost anyone else who was drawn into the textural New Paltz vacuum, Spencer's textural past and proclivity towards poetry allowed him to fit right in with the young activists while at the same time helped to legitimize their decisions to the larger public by his Republican vote of confidence.

Born on New Year's Day in 1945 in Tuxedo, New York, the young aspiring poet indulged his passions at St. John's University in Jamaica, Queens, where he graduated in 1967 with a bachelor's degree in English and a minor in philosophy. He then went on to enter the University of Maryland Law School in the fall of 1967, but said that he "quickly became bored and left."

After his first brush with law school he attended graduate school at Hunter College in New York City, where he pursued a Masters Degree in seventeenth century English literature, "and where I received all A's, thank you very much," he joked with me during an interview. Just before he was scheduled to take his comprehensive exam, he discovered that his wife was leaving him for his best friend. He never did take the exam. For someone who on the surface appeared to be such a solid part of "the establishment," Spencer had a colorful past. In between law schools he had worked as an eighth-grade teacher, a New York City cab driver, a customs inspector, an immigration officer, a sky marshal, security guard, and as Executive

Director of the NYC Neighborhood Stabilization Program and Executive Director of the NYC Commission on Human Rights under Mayor Ed Koch's administration.

I expressed my sympathy about the affair, even though it happened thirty years ago and he was now happily married with children.

"That's okay," he responded. "I wasn't much better myself back then. It was in the early seventies and I had just finished having an affair with a nun. Sounds like a Jerry Springer episode, doesn't it?"

As if he hadn't already piqued my interest, the bit about the affair with the nun put me over the edge. "Spencer, you're killing me! Can we talk about the nun?"

"Hey! It was the late sixties to early seventies. She was really cute and besides, she isn't a nun anymore!"

He told me that in his more Catholic moments he would look up at the altar and think, "I'm going to hell; I stole a bride from Christ!"

Spencer admitted that the opportunity to represent this newly elected village board, although not as exciting as an affair with a nun, was enticing for several reasons. "You had this iconoclastic group elected," he mused. Knowing that the new board which hired him would be there for at least four years—the length of their terms—he was excited to have the opportunity to be brought in as part of a team and start on the ground floor.

He also told me that he "lives" for environmental law. With his appointment as council to the New Paltz Village Board, not only did he have the chance to work with a board who had Green Party majority, but one that was enthusiastic about drafting and adopting a whole slew of new environmental/municipal laws.

"My first day on the job we're presented with a lawsuit from River Keeper!" he said, referring to the "friendly" lawsuit that River Keeper, a leading environmental watchdog group, headed in part by Robert (Bobby) Kennedy Jr., had threatened to level against the village if it didn't find a way to remedy the leaky water and sewer pipes so that raw sewage did not continue to flood into the Wallkill River and eventually find its way to the Hudson River.

"It was like finding a piece of chocolate on the pillow of your hotel room," he said with a boyish grin.

Besides handling the River Keeper suit, a proposed law which would all but ban trapping within the village boundaries, a Wetlands and Waterway Protection law, and a host of resolutions including ones opposing the war in Iraq, the Patriot Act, and calling for Indian Point nuclear plant to be shut down, Spencer was also asked by Jason to look into the issue of same-sex marriages and whether or not he had the legal right to marry gay couples.

"The initial research I conducted for the mayor took all of an hour and a half," said Spencer. "Apparently he'd been asked by two friends to officiate their marriage and he wanted to know what his legal options were. But he decided early on that I would not represent him on this issue, but that he would seek pro bono independent counsel."

Although a practicing Roman Catholic and a heterosexual, Spencer's experience working on New York City's Human Rights Commission unveiled a world he hadn't known much about. His unit was charged with researching various anti-discrimination laws as they applied to homosexuals and the newly developing AIDS epidemic. Almost all of his staff members were gay.

He ended up becoming close friends with his administrative assistant, Ray Tuite. "He was a wonderful man but when I first met him I wasn't sure if he was a man or a woman. He was that androgynous looking," he reflected. Through the work Spencer and Ray did on the council, and the education Victoria, his wife of 25 years, gave him, Spencer became, for the first time, acutely aware of how homosexuals were being discriminated against.

Spencer said he was still haunted by the image of Ray, who died of AIDS-related illnesses in his New York City apartment in 1988. "He used to tell me that his worst fear was dying alone. The tragic irony is that he did die alone. He was there for three days before someone found him. That still hurts me."

The Orange County lawyer admitted that there was a moral contradiction in his views on the same-sex marriage issue. "I'm an anomaly," he said with a laugh. "As a Roman Catholic, I don't believe in same-sex marriage, but I also don't believe in discriminating against anyone based on their sexual orientation. This is a choice that folks have made. It harms no one. And while I think that Jason did violate the Domestic Relations statute, it was also a well-reasoned act of civil disobedience and I say, 'hooray for him!'"

"For many of the members of my church, New Paltz is bizarro land," he said, recounting to me one particular Sunday when his priest was delivering a sermon about how horrible all of the gay-marriages in New Paltz were and how Catholics had to protect and defend traditional marriage. "I felt all of these heads turn and look at me," said Spencer as he stirred his coffee. While many of his fellow church-goers knew that he represented the village, few of them knew that he did *not* represent Jason on this particular issue.

Prior to having the opportunity to speak with the village attorney at length, I had observed that he had an appealingly scratchy texture to his voice. It was the type of voice that could have been cultivated from late-night jazz sessions in smoke-filled bars. While Jason always had a can of Red Bull Energy Drink faithfully by his side during the board meetings which could easily last from 7:30 p.m. to midnight, Spencer always had a throat lozenge, a lollipop, or something else to suck on.

I imagined that he might be trying to quit smoking, or had a canker sore. But I soon found out that he was battling throat cancer. "I'm almost finished with the treatments and they say that these treatments are one-hundred percent effective in ninety percent of the cases. But the odd thing is most people who get this particular form of cancer have smoked throughout their lives," he said to me. "I've never smoked. It's just one of those things."

While he projected a confident and courageous attitude towards the diagnosis, I knew that the treatments were incredibly painful. If he had a court appearance or a village board meeting, or something else scheduled where he might have to speak at length, he would try not to talk the entire day to save up his vocal energy.

"Imagine, a politician and an attorney for whom it is painful to talk? And who says God doesn't have a sense of humor," he joked.

Spencer did have a sense of humor, a surprising one that enabled him to get through long meetings, local controversy, and most recently throat cancer. He said that it was unfortunate to see the board so polarized with Bob Hebel on one end and the three newcomers on the other end of the table. But when it came to discussing Jason himself, Spencer was quick to give his stamp of approval.

"I really enjoy working with Jason," he said. "In the little amount of time that he has been mayor he has learned a lot and learned it fast. He listens to advice, he weighs decisions very carefully, and he is extremely mature for someone who is twenty-seven and has never held public office before. If he decides to stay in politics, he will make a great public servant."

He described Jason as someone who causes a catalytic reaction. "He reminds me of those lab experiments that we had to do in high school where you have a chemical solution with properties that normally co-exist peacefully together. Then you put in a catalyst which changes the very nature of these chemicals. It starts things spinning and forces change. Jason is a catalyst. When he is there things happen around him."

Things certainly were happening around Jason. Not only was he facing twenty-four criminal charges from the DA, but he had a temporary restraining order placed on him by Supreme Court Judge Michael Bruhn and the threat of another lawsuit from Bob Hebel and Liberty Counsel, one that would call for his removal as mayor.

Bob would make public charges that Jason had illegally used village taxpayers' money when he asked the village attorney to research the issue of same-sex marriages. "He had no authority to do that," said Bob for an article I was writing on his threatened lawsuit to have Jason removed from office. "It was an abuse of his position. He used taxpayers' money to further his own agenda. He never asked the board whether or not they would agree to have Spencer look into this."

"What's Andy doing there?" Deb asked me when I called her after the post-arraignment rally. "He's all over CNN standing right behind Jason at the courthouse. Is he representing him? Or the prosecution? Or is he acting as a bodyguard?"

She was referring to Andrew Kossover, a local criminal attorney whose offices are in the heart of downtown, right next to the mountain climbing store, Rock & Snow. Andy and his wife Vicki, a beautiful, petite woman with tight curly black hair, were the principle attorneys for the law firm Kossover & Kossover. The two could be seen at various times during the day or night holding hands crossing the street, eating at a local restaurant or bistro. Andy was often darting from his office towards Bacchus or the billiards hall, carrying a long linear case which held his cherished pool sticks.

I always smiled when I saw them. Although they had been married for years and had raised four children, they always appeared to be in a suspended honeymoon period as if New Paltz was their Paris and the Main Street Bistro was their Tour d'Argent.

"I don't know what he was doing there," I said. "But he certainly got his mug all over the evening news."

"That was bizarre," said Andy months later during one of our now weekly interviews at his office, referring to photos and news clips that showed him and the mayor across the nation and the world. "But it was fun for my mom. She loved it. My son was commuting on the subway in New York City when he opened up the *New York Post* and let out a shout! He called me up immediately and said, 'Dad? What are you doing in the *Post?*'"

Andy was not brought into the defense circle until the day of Jason's court arraignment. The second the news broke about Jason's plans to perform gay marriages Andy called him up and offered to provide him his legal services free of charge.

He told me that not only was he familiar with the local legal community and terrain, but that as counsel to Jason, he also believed in the underlying issue—the right for same-sex couples to be legally married.

"To be quite honest, it was part ego," he admitted to me. "I thought that any significant case in New Paltz that would involve criminal defense should be handled by my office. I've been here practicing criminal law for many years; I know all of the players and believed that I would be more zealous in the defense of the mayor than anyone else."

Just hours before the arraignment, Rosenkranz held a meeting with Andy and Jason inviting Andy to serve as the local counsel. Andy was familiar with the firm Rosenkranz worked for and the work he had done and had the utmost regard for him. He respected his approach to the law and felt that they would make a good team.

"Like me, he values greatly the need to maintain credibility with the prosecution and the court. We don't like to take cheap shots at our adversaries…and Josh's pedigree is unbelievable."

Rosenkranz was the law clerk for U.S. Supreme Court Justice William Brennan. He helped found the Brennan Center for Justice at the New York University Law School, "which is really a mini ACLU," noted Andy. In terms of their analysis on the case, he and Rosenkranz were completely in sync. "There has really been no dissent or friction between the legal team and the paralegals on this case. We all have a good rapport," said Andy happily, as if this was not a situation that lawyers from different firms found themselves in often while working together. Too many egos in one room, I guessed.

If a lawsuit from River Keeper against the newly elected, environmentally aligned village board was like a piece of chocolate on the village attorney's proverbial hotel pillow, then Jason's claim that he acted in accordance with the New York State and Federal Constitutions when he married those twenty-five gay couples was the biggest box of gourmet truffles ever to have been delivered to Andy's law office door.

"Most attorneys wait their entire lives for a case like this," he said, drumming his fingers against the desk as if trying to drum out just the right words to match what he felt was his great professional fortune to have been brought onto a case like this one. "This is a case that has the potential to change forever the national social landscape," he said passionately. "A case that has profound constitutional issues at its core. The odds of a country lawyer getting a chance to represent a case of such constitutional magnitude are unbelievable." It was as if someone had purchased a lawyer's lotto ticket for Andy and he had won, without even knowing he had entered the contest.

I felt a kindred spirit in Andy. We both had decided to dedicate our craft to the town we loved. Any delusions of grandeur—big-city law firms, or big-city papers—had been eclipsed by the desire to remain within the smaller constellation of New Paltz, a place we cherished, chose to raise our families, and worked, hopefully for the betterment of our friends and neighbors. So when a big story or a big case came from one of our own-homegrown from within the narrow boundaries we had accepted as our provincial refuge from the larger political landscape—it only made sense that we should remain positioned at the center.

Like Spencer, Andy looked like part of the establishment, dressed in suits at work, khakis on the weekends, and zipping around town in his 1982 vintage 911SC Red Porsche Targa with the license plate "CRIMPAYS." But he characterized himself as an "old-leftie," and you didn't have to scratch too far below the surface to smell the patchouli oil and incense. "I thought it was a hoot when Jason got elected," he said. "It was a real kick in the pants to the past administration who tried their best to stop the students from voting in local elections. Jason's heart is in the right place. He wants to help people, help the environment—and he's wise beyond his years."

Like many New Paltzians, Andy's hippie roots were not buried too deep into the ground. A SUNY alumnus like Jason, Andy had attended law school at SUNY Buffalo in the early 1970s. The now-seasoned lawyer admitted that back in the day, he was more interested in the political goings-on at SUNY Buffalo than the actual courses he was enrolled in. "I confess that I was more taken by the politics of the day than the academics," he said with a laugh. "I used to say that I was majoring in pharmaceuticals."

Besides working with the school's legal aid clinic, Andy also ran for and was elected to the SUNY Buffalo Student Government. At the time the college had approximately 20,000 enrolled students. "I enjoyed bringing in speakers who were opposed to the Vietnam War. As a student leader I was able to help bring in William Kuntzler, Jane Fonda, and Tom Hayden (who crashed at my apartment), Bernadette Devlin and Daniel Ellsberg—it was some cast of characters," he reflected, with a warm nostalgia glowing in his eyes. After a thirty-year hiatus from the revolutionary trenches, Andy found himself back on the front lines.

"Look at the fight for civil rights for blacks, the fight for interracial marriages to be legalized, for women to receive the right to vote, own land and have the same legal status as men. When you look back at these movements and all of the pain and suffering and sacrifice it took to advance a right and just cause forward, it begs the question as to why our government, our judicial system, cannot, for once, be evolved enough to stop discrimination without those who are being discriminated against having to fight for it at every level."

Before Andy became part of Jason's legal team, I really didn't know much about his political beliefs. But everything he said to me that day and in the subsequent months as this story unfolded, I tended to agree with wholeheartedly. He recounted to me something he had heard on National Public Radio just that morning. On the radio program they pointed out that Mike Tyson made more money in one fight than all of our Nobel Peace Prize–winners combined. "Can you believe that?" said Andy, throwing up his hands in exasperation. "Why do we reward barbarism and penalize tolerance? Where is the separation of Church and State? What about live and let live, for God's sake?"

Andy pondered the various personal, political and legal reasons why the DA would not only prosecute Jason for an alleged violation of the New York State Domestics Relation Law, but then prosecute two respected members of the Unitarian clergy for the same violation two weeks later.

"It's a question of discretion," Andy mused, shrugging his shoulders and raising his hands upwards. When he taught his criminal law course at SUNY New Paltz, the first lesson he always began with was the issue of "discretion." "I ask the students, *who* has discretion?" In Andy's veritable estimation, virtually every individual in the criminal justice system has discretion—the DA, police officers, the defense attorney, the defendant. "It is not a black-and-white system," he said to me emphatically, as if I were one of his students. "There is no barometer. The DA used his discretion in deciding to prosecute this case. He didn't have to. The law didn't require him to."

Andy went on to iterate what Rosenkranz had pointed out at the post-arraignment rally: Don Williams was the only district attorney in the country who brought this issue into a criminal court. While Andy said that he understood the DA's reasoning, he certainly did not agree with it. "I find his prosecution of the mayor and the two ministers to be unnecessary, overzealous. If he believes that the mayor does not have the legal authority to solemnize same-sex marriages without those couples obtaining the proper license, why not leave it at that? Let them have their ceremonies. If the marriages are deemed invalid, then they cannot invoke the rights that currently are available only to heterosexual couples. Where does the issue go from there? To *civil* court, where it belongs."

Seeing how passionate and animated Andy became when he talked about the issue of same-sex marriages, I imagined that he would make one hell of a teacher. When he began talking about the Constitution and *Brown v. the Board of Education*, he swiveled back and forth in his seat until I thought he was going to tip over. "Here I am reading these landmark court cases that I haven't read since I was in college thirty years ago," he said, asking his secretary to hold his calls. I could tell he was on a roll. "Not only am I reading them, but we're applying them to a case that is pending in court right now. That's the most exciting part. We have a case that has such broad, constitutional issues that you can't help but spout these clichés that you hear all the time about the Constitution being a 'living, breathing document.' It's alive for us right now, and it's exhilarating."

It was an exhilarating time—for the couples, the mayor, the local Green Party, the lawyers, the reporters, and the town and village of New Paltz. We never knew what was going to happen one day to the next.

Chapter 8
"No Honey, She's Not a Fag"

"There are people who might think that this same-sex marriage business is a flash-in-the-pan movement. But when you have waited most of your life for the civil rights that your straight friends had when they decided to get married for the first, second or third time—then it becomes a much more important movement to be a part of.... We have been silent a long, long time." —Reverend Kay Greenleaf speaking at SUNY New Paltz, after the Westboro Baptist Church protestors came to New Paltz

Not only was it Palm Sunday, and early, and cold, and rainy—but on top of that we were suffering from Daylight Savings Time. My alarm clock, which had been advanced only hours earlier, began bludgeoning its rooster-like rhythm into my already over-stimulated brain. It had been less than five weeks since Jason performed the first round of weddings, and while spring hung in the air like a promise, it hadn't, as yet, delivered.

"Gotta go," I said to Kazik, who had been jolted awake by the alarm clock. "The hate-mongers are here."

Everyone was snoring, even our dog, but I, the local scribe, had to get up, dress, inject myself with coffee, and prepare to head out into the freezing rain to cover the nine protests being staged at half-hour intervals around town by the Westboro Baptist Church congregation from Topeka, Kansas. Most of them were progeny of the Reverend Fred Phelps, a lawyer and minister so extreme in his positions that even the most right-wing fundamentalist Christian organizations condemned him and his hate-filled flock.

The group's first press release directed at New Paltz and Jason, which arrived at Village Hall just days after the marriages began, was so grotesque that it almost looked like a hoax. Handwritten at the top of the press release was "Attention Mayor Jason West." Besides the mayor, it also singled out two young lesbians who were married on that historic February day. The group named the couple, stated where they worked (at the Gilded Otter brewpub), and then had a caricature of two sows laying in the mud with the women's names written across the pigs' bellies, with placards above that said, "Fag-Dogs Wed Here" and "Dyke-Sows Wed Here."

"God is not mocked!" exclaimed the press release. Besides claiming that this "Sodom and Gomorrah whorehouse masquerading as the village of New Paltz" was doomed to hell, it went on to say:

God hates fags and fag-enablers! Ergo, God hates New Paltz, West, all sodomite 'newly weds' (Ugh! Gag! Puke!) like dykes Jennifer Smits and Dana Wegener, and the dog kennels / leper colonies pretending to be churches create New Paltz's sodomite zeitgeist! Fag/dyke sex = dogs eating vomit, sows wallowing in feces—see id, at 2:22.

Moses' Death Penalty. 'If a man also lie with mankind as he lieth with a woman, both of them have committed an act of abomination; they shall surely be put to death; their blood shall be upon them.' Lev. 20:13

There was another odd caption at the bottom of the press release which read, "Flash for Mel Gibson: Fags Killed Christ!" in response to Gibson's latest, controversial, chart-topping film, *The Passion of the Christ*. I had no idea what that meant.

We were all in the second-story corridor of the Village Hall while a meeting of more than a hundred volunteers was being organized by Trustee Walsh. The entire upstairs reeked of body odor

120

and stale coffee. While Walsh helped to divide the volunteers—many of them SUNY New Paltz students—into various committees, I tried to digest the WBC flier that had been handed to me.

"Do the police know about this?" I asked Jason.

"Oh yeah, they've been informed."

"It's absolutely bizarre," I said to him, not knowing whether I should laugh it off or take it seriously.

"You got that right," he said as we stared at the flier together, trying to make sense of it.

Just then Rachel squeezed her way into the narrow hallway. "Isn't this great?" she said. Student involvement in any aspect of government or political activism never ceased to put Rachel in a good mood. She would get that glassy-eyed look that many women get when shopping. Rachel's endorphins seemed to kick in when more than a dozen students could find enough inspiration about a cause to actually crawl out of their futons, slide on their bikes, and bring their fresh energy to bear on some local, national or even international issue that the Greens were championing.

My e-mail account was chronically filled with forwarded "alerts" from Rachel. There was either a protest being staged in front of Starbucks, trying to pressure them to sell only equal trade coffee, or a protest outside of Burger King or McDonald's, with people parading in cow suits, informing the mostly uninterested fast-food consuming masses of all of the health ills, loss of rain forests clear-cut for Big Mac cattle to graze, and poor wages for their young, pimply-faced employees who were busy flipping the hormone-charged hamburgers and plunging french fries into deep-fry grease bins.

Since, theoretically, I agreed with almost all of her protests, I would do my best to convince Deb to put in a news brief with an accompanying picture. When the war in Iraq broke out, the protests came faster than the rainstorms plaguing the Hudson Valley—with sit-ins and lie-downs and anti-war film festivals and radical lecturers on campus. The Women in Black organization was still holding vigils every Saturday morning outside the public library, just across from Starbucks, silently protesting the war in Iraq.

"Did you see this?" I asked Rachel, and handed her the charming flier.

"Oh, my god," she said, tears instantly welling in her eyes. "Do Dana and Jennifer know about this? Are they being protected? Who are these people? They're from Kansas? Is this a sick joke?"

It wasn't a joke, and soon we would all find out that the Westboro Baptist anti-fag flock was on its way to New Paltz. The dates changed several times, but eventually the group settled on Palm Sunday, April 4, to bring their message to Sodom and Gomorrah land. Their protests were not limited to the "infested" SUNY New Paltz campus or the site of the "sodomite weddings" outside of Village Hall, but they also included the restaurant where Dana and Jennifer worked, and six local churches that they dubbed "dog kennels and leper colonies." Their website, www.godhatesfags.com, was almost laughable if it wasn't so deadly serious. It seemed like a satire of a religious extremist group—only they were real, and not even *Saturday Night Live* would dare to joke about the things they were preaching.

"They're known for protesting at the funerals of AIDS victims," said Jason, disgusted. "But I've read about counter-protestors who create these gigantic angel wings and open them up around the site of the funeral to block the Phelps protestors." Other counter-Phelps protestors would hold "Fred-a-Thons" where they would raise money from people for every minute that the WBC protestors were in town and then donate the proceeds to one of the Phelps family's most despised charities.

Jason told me that the WBC even protested the funeral of Matthew Shepard, the young gay man from Laramie, Wyoming, who was pistol-whipped, beaten, and then lynched by two bigots for his sexual orientation. On the website, the group depicted a monument dedicated to Shepard that marks every day that he has "been in hell" since he was brutally murdered. They considered themselves to be Calvinists, to have been chosen as God's elite, and thus obligated to spread the message that the majority of the population was destined for hell, particularly, but certainly not limited to, homosexuals.

"How are you preparing for the visit from the WBC, Chief?" I asked Ray Zappone as the visit grew closer.

"Well, we've been gathering intelligence on them," he said.

The word "intelligence" coming from our local police chief took me a bit by surprise. I reserved the word "intelligence" for the FBI or CIA, never thinking that it had its right and lawful place in a small-town police force. What the police and other researchers quickly ascertained was that while the WBC was not known for being *physically* violent, they were known for provoking emotional reactions in people who might then lash out and hit them, enabling them to sue the municipality for not having adequately protected them.

"They have more than a dozen lawyers in their family," said the chief. "Our main objective is to guarantee the safety of our residents and to guarantee the safety and welfare of the Westboro Church protestors. We are trying to educate the public and encourage them not to react to the protestors in any physical way." To this end, a local group of Peace Keepers was assembled and trained by local Green Party member and political activist, Jim Gordon, who also happened to work for my newspaper's publishing company and various regional papers.

Several clergy members from the churches being targeted by the WBC protestors agreed to meet with members of the newly formed New Paltz Equality Initiative, Green Party members, Democrats, various local officials and concerned residents to try and gracefully counter demonstrate the WBC's visit.

"It was great," said Rachel, after one of the meetings with the clergy. "Several of the churches agreed to make banners that will say, 'God Loves Everyone.' We agreed to put posters up in all of the local businesses that say, 'Love is All You Need.' Even pastor Greg Ortiz, from Christ The King church, who admitted to us right off the bat that he in no way supported gay marriages, was totally willing to work with us to find peaceful ways of condemning the Phelps family's protests."

Deep Love was again in her element. "The hate-mongers have met their match in New Paltz," she said proudly.

The night before their arrival, I must have talked to Rachel four times to try to get an idea of the exact schedule of the "Civil Rights Day" that Walsh and the NPEI had organized on campus. The event was slated for 12:30 p.m., just after the Phelps family would head out of town and make their way to Nyack to protest the openly gay mayor, John Shields, who had also become a familiar face in New Paltz ever since he jumped on the same-sex marriage bandwagon that West got rolling.

While Mayor Shields considered following suit and solemnizing same-sex marriages without a license, in the end he decided instead to take the issue to the courts. He and his partner filed an Article 78 lawsuit against the town clerk of Nyack for refusing to provide same-sex couples with marriage licenses. He also leveled a lawsuit against the New York State Health Department for refusing to provide those licenses to gay couples and for ordering town and city clerks not to do so.

He was cute, Mayor Shields. Always smiling, always dressed in typical mayoral fashion with a suit and tie and a long, black wool overcoat. He had thinning gray hair and red cheeks and his boyfriend was rabidly supportive and defensive of him. Mayor Shields, like Billiam van Roestenberg, was someone who was almost impossible not to like.

There was no time for a shower. I rummaged around in the pre-dawn gray light of our bedroom for a clean sweater and a decent pair of pants. Trying my best not to wake anyone, I searched in and around my disheveled desk for a notebook. I hadn't been to the office in weeks to pick up supplies and I soon discovered that I had no pages left in my steno pads, barely any ink left in my pens, and certainly no paper in the printer. Then I found my half-used notebook and grabbed my new black purse that still had the price tag hanging off it, and headed out the door, shutting it quietly so as not to wake the kids.

The streets looked sleepy. The rain felt cold and mean, and everything was oddly quiet. Part of me still didn't believe that these protestors really existed. Or that if they did, they would certainly turn around and head back towards Kansas when they saw the forecast. But when I turned up Main Street, just past the Trailways bus station at the corner of my block, I could see a swell of police officers, police cars, K-9 units, and a dozen or so neon-colored signs poking out from the fists of the Westboro Baptist flock, which included a five-year-old boy and a twelve-year-old girl. The boy carried a yellow and black sign with a smiley face that said, "God Hates Fags."

On the other side of the road I could see at least seventy-five counter-protestors carrying signs and sheets and boom boxes trying to drown out the sounds of the Westboro Baptists' ballads which included, "Hey Ho / Feces Eating Has Got to Go" and a new riff on the national anthem, "God Hates America / Home of the Fags," to name a few. As I moved closer and the rest of their signs came into view, I had to stop in my tracks. They said, "God Blew up the Space Shuttle" and "Fags= Feces Eaters" and "God Hates America." Then there was, "Thank God for September 11th."

Not only did they exist, but they bore professionally printed and silk-screened signs, were screaming, and were so above and beyond what I had ever encountered or imagined that I kept rubbing my eyes to make sure that what I was witnessing was, in fact, in front of me.

One man, in his mid-thirties, wearing Ray-Bans and heckling the counter-protestors, was dragging an American flag in the mud as parishioners filed into the New Paltz Methodist Church for the Palm Sunday service. "Get that flag off the ground," said one elderly parishioner as he entered the church. "Get it off the ground!" I could see him shaking. Quickly, two representatives of the church shepherded him inside.

I knew this group's position on homosexuality. But I was wholly unprepared for their celebration of the September 11 terrorist attacks on New York City and Washington, D.C., which left nearly 3,000 innocent people dead just seventy-five miles south of us. Nor could I fathom their contention that the fallen American soldiers in Iraq were the direct result of God's wrath against our "feces-eating nation." A family in our neighboring town of Highland had just buried their twenty-four-year-old son who died the weekend before in Iraq.

"This is what they do," Chief Zappone had warned me. Their shtick was to push every button imaginable. The chief told me that he very carefully selected the officers who would be responsible for protecting the hate-mongers that day. He had them read the WBC literature and watch videotapes of their past protests so that they knew what to expect. "I know that some of them felt sick when they first saw the signs and heard the chants, but they are professionals," he said, obviously proud of his boys.

Jim Gordon, our reporter by night turned Peace Keeper by day, was moving back and forth across the street with his clipboard held tight. He encouraged the counter-protestors to just laugh and smile and not give into the provocations. There were two Lutherans from Poughkeepsie with a large sheet and the biblical quotation, "'Nothing can separate us from the love of God' Romans 8:39."

"We're all going to glory," said Carol Riechert, SUNY New Paltz alumn, class of 1963, "and we're bringing you with us! We have an eternity to discuss this. Some of us may get there faster, some of us may have nicer rooms, but we're all going to be there together."

Just then Rachel came riding up the middle of Main Street on her bike with a camera and backpack strapped over her shoulder. She was rain-drenched and disheveled and looked as if she had no idea where she was going.

"Good morning, Rachel!" some of the counter-protestors called out.

"I was up most of the night preparing and then we met at The Bakery at 6:30 a.m. I'm exhausted," she said to me. But somehow I could tell that she was in her element, even if half asleep, and she was prepared to defend the constitutional rights of her comrades against this live spectacle of intolerance and sideshow of religious extremism.

The New Paltz town supervisor, Don Wilen, came walking up Main Street with his baseball hat and windbreaker. "I think you're missing the biggest story," he said to me. "We'll have the largest pizza order in the history of New Paltz today." There were approximately 110 law enforcement officers on duty this day, and at 3 p.m. they were scheduled to de-brief at New Paltz Middle School and have lunch.

Our police department had a fulltime staff of twenty-one. So Chief Zappone had to recruit the aid of other enforcement agencies including the New York State Police, the County Sheriff's Department, the SUNY New Paltz Campus Police as well as neighboring municipalities and various State and County special operations and SWAT teams. The bulk of them were back at the station house or at the local middle school waiting to be called in on back-up if a situation arose.

"This sort of demonstration has a way of bringing out the whackos," admitted the chief. He told me that he had no way of knowing how many people were going to show up to counter-protest and that there were likely to be busloads of college students coming up from New York City. Part of his goal was to be prepared for crowd control, to prevent any altercations, and to make sure that both the Phelps family and the rest of the public were safe.

I kept staring at the dozen members and extended members of the Phelps family and waited for them to crack. They couldn't be serious. They looked normal, incredibly normal with their synchilla jackets and brand-name sneakers. They could have been a family coming into town for a hike up at the Mohonk Preserve or on their way to have breakfast at The Bistro, but when they opened their mouths, their displacement was obvious. What were they doing in New Paltz, a town and village which probably supported more head shops, tie-dye vendors, and student bars per square foot than any other place in America?

While the counter-protestors were quick to label the inclusion of the Phelps grandchildren as a form of child abuse, I had to wonder if it was any different than the young children attending peace marches on their parents' shoulders or rallying in Washington, D.C., in defense of a woman's right to choose. Rachel herself had her nine-year-old daughter Sylvie in tow at almost all of the protests, rallies,

127

and marches she engaged in. I would see Sylvie on campus, along Main Street, out in front of McDonald's handing out literature to passers-by. She was sort of the "Eloise" of the SUNY New Paltz campus. The message the Phelps family was delivering was disconcerting to many but their decision to involve their kids was not unprecedented by members of the Left or Right.

"September 11th was God's rod," said the Ray-Bans-wearing protester. "It was God's rod coming to bear on America for their fag-loving ways. Every time a soldier dies in Iraq, it's on the backs of you perverts."

Under the eave to the entrance of the church, the Reverend Dorothy Caldwell led the choir in a half an hour hymnal session dedicated to songs that spoke of love and brotherhood and sisterhood while the protestors peddled their message.

I crossed the street, feeling compelled to talk to the WBC members, to get a sense of who they were and what exactly they were trying to achieve. I was nervous at first, but they apparently are very used to press and welcome it. I approached twenty-one-year-old Sarah Phelps first. She is a granddaughter of the Reverend Fred Phelps, who they claimed was busy conducting another protest tour.

"Why did you decide to come to New Paltz and protest?" I asked, always picking a very general question just to get the subject talking.

"Because we need to preach against people acting like man and man or woman and woman being together is okay," she said. "The Bible clearly says that it is an abomination. So we just decided to come here today and do a little preachin'."

Sarah, who noted that she would be twenty-two in eighteen days, said that her grandfather was "the best that anyone could ever hope for" and that she had been attending the Westboro Baptist Church since she was born.

"What are your religious beliefs and why have you chosen to share them with the public?" I asked.

"I feel that I have the grace of God and it is my responsibility to cry aloud and show people the error of their ways and their transgressions against God. What I believe is that God loves his chosen elect. He has pre-destined only a few of us to go to heaven and everyone else is going to hell. Remember there were only eight people on the ark and the rest God destroyed. Look what happened on September 11th. No one was listening to God's warnings and they were doomed for hell."

"Since so many of us, in your estimation, are already hated by God and doomed to an eternity in hell, what do you hope to achieve by protesting and preaching to the unloved masses?"

"I don't hope to achieve anything," she said. "But now they can't say 'I didn't know' when they're sent to hell. There's no excuse."

This was a young, pretty, blonde Kansas girl who had all the external innocence of Dorothy but with the words of the Wicked Witch of the West. I just kept imagining that she would give me a wink and let me know that this was all for show, that really she was a closet lover of classical literature but had to appease her family and do a hate tour every now and again, or that they made incredible amounts of money suing municipalities when they were assaulted and she was only playing her obligatory role in the family business, corrupt as it may be. But no matter how many questions I asked her, she just came back with more damnation and abomination talk.

"What do you want to do with your life?" I asked her.

"Continue serving the Lord, of course," she said. "Most of my aunts and uncles and parents are lawyers. I work in the health-care field. We work and live like everyone else and pay our own way to do these trips."

I asked her if she or her family members had ever been assaulted during their "trips."

"Numerous times," she said. "Not me personally, but we've had our cars and our houses vandalized. We've had many people hit us. But we are in the hands of the Lord and we will be delivered. Our business is serving the Lord. We do not control the hearts of men and if Satan has gotten into their hearts there is nothing we can do to stop that."

I was determined to find out more about Sarah Phelps: What did she like to do in her spare time? Did she listen to music and what were her favorite movies or books? What was her earliest memory as a child? What had been the greatest highlights or disappointments in her life? Did she have a boyfriend? Prefer baths to showers or the other way around?

While I was imagining a Barbara Walters–type interview with the young zealot, her family began filing past us towards their SUVs. I saw Jim Gordon sprinting towards his car and the counter-protestors folding up their sheets and heading to the next WBC protest destination, just two blocks up at the New Paltz Episcopal Church.

"Is there somewhere I can call you?" I asked Sarah quickly. "A phone number you can be reached at, because I'd like to talk with you more."

She seemed flattered and eagerly gave me her cell phone number, repeating it to me twice to make sure I had noted it correctly. Even young Calvinist fanatics have cell phones these days, I thought to myself, as I walked towards one of our former town supervisors and my neighbor growing up, Carol Roper, a pillar of the Methodist Church.

"From our perspective it went beautifully," she said. "We sang our hymns that focused on love and acceptance. The police were incredible. They have consistently and repeatedly asked us if there was anything we needed, if they could be of service in any way. Of course I know most of the officers, so that's a comfort. They made us feel very secure. But it is definitely hard to take, seeing signs that say 'Methodist Fag Church' on our sidewalk."

"I certainly didn't like their signs," said Craig Haight, a retired reverend of the Methodist Church who presided over the congregation in the 1970s. "It's a form of religious perversion at its worst."

"Are you a journalist?" one of the counter-protestors asked me.
"Yes," I said.

"Can you ask one of them for me why they are calling us all 'feces eaters'? I'm just confused. What does feces and feces eating have to do with the Episcopal Church or gay marriages?"

I went back to Miss Sarah Phelps to ask her this question, as uncomfortable as I was asking it; but I felt that this woman had the right to an explanation.

"We all know that fags lick each other's anuses and penetrate each other's anuses," she said without blushing. "That means that they have fecal matter on their tongues and swallow that. They also conduct 'golden showers' on each other, where they are drenched in the other's urine. They are slovenly and disgusting and roll in their own shit like pigs and sows."

Well, that was the answer. Instead of repeating it, I just showed the curious counter-protester my notes and she shrugged her shoulders and said, "Oh, now I get it." But I didn't get it. I didn't get any of it really, and where in the hell was Jason? He was the one who started the whole damn thing and he was nowhere to be found. "He's probably sleeping," said Rachel. "Why don't you call him?"

But there was no time. The WBC were on their way to the Village Hall. I had run home to change my sweater which was now soaking wet from the freezing rain. I ran as fast as I could towards the Village Hall, my new purse sliding off my shoulder. I cursed myself for not choosing one with a long strap so that I could sling it over my shoulder and have my hands free.

The crowd of counter-protestors had grown again. There were now approximately 175 people standing vigil against the WBC's message. I stuck to the side of the WBC, not because I had some great affection for them, but because they were the ones I had to get the quotes from. The people on the other side of the street were the people I talked to every day. I could almost anticipate their quotes, make them up if I had to, and have them tell me later that I made them "sound much more articulate" than they really were.

"I can always relax when I talk to you," said Jason, midway into the wedding drama. "You always make me sound intelligent."

"You are intelligent," I offered, and I meant it.

"But with you I don't have to worry about the sound bite or about statements I make being taken out of context. The *New York*

Post is impossible. They'll take a string of three words from a complete sentence and just insert it where they want."

It had been more than four weeks since he began speaking to the public and the press on a daily basis and his voice still sounded exasperated, as if each word he uttered caused him great physical and emotional pain. "What did you ask me?" he would often say, confused as to who he was talking to and what the question had been.

I understood his frustration with the papers. It was exactly why I hardly even liked journalists. I, like Jason, landed my job on a fluke. I returned to New Paltz after completing an undergraduate degree in literature at the University of Oregon and traveling throughout Europe. I began dressing up as various Disney characters for wealthy children's birthday parties in Westchester County on the weekends. During the week I would work on short stories and a novel.

While at the local post office I ran into a wild, gray-haired man, an artist, writer, poet, sports enthusiast and activist. He was married to a childhood family friend of mine, Julie O'Connor, who happened to be the editor and assistant publisher of the *New Paltz Times* and the *Woodstock Times*. We swapped stories. Unbeknownst to me, he passed along one of my short stories about deer hunting to his wife.

"She's always looking for quality writers for the paper," he said. "Why don't you talk to her?"

I agreed to write a feature on a popular area restaurant, The Egg's Nest, and its colorful owner, Richard Murphy, who was married to a former model from the U.K. His flamboyant artistry turned what could have been an average pub into a Who's Who dining venue in upstate New York. While The Egg's Nest served as a Monday night football intoxication landmark during the 1970s, it evolved, subsequent to Murphy's recovery from alcoholism, into a prime lunch and dinner venue for locals and tourists who appreciated its artistic backdrop. Murphy, armed with a glue gun and various pieces of collected and purchased fabrics, papers, artifacts, antiques, and relics, would redecorate the walls, ceilings, restrooms, and terrace on a bi-monthly basis. When you entered The Egg's Nest, you entered a world unto its own.

The story went over well. Soon Julie brought me into the fold and had me writing news articles. I remember sitting at her desk and practicing "leads"—a concept that was strange and challenging for me as I was used to setting up the story without announcing its conclusion in the first line. Eventually, I got it. Or I understood the technique well enough to fake it.

For me, local town and village board meetings were like morality plays, each character exposing his or her own viewpoint on the issue at hand and the audience, the readers, deciding who was the most informed and righteous. What was happening in New Paltz that Palm Sunday was theatre, that's for sure, but I couldn't decide if it was supposed to be a comedy or a tragedy. As the minutes clicked by, I leaned towards the latter.

Before I gathered up the nerve to interview more of the WBC's protestors, I decided to congratulate my old friend turned New Paltz police sergeant, Robert Lucchesi, on his first baby who was only a few weeks old. Rob was dressed in a long wool trench coat with his hands placed casually in his pockets. I could easily see why he would have been one of the chief's first choices to put on duty for this event as his demeanor was calm, non-judgmental, and friendly.

"Thanks Erin," he said. "So far so good. And we've been lucky because she's a good little sleeper." He looked like he would rather talk to me about his new baby than have to deal with this bizarre protest. But, being a professional, he had to turn back into a bodyguard for the Phelps family.

When Rob was little we were on the local swim team, the Sea Hawks, together. We were basically a group of aquatically acute pool brats from the Moriello Public Pool, named after Mike Moriello's great-grandfather who donated the money for the original pool, but then died in a plane crash while spraying his apple crops.

Luch, as he was called then, was younger than me, and I can still remember him up on the diving blocks when he was only seven. He was this little Italian butterball—all belly and no legs. But he was as dedicated as he was determined. And his mother used to run up and down the side of the pool screaming, "C'mon, Robert! You're gaining on them! Keep it up, Robert, you can do it!"

Not only was he generally a half a length behind every other child in the race, but he swam so far underwater half the time that there was no way he could have heard his mother's encouraging words. But as he grew older, he turned into quite the jock. Now, pushing six feet, with long sculpted legs, Luch is a triathlete and can be seen off-duty running at a fast clip through the streets of New Paltz with Mike Beck, the owner of P&G's. He is honed, handsome, and a dedicated high school coach.

The five-year-old protester, whose name I learned was Noah, had dropped his sign altogether and was attempting to catch raindrops in his empty water bottle. "I think I got one," he said to no one in particular. "I think I caught a raindrop."

"Do you mind if I ask him a few questions?" I asked the woman standing nearest to him.

"No, go right ahead. But he says he's tired."

First I asked him his name and his age. I felt awkward doing this. I had seen other reporters interview him earlier and while it seemed an exploitive move on their parts, once they finished, I felt a nagging journalistic responsibility. The way I resolved this conflict was just to be as friendly and nice as I could towards him. "You know, my son Seamus is almost five years old," I said. "He'll be going to kindergarten next year. I keep telling him that I'm the one who is going to be crying when he gets on that big yellow school bus for the first time. And he'll just wave and say 'Bye Mom, I have to go to school now!'"

"I can't start crying now, because I still have my three-year-old left," interjected Noah's mom, Reverend Phelps's daughter, who, if you took away her placards and placed her in a playground, would seem like any other mother I would strike up a conversation with while our children ran around the park.

"How many children do you have?" I asked.

"Eleven," she said.

"Eleven?" I responded. "You deserve a medal. Don't you think your mother deserves a medal?" I asked Noah.

He stopped catching raindrops for a second and looked at me. I thought I had peaked his interest somewhat but then he said, "God hates fags and you're a fag."

His mother, who looked slightly embarrassed for the first time, corrected him. "No honey, she's not a fag, she's a reporter."

"I'm sorry," she said.

"It's okay," I said.

When I saw Jim Gordon make the move towards his car, I went with him. "Can I catch a ride with you to the Reformed Church?" I asked.

"Sure," he said, very seriously. "We just have to move fast because I want to get there first."

The Reformed Church of New Paltz is located on Huguenot Street in the heart of the village's historic district. Its bells sound every hour, and it carries within its large steeple a sense of nobility, permanency, and stability. The chapel began as a small stone French church in the 1600s and gradually became the house of worship for the Dutch settlers that followed the first wave of French religious immigration to the New World. It moved from its small, austere stone building down the road to the large red brick church it is today, with massive white columns and a white clock-tower steeple.

Jim and I were not the first to arrive. There were already counter-protestors outside the church, including my mother who lives just a few doors down the road.

"I was so worried about you," she said to me. "These people are crazy!"

"Don't worry, Mom, they're vile but not violent."

My mother, like me was a very sensitive soul who could not tolerate any type of discrimination, indignity or violence towards others. Although I was married with my own children, she still considered me to be a fawn at times, lost in the woods, and felt compelled to make sure that I hadn't accidentally wandered down a dangerous path.

The pastor of the church, Reverend Howard Major, was outside, looking nervous and somewhat tweaked.

"Do you mind if I ask you some questions, Howard?" I didn't want to bug him, especially on Palm Sunday, knowing what he was about to face, but it was my job.

"No," he said, but I could tell he'd rather be somewhere else at the moment than where he was as the Phelps family began filling up the sidewalk in front of his church.

"What's your reaction to the protest?"

"I think it's disgusting," he said as he greeted and welcomed parishioners who were forced to walk past the protestors. "But we have agreed to ignore them. The original Palm Sunday also had protestors. They were not carrying signs, but there was certainly not a universal popularity for Jesus. So in some ways I don't think that it's so bad for the children of our church to see this."

It was 10:30 a.m. The Sunday school was preparing for its scheduled Palm Sunday parade, which would lead participants from the church's education building across Huguenot Street past the protestors and into the church's cathedral entrance. As the children began to walk from their education building towards the church, the counter-protestors gathered a lot of steam.

"Amazing Grace / How Sweet the Sound / That Saved a Wretch Like Me."

"Those dead reeds aren't going to save you," screamed the protestors at the parade of children carrying their palms. "They aren't going to get you into heaven!"

Then towards the counter-protestors they began their usual diatribe. "You're all a bunch of dirty feces eaters and fag enablers…."

The counter-protestors began to sing louder. Jim Gordon ran alongside the children and kept saying, "Happy Palm Sunday." Others joined him, trying to smile and encourage the children and keep the rhetoric of the WBC from reaching them.

I could hear my mother's definitive soprano voice start a new song. "He's got the whole world in his hands / He's got gay couples in his hands / He's got gay couples in his hands / He's got gay couples in his hands / He's got the whole world in his hands/ He's got the Phelps family in his hands…."

136

Like most of my adult girlfriends, there was something about hearing your own mother sing or chew that was grating. Although she had a beautiful voice, I couldn't help but cringe.

"I love a good fight," she said to me afterwards. "This reminds me of the seventies when we all joined hands and circled Carol's Fast Food hamburger joint on Main Street. Of course, many of us were half drunk at the time."

The children carried their palms low to the ground and seemed confused by all of the attention as they filed in towards the church.

When their thirty minutes were up, the WBC members marched quickly towards their vans. Jim Gordon was already speeding away towards the Lutheran Church out on Route 32. My hands were so cold that I had to stop at my mother's house and borrow some gloves. I looked at the dripping chicken-scrawl notes I had taken in the margins of my already exhausted notepad and wondered how in the hell I was going to be able to make any sense out of it. For the second time that morning, I had to go home and change shirts as my second and only other clean sweater was soaked from the freezing rain.

I rejoined the two camps and fleet of police officers out in front of the main entrance of SUNY New Paltz off Route 32 South. This segment became like a call and response protest between the two groups.

Billiam could no longer contain himself. He was dressed in his usual button-down oxford, sans bow tie, a tweed blazer and pleated trousers. "You lost!" he shouted at them. "I'm already married." And then he flashed them his gold wedding ring. "You can go home now. It's too late. We won!"

"You didn't win, you're going to hell!" shouted Fred Phelps's daughter.

Luch asked Billiam, who was in the middle of the street, to step back onto the sidewalk. Jeremiah was there talking to Butch Dener, who could be seen driving through town in a white Saab convertible with an American flag on the back. Dener, who was the manager of The Band, immortalized more than three decades ago by Martin Scorsese's rockumentary "The Last Waltz," had chronic health problems with his liver, and was the former chair of the New Paltz town planning board during the controversial Wal-Mart proposal, which he had been in favor of. From what I gathered, during the late 1960s and the 1970s, Dener was thick in the psychedelic mix of Woodstock and New Paltz; his right-wing leanings were born sometime after his drug and alcohol rehabilitation. Still, it was always ironic to imagine this militant pro-police, pro-development, anti-liberal, olive-skinned conservative as the manager of The Band.

"What do you think about all of this, Butch?"

"What do I think?" he said with a laugh. "I'm surprised there aren't 5,000 people here. I mean this is New Paltz. Where are all the liberal supporters now?"

"All local officials, including the mayor, the town supervisor and the police chief encouraged people to stay at home and not come out and give the WBC an audience," I explained.

"I think it's grotesque," he said. "But I think the police are doing an excellent job."

I walked over and spoke with Mayor Shields, introducing him to Susan Zimet. She handed him one of her t-shirts and a button which read, "New Paltz: Somewhere Over the Rainbow" and had an image of the gay and lesbian rainbow logo as well as the silhouette of the Shawangunk Mountains and Mohonk Tower. "This is for you. It's a pleasure to meet you," she said.

"What do you think about the fact that Jason's probably home sleeping and you're out here in the pouring rain?" I asked Mayor Shields.

"He's sleeping?" he asked. "Well I think we should direct this counter-protest right through his living room!"

The rain would not let up. I wondered if spring, which had a habit of avoiding the Hudson Valley altogether, would ever arrive. There were many years when we went from a snowfall or freezing rain in April to a heat wave in June that kept a steady pace through the middle of September. It was always tricky for our local fruit farmers. Spring was such a precarious time for them. Only two years

138

earlier they had collectively lost more than eighty percent of their fruit crops because of the unpredictable spring weather. There had been a string of 90-degree days in early April which caused the apple trees to blossom, and then two days where the temperatures dropped below freezing. I remember driving by many of the farms along Route 208 in both New Paltz and Gardiner, the neighboring small town to the south, and seeing enormous generators and fans trying to keep the trees warm and the impending fruit from freezing. They were up against so many obstacles, both natural and commercial. They had little control over either. It was now April, and cold, and there were few tourists, except for the Phelps congregation.

I was looking for a ride down to the Gilded Otter brewpub, the site of the next-to-last WBC protest, and a fairly new addition to the local bar/restaurant scene that had coincidentally hired two young, attractive female waitresses who happened to be the second same-sex couple that Jason married on that fateful February 27. For some reason, these women, both in their twenties, had become the focal point for the WBC's protest. In an effort to combat the WBC, or to help promote their newly brewed "Nuptial Ale," the Gilded Otter had its animal mascot outside waving and encouraging people to come in and have some food and beverage after their protesting was concluded.

I saw Jeremiah moving towards his car. "Jeremiah, can I catch a ride with you?" I asked, realizing that while we covered many of the same subjects and events, we had never spoken more than a few words to one another. But today felt like a day for camaraderie, and I welcomed the stale, dry air of his little Honda.

Jeremiah almost always wore a baseball cap of some kind. He also wore a trench coat and a button-down shirt. That was part of the *Times Herald-Record* dress code. All of their reporters had to wear oxford-style shirts. I'm not sure what the requirements were for the women, possibly silk blouses only, or rayon and cotton blend shirts without a plunging neckline.

Somehow our conversation, in the short, one-mile drive to the Gilded Otter turned towards his good fortune to have broken the same-sex marriage story. He was sweet, with a gray goatee, and he honestly sympathized with me that it was his paper which had broken the story and not ours.

We parked by Cookies and Cream, a little ice-cream parlor just up the street from the Gilded Otter. As I climbed out I saw my friend Kristen and her brother Steve parking next to us and heading down to the Otter.

"So God hates beer too?" asked Steve.

"Apparently he hates otters as well," said Kristen.

"And the space shuttle?" asked Steve with a bemused look on his face. "There was a lot of hanky-panky going down on the space shuttle. They have these special little holes cut out in the back so that the astronauts can get some super space sex in!"

But then our banter was overwhelmed by the sound of an approaching helicopter. As it passed overhead we could see that it was a State Police helicopter. We approached the growing number of counter-protestors lined up on the edge of the Blueberry Fields. Throughout the day a lot of people were mumbling and grumbling about "overkill" in terms of the police protection, which really culminated with the addition of the helicopter, hovering noisily over head. "Maybe it is overkill but I feel very protected," said Kristen.

I lingered with friends on the opposite side of the protest for a while, admiring the ridiculous juxtaposition between the human-sized otter costume waving and soliciting motorists, and the hate rhetoric of the protestors, who were becomingly increasingly difficult to hear because of the State Police chopper. "I'm calling Jason," I said as I pulled out my cell phone and dialed his number.

It was his voice mail. "Hi, this is New Paltz Village Mayor Jason West. If you are a member of the press you must hang up and dial 255-1413. Messages left by the press on this phone will not be returned. For all other calls please leave your name, number and brief message. Thank you."

"I hope you're getting your beauty sleep, Mr. Mayor, while the rest of us are standing out in the freezing rain listening to the lovely and enchanting rhetoric of the Westboro Baptist Church protestors.

I think it might behoove you to get your mayoral ass out of bed and come down here, since you're the one that started this whole thing! Even the mayor of Nyack is here!"

I saw other friends and neighbors outside the Otter: Kristine Harris, a professor of Chinese language, culture and history at SUNY New Paltz, and her husband Robert Polito, the director of the Graduate Creative Writing Program at the New School in New York City. They had been on their way to The Bakery for coffee and bagels when they saw the crowds and signs and protestors heaving down Main Street.

Robert's wardrobe was entirely black. Even his outfit for the gym uptown consisted of a black t-shirt and black sweatpants and black high-tops. He was possibly the most well-read person I had ever encountered, and talking with him on any subject for only a few minutes made me feel one of two ways: either completely edified and smart and in possession of some new and profound knowledge, or like a washed-up intellectual with too many babies and too few brain cells.

As we were discussing the cohesive ideological approach of the protestors, my cell phone rang. It had a way of always startling me.

It was Jason. "I thought we were supposed to ignore the right-wing fascist zealots!" he said.

"Well, they're here," I said. "And so are we hungover?

"No. I was yesterday, but not today. Where are you?"

"At the Gilded Otter. But they'll be heading to the Catholic church for their final protest in five minutes."

"Okay. I'll be there."

Robert, Kristine and I walked up the steep hill towards the Catholic church. By the time we arrived, the counter-protestors had grown in numbers once again. The priest who was protecting his flock and welcoming a second Palm Sunday Mass congregation smiled at me. At first I thought he recognized me from a funeral I had recently attended that he had ministered. It was the funeral for a nine-day-old boy, Beckett, a twin, and the son of our friends Shari and Paul Carroll. But as he approached me his smile faded. "I do not want any of our parishioners interviewed," he said severely. "Please, no press."

141

I wanted to scream out that I wasn't the press, not the kind of "press" he alluded to, but instead I refocused my attention on the protestors, who were parading towards the church with a new slew of signs and banners.

"Zero Tolerance for Child Molesting Priests" was one.

"Hail Mary Fag Priest" was another. This sign had the silhouettes of two priests engaged in anal sex.

"These people are unbelievable," Robert Polito whispered. "What *do* they believe in?"

"They claim to be Calvinists and God's chosen elite," I explained, although I myself was still unsure what that meant. So I decided to walk over to the dark side of the street and try to get a better handle on their religious viewpoints, which were sketchy to me at best.

When I crossed over, Luch approached me apologetically.

"I'm sorry, Erin, but I have to ask you to be brief because we have some security issues here."

"No problem," I said, suddenly more intrigued by the "security issues" than the breakdown of the Phelps's home-spun spiritual belief system.

The helicopter was flying lower and lower. I thought it was preparing to land at the Hasbrouck Park just east of St. Joseph's Church. The noise lent a certain maliciousness and foreboding to the scene.

"What security issues?" I asked Luch.

"Of all the protest sites, this is the one we're most concerned about," he said quietly, already appearing to be on high alert. "The chief believes it has the greatest potential for conflict."

I could see the chief's point. It was Palm Sunday, and the priests, while greeting and releasing their flock from Mass, were faced with slanderous and vulgar depictions of themselves and their faith. It was an odd contrast to look at St. Joe's parking lot and the streetfront, now filled with protestors, and to think about the annual summer "Italian Festa" its congregants hosted each July. Besides the library fair, and the Fourth of July fireworks show, it's the event which draws the biggest crowds in New Paltz. Catholic, Buddhist, atheist, gay, straight, single or with family—almost no one can resist the draw of sweet pepper sausages, homemade cannolis, a Ferris wheel ride on a summer night, or a shot at sinking their most loved or despised public official in the dunking booth. But it was the tail-end of winter, it was raining, and there was no fresh red sauce doused with basil to sweeten the air.

Out of the corner of my eye, I saw Jason walk towards the church, a cup of coffee clenched in his hand and a baseball hat and windbreaker guarding him against the rain.

"Nice of you to show up," I joked.

"I would have come, but I was told we were all supposed to stay home. So these are what the right-wing fascist gay-bashers look like? Hmm. I bet they don't even know who I am."

"Introduce yourself," I said.

"Welcome to New Paltz," Jason shouted to the Phelps family. "How do you like our little village?"

The Phelps brigade did not recognize Jason, but everyone on this side of the street did.

"Hey, Mayor West, I grew up here and I came all the way from Cincinnati to lend my support to you and New Paltz and the gay couples that have been married here," said one man shaking Jason's hand. "I just want to thank you. My parents still live here and they want you to paint their house."

"I have to get back to house painting because I'm going into debt!" Jason replied. Although he said this with a laugh, I knew it was true.

Once Jason was consumed by the crowd and the Phelps protestors lost their voice under the hornet-like buzz of the helicopter, the climate seemed to change. Within minutes of the WBC's dropping their signs and heading towards their cars, departing for Mayor Shield's Nyack and their next scheduled protest, the sun poked its ambivalent head through the clouds. The rain stopped and Jason looked up, turned up his palms towards the sky, and said, "Look at this. The sun is finally shining and the rain has stopped. It looks like God is on our side."

Chapter 9
If That is the Law then the Law is an Ass

I received a phone call from Jason telling me that in ten minutes the oral arguments would be presented before Judge Katz on the criminal case against him. It was the first week in May, less than a month after the Phelps family had returned to their natural habitat in Topeka, Kansas. Sometime after Jason's arraignment back in March, his lawyers had filed a motion asking Judge Katz to dismiss the criminal charges leveled by the DA against the mayor. Their argument was that the Domestic Relations Law statute, which denied same-sex couples the ability to obtain marriage licenses, was unconstitutional as applied. Before Judge Katz could schedule a trial, he had to first decide whether or not to grant the defense's motion to dismiss the charges. Rosenkranz and Kossover requested and were granted the opportunity to present their oral arguments before Judge Katz. The DA's office would also be present to counter those arguments, and to try to convince the judge that the constitutionality of the law was not the issue, but instead, Jason's conscious decision to break the law.

At the same time, State Supreme Court Judge Michael Kavanagh would have to consider whether or not he, too, would hear oral arguments on the civil suit being brought against Jason by Bob Hebel and Liberty Counsel. While Bob had successfully convinced Ulster County Judge Vincent Bradley to place a temporary restraining order on the mayor, barring him from marrying same-sex couples, Judge Kavanagh would now have to determine whether or not that restraining order should be lifted, or made permanent.

I called my father, who was luckily at his office and not too busy, to see if he could watch the kids on such short notice. Once he picked them up, I jumped into the shower, barely dried myself off, and dashed down to the courthouse, hair still wet, to make sure I had a seat. As I ran towards the court, I kept imagining that I would be confronted with another parking lot full of satellite trucks and TV reporters. But to my surprise, the only other people there, besides my old neighbor and veteran court clerk, Al Bouchard, were Jason, Andy Kossover, Joshua Rosenkranz, and Paul O'Neil once again representing the district attorney's office.

"Where is everyone?" I asked Jason.

"I don't know," he said. "I guess someone should have gotten the word out."

Andy and Rosenkranz were whispering to each other and trading papers back and forth. Al Bouchard motioned me to sit up front, next to the judge's bench, where I would be able to hear. Jason, while looking freshly showered and clean-shaven, had dark circles under his eyes. I wondered if they were from worry, or from a late night at the bars.

Soon Judge Katz walked in and all six of us stood. I was very curious as to how he was going to deal with this case. I imagined that he felt an enormous amount of pressure. Here he was a liberal Democrat who now found himself with a high-profile case, which, even Jason's closest supporters would privately confess, was fairly cut-and-dry. If Katz chose to stick to a narrow interpretation of the case and ignore the constitutional issues, as the *prosecution* wanted him to, then Jason would be put on trial. But if Judge Katz allowed himself to consider the constitutional issues in this case, as Jason's attorneys wanted him to, then he would be in the position, not only to dismiss the criminal charges against Jason on the grounds that the

Domestic Relations Law statute as applied was unconstitutional, but also to make a landmark civil rights decision.

The judge invited me to sit up front so I could hear the arguments. The last time I had been in the courtroom was back in March for the arraignment of the two Unitarian ministers the DA had also prosecuted for solemnizing gay marriages in New Paltz. There had been a swarm of journalists inside and a sea of supporters singing hymns outside. But this Friday morning, all was strangely quiet. I couldn't understand why no other reporters were there. Had Jason's sex appeal worn off? Were gay marriages no longer a topical issue? I thought it odd that all of the fervor displayed when he conducted the marriages and then pleaded not guilty to the charges had ebbed to the point where the actual decision of whether or not to have a trial was largely ignored. The only other person there was Jason's girlfriend at the time, April, who Rachel described as a vegan. "She won't even eat honey because it comes from bees."

"What does she eat then?" I asked.

"I don't know but she likes to drink."

"Well, at least she's getting her grains."

Jason asked the judge if it was all right if his friend recorded the arguments with her camcorder. The judge denied the request. Halfway into the arguments, Jeremiah stumbled in, giving the impression that he, like me, had just rolled out of bed. He sat next to me and I tried to catch him up to speed. "I just got the message," he whispered to me. "So did I," I said.

And so it began. Judge Katz went immediately after Rosenkranz, asking him how he could possibly get around the fact that the mayor violated the Domestic Relations Law. "I don't know if you can get from me what you want to get from me," said the judge. "You've sort of painted me into a box here and I'm not sure how I can get out...I do not foresee my ruling predicated on your contention that New York allows for same-sex marriages. That would be a tortured reading of the Domestic Relations Law to say that it recognizes same-sex marriages."

"With all due respect your honor," said Rosenkranz, not yet willing to give up the argument that the DRL statute was gender-neutral, thus making Jason's actions sanctioned by law. "There is no explicit prohibition of same-sex marriage in the DRL statute." Rosenkranz took a deep breath and continued. "The two regulations the statute provides is that the parties must satisfy requirements of age and capacity. There are stray references to 'man' and 'woman' but no statutory requirement that the applying parties be one man and one woman. Even if the State law did prohibit same-sex couples from marrying, that prohibition would be unconstitutional. The right to choose one's partner in marriage is a fundamental right. The prosecution has given no compelling evidence for the prohibition of same-sex marriages, except a statement that says the State has an interest in preserving 'traditional marriage.' Well, what is the evidence?"

"What was the emergency?" Judge Katz asked. "Why did he have to perform the marriages on that day? Why not pursue other remedies?"

"That is fair, your honor, and you're right," said Rosenkranz. "No one would have died had the mayor refused to marry them, but they would have experienced longer periods of invidious discrimination. Rosa Parks could have filed an Article 78 to argue the case that she had a right to sit at the front of the bus, but she did not. Why? Because she was tired that day. She was tired of the ongoing discrimination."

Katz asked O'Neil to present the prosecution's argument, or the "people's argument" as it is referred to.

"Your honor, we are here today because Mayor West unilaterally decided what laws he would follow and which ones he would not follow," argued O'Neil. "We are in a precarious position if we allow duly elected officials to determine which laws they will follow and which ones they will not. We have a system, a good system that allows for us to challenge laws that are deemed incorrect or unconstitutional. The DA's office is not taking a position on same-sex marriages; we are here because Mayor West officiated those marriages without having been provided with a valid New York State marriage license, as required by law."

Paul had this nervous habit of clicking his pen cap on and off. It was making me crazy. I wanted to whisper to him to stop it, partly because it was irritating but mostly because it made him look bad. Although I didn't agree with his arguments, part of the hometown girl in me wanted him to at least present those arguments professionally. Regardless of my inner pleas to Paul to stop, the clicking continued.

Judge Katz said that he would not buy what he deemed as the prosecution's "superficial" argument that this case was based solely on West's officiating the marriages without a license. "I think we need to look beyond that," he said.

"Your honor," responded O'Neil. "What if a group of adults came forward and asked to be married? If we allow Mayor West to marry members of the same-sex without a proper license, then what is to stop an elected official from marrying several people at one time if they believe it is the right thing to do?"

"I think that case would most likely take place in Woodstock," joked the judge. "But what is the people's interest in this case? Would the prosecution act the same had this been an interracial couple? Is the people's argument a defense of the traditional definition of marriage?"

O'Neil continued to repeat that the prosecution's case was based solely on the mayor's violation of the Domestic Relations Law statutes 13 and 17—requiring a valid marriage license before an officiate can solemnize a marriage—and on the mayor's "subjective interpretation of the law."

"Well, the response to that is obvious, isn't it?" said Judge Katz. "To quote Charles Dickens: 'If that is the law then the law is an ass.'"

With this opening Rosenkranz literally danced constitutional circles around O'Neil, heavily referencing whole paragraphs of U.S. Supreme Court decisions on landmark cases including *Loving v. Virginia*, *Brown v. Board of Education*, the Under 21 Law, and the court's reversal of the Jim Crow laws.

"You know what's a great perk about working on this case?" said Andy during one of my many follow-up calls to him trying to get my presentation of the legal issues just right. "It raises your game. I'm playing with the big boys here. There are national and constitutional issues at stake. It's like being in the NBA playoffs."

O'Neil continued to press his case. "To this day, your honor, no Article 78 has been filed by any of the couples that the mayor married against the New Paltz town clerk or the State Department of Health for denying them a marriage license. There is a judicial process to follow if someone believes that the law is incorrect. But Mayor West has no authority as a member of the executive branch to declare statutes unconstitutional. He also has no authority to make a new law that says 'As mayor, I can issue my own licenses to couples,' which is what he did. Never once did the mayor contact the attorney general for his opinion before marrying the couples. He did not attempt to change the law through the State legislature. He contacted the national media before he contacted the New Paltz police who were forced to exercise ground control at the last minute without any preparation. If we all did the same then I'm afraid our world would become a lot more chaotic than it already is."

In his closing argument, Rosenkranz pointed out that this was the only case in the country where criminal charges had been brought against an official for solemnizing same-sex marriages. "No other district attorney saw fit to bring criminal charges against an officiate of same-sex marriages except the Ulster County district attorney," he said. "Not in Oregon, Massachusetts, San Francisco. There have been more than 6,100 same-sex marriages recently officiated throughout the United States and there has been no mayhem in the social order of our country."

"He's not a crook," said Rosenkranz during the final thrust of his oral arguments to have the criminal charges against the mayor dismissed. "He researched this, spoke at length with the couples, the attorneys, with constitutional experts before he made his decision. He is not putting himself above the law; in fact he is holding his actions accountable to the Constitution of New York State. And I believe that is what we ask and we expect from our elected officials. To serve us in the honor of justice."

"I think it went well," said Jason.

I, too, thought it had gone well for Jason. Katz was obviously interested in hearing the constitutional reasons behind Jason's actions while Paul, speaking on behalf of the DA, was trying desperately to avoid the constitutional issues, which were central to this case. The couples didn't have licenses because of their sexual orientation. That was obvious. And what Rosenkranz had made even more obvious was that denying gay couples marriage licenses was a clear violation of the New York State Constitution's equal protection clause.

The mayor was off to the airport to go on yet another fundraising and speaking tour. Rosenkranz and his colleagues allowed Jeremiah and me to interview them and then they climbed quickly into a chauffeured black sedan back to the city. I imagined Andy went to meet his wife for lunch and Jeremiah had to write the story for the next day's issue; I had to run home to my flock.

Chapter 10
Hebel v. West

"Marriage is a great institution, and no family should be without it."—Channing Pollock

Only a week later, on May 17, State Supreme Court Justice Michael Kavanagh announced that he would be hearing the oral arguments on the civil case leveled against Jason by Bob Hebel, who was Jason's fellow board member, but in this case was acting as an ordinary citizen exercising his right to request that a restraining order be placed on someone he believed to be dangerous. Bob was dragging the mayor back to court again, this time in an attempt to convince Judge Kavanagh to make the temporary restraining order permanent, thus barring Jason from marrying any gay couples now or ever.

I asked Andy if I could ride with him to the Kingston courthouse where the oral arguments would take place. I didn't necessarily want to admit this to Andy, but I hated to drive. I could manage well inside a small radius, but when I had to move away from the boundaries of New Paltz, my palms would get sweaty and my heart would start racing. Jason was also looking for a ride. I gathered he didn't want to risk making the twenty-five-minute trek with his Toyota truck, the hood of which had recently blown off and was held in place by two bungee cords. Andy told Jason and me to meet him at his office no later than 10 a.m. He and Jason were scheduled to meet up at the Kingston courthouse with Rosenkranz, who was driving up from Manhattan, to go over some legal strategies before court went into session.

Andy's office was air-conditioned and clean. Everyone working there looked very serious and purposeful. I was trying to look important as well, toying with the handheld recorder Rachel had lent me for the court proceedings. I met her outside of the Old Main Building on campus just five minutes earlier so that she could deliver the recorder to me. "It's really easy," she said. "You just push this button and it records." Although most people might not have found this common-enough device daunting, it made me feel like I was engaging in espionage. I always took notes by hand.

Andy stepped out of his office. "I heard Jason was going to give you a ride up to Kingston on the back of his bike," he said to me with a laugh.

"We were planning on it but he got a flat tire," I said.

Andy had this jovial nature that was pleasant to be around. He could find something in common to talk with anyone about—law, sports, taxes, traffic, *The Daily Show* with Jon Stewart. "*The Daily Show* has been going crazy with the same-sex marriage issue," he said. "Jon Stewart keeps flashing clips of the Senate debate on the proposed 'defense of traditional marriage' amendment. This one senator was arguing that marriage would encourage gay people to procreate. Jon Stewart said, 'If you put this thing in that hole you get a baby?' It was hysterical. Then he showed a clip of the mayor with Billiam and Jeffrey getting married and said, 'Where is the compassion?'"

"Have you seen this?" I asked, showing Andy a copy of the *New York Post* article that featured the controversy over fashion designer Kenneth Cole's window design at his Rockefeller Center store. The window display showed two women linking arms and two men holding hands with suitcases in their hands. Written above the mannequins was the phrase "We See A Pattern Here" and arrows pointing towards "San Francisco 1,943 miles" and "New Paltz, N.Y. 90 miles." Below, a sign read "Marriage Licenses Obtained Here."

"That's great," said Andy. "Can I make a copy of this?"

"Sure. My dad gave it to me. He is the only person I know who reads the *New York Post*."

Just then Jason walked in. I had to laugh. While I could tell that he had made an effort to clean up, he could never quite pull it off. He was wearing the same suit that his friends had purchased for him months ago, a nasty pair of shoes that looked like something he picked up at the Goodwill, and his army surplus green canvas sack slung over his shoulder with various buttons pinned to it and unraveling threads dangling from the bottom.

"Good morning, Mr. Mayor," I said.

"What? Do I look okay?"

"You look...like you."

"Let's get going. Josh is going to think that we're not showing up. We're supposed to meet him at the courthouse in fifteen minutes," said Andy. Off we went in Andy's very plush and comfortable BMW sports car. It was the first really hot day of the spring and I was happy to be resting easy in his air-conditioned car. Jason reviewed the briefs that the lawyers had prepared. I fiddled with the recorder and Andy talked. He asked Jason about his book.

"Who's publishing it?" he asked.

"It's with Miramax Books," he said, looking slightly uncomfortable. "It's going to be a political, philosophical book."

"I heard that Harvey Weinstein wants to buy back Miramax," said Andy. "You know I helped fund Harvey's first capital venture?"

"Harvey Weinstein?" said Jason.

Andy told us that he and Harvey were in college together at SUNY Buffalo. They were friends, and one day Harvey approached Andy and nine other friends and asked each of them to lend him $2,000. He said that he'd pay them back double within the month. Shortly before a Grateful Dead show at Buffalo's War Memorial Auditorium, Andy learned the money Harvey had borrowed from them was the $20,000 seed money he needed to promote the concert. The day before the show he asked Andy to be house manager. It was a very successful concert and the next day Harvey gave Andy and his friends $4,000 each.

Andy went on to serve as Weinstein's house manager for a series of concerts that he promoted in Buffalo, Syracuse, and Rochester. "I did that for a number of years," said Andy. "Harvey was a formidable person and I was one of the few people that could deal with him. He wasn't necessarily easy. He pissed a lot of people off, but we always worked well together." Andy had a real finesse for dealing with complex and powerful individuals, which made him the perfect lawyer for this case.

Andy said the rock concerts slowed down and Weinstein went on to purchase the old Century Theatre in downtown Buffalo, which was equivalent to our Upstate Films, an independent cinema in Rhinebeck, New York. "He developed this skill for identifying quality independent films and producing them," Andy explained to us as we drove. "He had a great vision and saw a niche in the film industry to promote and distribute quality independent films, which we all know now as Miramax."

"You know what Miramax is?" he asked us. Jason and I both shook our heads. "Most people don't know this, but Miramax is a combination of his parents' names, Miriam and Max."

At one point, Harvey encouraged Andy to forget the law and come work for him. "He asked me if I wanted to be one of his partners on this venture. I'm thinking, this guy has the Midas touch. Everything he touches turns to gold. But then I thought about my parents. What would they say? 'You're not going to become a lawyer?' Telling them I was going to help promote independent films would be like telling them I was leaving law school to go join a rock band." Jason and I started to laugh.

While Andy admitted that he still thinks about what might have happened had he taken Weinstein up on his offer, he said he regretted absolutely nothing. "What is there to regret? I have a wonderful life, a wonderful family, and a great law practice. It might not be Hollywood, but I'm happier than I ever dreamed I could be."

When we got up to the courthouse Jason turned to me and said, "I'd like to think that Judge Kavanagh consciously scheduled these arguments on the 50th anniversary of *Brown v. Board of Ed*, but somehow I doubt it." He always impressed me with the way history was right at his fingertips. I began to think about that. I realized it was also the same day that gay marriages were to be performed legally in Massachusetts after the State Supreme Court refused to step in and block municipal clerks from issuing licenses to gay couples, clearing the way for the nation's first State-sanctioned same-sex weddings.

The courthouse, located on Wall Street in Kingston's historic district, is an impressive building. It was where a New Paltz–born slave, Sojourner Truth, turned to win back her son from his slave owners once she herself had become freed. This building was the first stop in what would become Truth's lifelong advocacy for abolition, the rights of freed slaves, and women's rights. Her public oration began here, I reflected, on these court steps, and she would go on to become one of the most famous civil rights and women's rights advocates in American history. She couldn't read or write, her voice was her most powerful tool.

I remembered one of the *New Paltz Times* copyeditors saying that if Sojourner Truth had been a man they would have erected a gigantic statue on Main Street in downtown New Paltz and forced traffic to be re-routed around it. But since she was a black woman, all we had was a "lousy plaque." The SUNY New Paltz library was also dedicated to the heroine, and one of the final events of former Mayor Nyquist's term was to dedicate a small riverside park in honor of the "most famous person, man or woman, to have come from New Paltz." Although he was so well-versed in American history, I wondered if Jason knew of this bit of local history, about what type of fertile soil his political career had risen from. I began to believe that there was a continuum here, and that New Paltz was a place that could nurture great leaders.

Joshua Rosenkranz was waiting at the side entrance of the courthouse with his wife—a beautiful woman, very thin and chic and slightly taller than her husband—and members of his legal team. "I think this is personal for Josh," Jason said to me once. "He's married to a black woman and I'm sure he thinks about the fact that if they had attempted to be married only twenty-five years earlier, they wouldn't have been able to because interracial couples would have been denied the right to a marriage license. He's a brilliant civil rights lawyer, but I think that this particular case means more to him than others."

As we entered the cool basement of the courthouse, where everyone had to go through a security check, I wondered how Kavanagh would navigate this case. He was a bright man and a brilliant prosecutor. But he was also a staunch conservative. I had interviewed him once when he was the district attorney. It was during one of my true-crime phases when I was obsessed with all kinds of dark tales. My dad had always told me how impressed he was with this young DA whose first big case was to prosecute the mobster, Tony Provenzano. The DA had to prove that Provenzano ordered his men to murder an Ulster County man more than twenty years after it had happened. My dad had gone to the courthouse every day to watch the trial. "I didn't know that ten years later we would become good friends," he told me. Kavanagh was often at my dad's house for barbecues and dinners or big PGA tournaments. He was as Irish as they came. A tall, handsome man now in his early sixties, he had a real Robert Redford quality to him with his strawberry blonde hair and sophisticated roughness. My dad often characterized him as the "consummate politician." Now Kavanagh was to hear the oral arguments from both Liberty Counsel, which was swiftly losing every battle in Massachusetts, and Jason's team, on whether or not a permanent injunction should be placed on the mayor's same-sex marriages.

Andy led us into the court library on the bottom floor. There was a lot of handshaking and introductions between Rosenkranz's wife, his legal assistant, and Jason's team. I offered to step out and let them have their pre-game meeting but they declined. After some brief lawyer talk, Andy suggested that it was time to head into the courtroom.

"I think we're ready," said Rosenkranz, gently placing his arm on Jason's back.

"Let's do it," said Jason.

The elevator was jammed so we walked up the three flights of stairs to Kavanagh's chambers. In the hallway, at the top of the stairs, just outside of courtroom, Jason was greeted with several camera flashes, anxious journalists, and a handful of supporters including Billiam, who was dressed head to toe in cowboy regalia. Billiam was always dressed either one of two ways: in a suit with his signature bow tie, or like a cross between a gentlemen farmer and a cattle rancher on his way to do some serious line dancing.

"This feels like a high school reunion," joked Jason, as he shook hands with the reporters and paused briefly for photos. "We haven't all been in the same place for a while."

I sat next to Vicki Kossover, who had come to watch the arguments. "I think this is going to be fascinating," she said. I reached for my recorder. It wasn't there. I had been so diligent about testing it out on the car ride that I completely forgot it on the front seat of Andy's car.

"Crap, I forgot it."

"Forgot what?" Vicki asked.

"Never mind," I muttered, "Do you have a pen I can borrow?"

"All rise for the Honorable Judge Michael Kavanagh."

Bob Hebel had not shown up. There was a rumor floating around that he had gone with the Liberty Counsel co-president, Michael Staver, to Massachusetts where Staver was making last-minute appeals to the State Supreme Court to stop the gay marriages. Regardless, his interests were well represented by Rena Lindavaldsen, another attorney with the right-wing law firm.

"This case is not about the constitutionality of law," she argued. "It is about whether or not Mayor Jason West had the power and authority to violate New York State law because he didn't like it, didn't believe in it or interpret it as being constitutional. There are three separate court cases in New York right now that will determine the constitutionality of same-sex marriages."

"Let's get to the issue," Kavanagh said abruptly. "Liberty Counsel is not here because you're so terribly upset that Mayor West performed a marriage without a valid license. You're here because he married two members of the same sex. What is the legitimate State interest in barring same-sex marriages?"

Lindavaldsen responded, "Various studies prove that a marriage which includes one man and one woman provides the optimal benefits for children...."

The judge cut her off again. "Well, in New York State we already allow same-sex couples to adopt, have their own children, and have full parental and custodial rights. So the State would not be served by that argument."

"Marriage has always been, always understood to be, a union between one man and one woman," Lindavaldsen continued, but was once again cut off by the judge's questions.

"If two people, of proper age, are willing to assume the enormous responsibility of marriage, why not let them?" asked the judge.

"West is not a lawmaker, he is not a judge, he disobeyed the law and he took an oath to uphold the law; that is what this case is about," repeated Lindavaldsen.

"What is the legitimate State interest in upholding what is clearly a *discriminatory* statute?" said Kavanagh.

I kept thinking that this case was sewn up, that Kavanagh would shock the local Republican and conservative world and dismiss the case. He grilled Lindavaldsen with such intensity that I almost began to feel sorry for her. She looked tired with her greasy, dirty-blonde hair falling in her face as she repeated the same response over and over again. But just as I imagined that Jason would be back singing "Going to the Chapel," the judge turned his scalpel on Rosenkranz.

"Was there not a more responsible course of action for the Mayor to pursue rather than break a law?" asked the judge. "He, or more likely one of the couples wishing to be married, could have applied for a license from the town clerk and when they were rejected filed a civil suit."

"There were several available courses of action to take," agreed Rosenkranz. "But Mayor West, who was asked by Billiam van Roestenberg and Major Jeffrey McGowan to solemnize their marriage, believed that he would be complicit in a violation of the Constitution of New York if he were to reject them. Faced with the conflict between a technical licensing provision that makes random references to 'man' and 'woman,' and the New York State Constitution, Mayor West chose to abide by and uphold the highest law of the land which was and is the Constitution."

"What you are proposing would set a dangerous precedent," countered Kavanagh. "You're saying that if an executive officer of government disagrees with an existing law, they are obligated to commit a crime if it is consistent with their belief. What if someone with that same authority decided that children ten years of age should be permitted to marry? Are you telling me that if that official believed that they were right and were acting in good faith based on their beliefs and their interpretation of the Constitution that they would be right?"

"If the official was wrong and had no good-faith basis, then he would be exposed to the criminal consequences, which is a risk that Mayor West took in this instance. Then the courts would decide whether or not the interpretation was correct. This court has to decide whether or not West correctly interpreted the Constitution."

Kavanagh expressed on several occasions that to set a precedent through which a duly elected official could violate the law if he or she believed the law unjust was "dangerous" and "disturbing."

Rosenkranz argued that such actions are part of the very fabric of the greatest civil rights cases. "There is a time-honored tradition of executive officers setting up test cases for the courts to determine the constitutionality of a discriminatory provision or statute as applied," he said to me after the arguments were concluded. "While the courts have the final word, they do not have a monopoly on constitutional issues."

It was an oddly celebratory moment outside the courthouse. I did not know why. But we all stood in the parking lot, in the piercing late May sunshine, conducting an informal, post-court analysis. I quickly realized what I thought Kavanagh might do. While he would agree that a statute that denied gay couples the ability to receive valid marriage licenses was discriminatory, he would, at the same time, penalize Jason for taking the law into his own hands.

Rosenkranz and his wife stood off to the side talking while Jason spoke to the reporters. I felt bad intruding upon what seemed to be an intimate moment, but I knew I could talk to Jason on the car ride home and wasn't sure when I'd get the chance to talk to Rosenkranz again. I couldn't think of anything brilliant to ask him, so instead, I just solicited his reaction to the arguments.

"Judge Kavanagh was very engaged and did not seem to be prejudging the case," he said, slipping on his sunglasses. He did admit that Kavanaugh's comments appeared to be more favorable towards the defense. "Judge Kavanagh kept his cards very close to his chest. It was difficult to know what he was thinking."

"I'm confident that the injunction will be lifted," I could hear Jason boast to the various members of the press gathered around him. "This is an auspicious day for many reasons and we will have marriage equality in New York State within a generation. February twenty-seventh was the best day of my life. When I looked into those couples' eyes and saw the love between them, it moved me...I look forward to the injunction being lifted so that I can solemnize marriages for more couples who have suffered discrimination for way too long."

He repeated, ad nauseum, the part about February 27 being the happiest day of his life when he "looked into those couples' eyes and saw the love between them." While I'm all about the love, Jason repeated this line and a few of his other greatest hits time after time. "Jason, you have to drop that part about the 'looking into their eyes,'" I said at some point.

"I know," he said sheepishly, "I've had to become a master of the sound bite."

"Well, if you only have three words then just say, 'Justice will prevail.'"

"That's good," he said and pretended to write it down on the palm of his hand: *Justice will prevail.*

"It works for everything. 'So Mr. Mayor, what do you think about the Bush administration's announcement today that they will be sending more troops into Iraq?' and you respond..."

"Justice will prevail," he repeated.

As Judge Vincent Bradley drove by in his pick-up truck, someone pointed him out to Jason. "So that's the one that put the restraining order on me. I wonder if he would even recognize me. He certainly believes I'm dangerous.... Hi, Judge!" he said with a large wave. The truck drove out of the parking lot.

Sometimes he could be so arrogant, I thought.

The photographer from *The New York Times* had just shown up. He began clicking away as Jason and Rosenkranz were being interviewed by Tom Crampton of *The New York Times*. Although the photographer took what seemed to be a hundred shots out in front of the courthouse and then again outside of The Bistro where we would have lunch, the picture he used was of Rosenkranz, Jason, and my ear.

"Erin, was that you in *The New York Times* photograph?" Mala asked me later in an e-mail. "You were wearing a pearl necklace and a black dress?"

I had gratefully managed to stay out of any pictures in this high-profile story. I saw many of my fellow journalists unwillingly make the papers with double chins, eyes closed, paunches protruding, or their tongues hanging out while interviewing the mayor, the clergy, or standing by idly. The local public library board president, Sally Rhoads, was kind enough to send me a nice letter that said, "Just thought you might enjoy these for your records—you're always covering other people so I thought it might be fun to have a picture of yourself." She had enclosed two pictures of me she had taken amidst a throng of journalists, as we covered the first round of gay marriages performed by the mayor back in February. I had remembered feeling good that day in my faux-leather jacket and light blue turtleneck sweater with my hair pulled back in a smart fashion.

That image of myself may have rested pleasantly in my mind forever had I not seen the physical proof, which proved so painfully to the contrary. There I was, hunched over, writing notes, my just-out-of-the-shower hair looking greasy rather than wet, my pants sagging and the expression on my face one of pinched concentration rather than carefree beauty.

While millions of everyday folk have had their picture in *The New York Times*—passing by on a street, or their face in a subway window—like an unending cast of extras walking by as the news unfolds around them, I still couldn't resist taking a look.

"I'm just going to run down to the corner store and get a paper," I said to Kazik after receiving the e-mail from Mala late at night.

"At this hour?" he said surprised. "You never buy the paper this late."

"I know," I said. "I just heard there was an interesting story on Jason in the *Times*."

I flipped through the pages anxiously. There it was, the picture of Jason, Rosenkranz and me just below photos of the first married gay couples in Massachusetts. My grandmother's pearls, albeit fake, made the shot as did my pulled-back hair, gesticulating hand...and my ear.

"Oh honey, I saw your grandmother's pearls in *The New York Times*," said my mother the next morning. "If only she were here to see them."

Outside The Bistro, while waiting for the others to arrive, Jason and I shared a cigarette. He asked me how I thought it had gone.

"I don't think it went well," I said. "I mean, Josh did a great job, it's not that..."

"I think you're right."

The problem is, I told him, as we passed a Camel Light back and forth, keeping an eye out for the rest of the entourage to arrive, Judge Katz will probably rule to dismiss the charges while Kavanagh would most likely rule against him.

"For the 'movement', the reverse would be better," I mused, trying to think the whole thing through to find some way we might come up with a flashy trial. I could feel the sunburn on my shoulders, and I put my hands on them instinctively as if to ward off greater penetration. "If Kavanagh ruled to lift the restraining order on you, then you could continue to marry same-sex couples. And if Katz refused to dismiss the criminal charges and order a trial, that would create another media windfall and put the issue back on the front burner."

"I know," he said, unbuttoning his suit jacket. "Part of me wants to just rescind my motion to have the charges dismissed and go directly to trial. What could they do to me? They won't put me in jail and I've had offers from people around the country to pay for any penalties I could be charged with."

"You *rescind* that motion," I ordered, playfully. Just then, someone called out to Jason. He walked around to the front of The Bistro, then darted back towards me.

"Here, take my cigarette, the *Times* photographer wants a shot of me in front of The Bistro with Josh."

"Another 'Jason in his natural habitat shot?'"

"Yup."

I crushed out the cigarette with my heel, squeezed some lotion on my hands, and went inside.

During lunch, Jason and I tried to encourage Rosenkranz to rescind the motion to dismiss. While I could see that he wanted to entertain it, the professional defense attorney in him would not even joke about it, especially with members of the press around. "My main priority is seeing that the charges against my client are dropped," he said.

"Although it would be unfortunate for Jason, a trial would advance the movement" Andy suggested. "And we'd certainly have fun!"

Nothing galvanizes a movement like having a victim. While the gay couples themselves were the true victims of a discriminatory statute in New York and in most states around the country, Jason, a young, white, straight guy, had ironically become the victim in this particular drama. He was also the only elected official in the country to have criminal charges brought against him: twenty-four charges that could each carry up to one year in prison or a $500 fine.

I could only imagine the amount of support that would flood in when people saw this young, left-leaning idealistic mayor put on trial for marrying gay couples.

Chapter 11

Public Enemy Number One
and Two (and Three)

"A wise man gets more use from his enemies than a fool from his friends."—Baltasar Gracian

The Ulster County district attorney is an elected official. And this DA, Don Williams, ran in very conservative circles. He was endorsed by both the Democrat and Republican parties in his last election, in which he ran unopposed. But he was well aware that the political climate of Ulster County was rapidly cooling from a Republican hotbed to a Democratic lakeside retreat.

Williams graduated from Albany Law School in 1978 and promptly returned to his hometown of Kingston, New York, where he landed a job as an assistant district attorney. He had worked in the district attorney's office in the county courthouse—half a block from the house where he was born—ever since. As former District Attorney Michael Kavanagh's chief assistant for sixteen years, Williams faced plenty of challenges, including the prosecution of the State's first death penalty case in more than two decades. In 1996, Williams helped put Larry Whitehurst in prison for life, without a chance of parole for the brutal murder of his neighbor, seven-year-old Rickel Knox. When Kavanagh left the office to take a seat on the State Supreme Court bench in 1999, Williams filled the post. He was then re-elected without opposition in November 2003, imagining that 2004 would be the year where he could turn his attention to the younger members of his staff to teach them how to try cases. "It hasn't worked out as I planned," he said during an interview I had set up with him in Kingston, while we awaited the decision on the appeal.

The morning of February 27, 2004, the DA was contacted by New Paltz Police Chief Ray Zappone who informed him that the mayor was planning to perform same-sex marriages at noon and that these couples had no valid marriage licenses. Chief Zappone believed that there was some criminal violation involved in this action, under the penal code, but asked his office to look into it because the police rarely deal with violations of this nature. According to the DA, because the police have the power and authority to arrest, they rarely contact the district attorney's office for guidance or authorization to arrest someone. This was reserved for the most violent crimes that may involve very complicated legal issues.

After spending a brief period researching the Domestic Relations Law, the DA informed Chief Zappone that his initial interpretation of the code was accurate and that it would constitute a criminal act if the mayor went ahead with his plans. The DA directed the chief to tell the mayor that if he were to go forward that he would be "knowingly and consciously breaking the law." Chief Zappone then informed the DA that the mayor had been warned, but that he indicated that he would go forward regardless. To make sure that there was no ambiguity, the DA served Jason with a letter.

The DA leaned back in his leather chair as he explained his side of the story from beginning to end. "The next phone call I received was from Mayor West's attorney, Mr. Rosenkranz," he said. This phone call had obviously served to incite the DA. In fact, Williams became angered even as he recounted what happened that day: "He called this office to say, with a very thinly veiled threat, that if I were to go forward with an arrest of the mayor or authorize an arrest that I would suffer the political ramifications and that he would use the force of his eight-hundred-member law firm to bring the operation of my office to a grinding halt." The DA admitted that although he was offended by Rosenkranz's suggestion and tone, he "calmly and clearly explained to Mr. Rosenkranz that his insinuations would not benefit anyone, particularly his client, and I also said that I do not allow personal or political ambitions to influence my lawful obligations."

The DA emphasized that he was motivated not by politics, but by a deep respect for the law. "I grew up two blocks from this courthouse and have no desire other than to serve the people of this county as long as they would like me to serve. I could make three times as much money in a private practice and reacquaint myself with my family if that is what I wanted to do. But instead I chose public office."

I remembered taking a walk with my childhood friend, Kristen, now a fifth-grade teacher in the Kingston Public Schools system. She was raving about this one child in her class, Collin Williams, and how delightful he was, particularly how fair he was when it came to choosing boys and girls for his team in a game of soccer. I don't think she was even aware that he was our local Elliot Ness's son. "Colin was the most insightful, feminist child I'd ever had in my class," she said. "We were dealing with a real 'soccer scandal' that year. Either the girls weren't being chosen for the teams during recess, or if they were chosen they weren't being given the opportunity to have the ball. Colin was absolutely adamant that this was unjust and advocated for the girls and their rightful inclusion into the game."

"Chip off the ol' block, Don?" I asked him, recounting my friend's affection for his son.

"No, he's nothing like me, he takes after my wife. Now my daughter, on the other hand, *does* take after me. She's a handful."

It may have been easy and certainly convenient for Jason's supporters to villainize the DA, but he was a tenacious, bright and seemingly sincere prosecutor who also adored his family, his hometown of Kingston, and putting the bad guys away.

While the marriages were taking place, the DA had requested an opinion from State Attorney General Eliot Spitzer on whether

Jason should be charged and prosecuted. When Spitzer's office declined to provide an opinion, the burden lay on the DA's shoulders. "We didn't want to further fan the flames of the circus atmosphere and have the mayor arrested during the marriage ceremonies," said the DA. "But what my office did see right away was the significance of a public official violating a law. That aspect made it a more compelling issue and one that merited close examination." Left without guidance from Spitzer's office, the DA, with the assistance of his staff, pondered the case for three days and finally decided on March 2, 2004, to authorize the arrest of Mayor West with a criminal summons from the New Paltz Police Department.

From the moment that the DA woke up on February 27, his phone never stopped ringing, nor did it stop for the next several weeks. Little did he know that he had joined an elite club—along with Jason and his pro bono team—as the people the press most wanted to speak to. "Thankfully, my calendar was pretty light that week," he admitted. "Because part of what I pride myself on is returning all legitimate calls from the press to the best of my ability."

And thankfully for me, Jeremiah, and a few other regional reporters, the DA prioritized calls from the local press before he returned those of the *Daily News* or the *New York Post*. "I probably have spent more time talking with you on this case than anyone else," said the DA during an interview months later as we awaited the results of the appeal. "But seriously, I am elected by the people of this county and they are the ones I have to answer to first."

Although the DA did become a big hit with the more conservative *New York Post*—where he appeared on the front page even more times than the mayor himself—he was also popular with the more liberal *New York Times* where he was featured in the "Public Lives" column. "I received requests to appear on the *Today* show, the Bill O'Reilly show, CNN, and the Greta Van Susteren show, and believe me, I was flattered and honored to have been contacted by these organizations, but it would have interfered dramatically with the operation of this office. And this office and this county are who I'm beholden to.

"Having to decide whether or not to prosecute the mayor was a position that was very distasteful to me," continued the DA. "It was a position that I did not want to be in. But what I was taught by Judge Kavanagh is that we must make decisions that may be unpopular. And we have had many, many hateful and negative responses. Does that hurt? I'm a human being, of course it hurts."

The DA went on to share with me what he considered the most challenging part of his job. "What's hard is telling the family of a victim of a brutal crime that I am not able to hold accountable the person who is responsible because of some technicality in the law. That's something that haunts me forever. So in all honesty, this case, while it has received a lot of national attention, is not the most significant one this office has had to deal with." During the months that the *People v. West* case worked its way through the court system, the DA's office was responsible for prosecuting two murder trials.

When the DA first announced that he would level charges against the mayor, I had many off-the-record talks with him, trying to paint Jason in a human light. "I do not know the mayor, I've never met him, I hope for his sake that he is not furthering his own agenda but is instead following a deeply held belief," he said to me.

"Don. He's young, he's idealistic, he's really a nice guy," I said. "His intentions are in the right place. I'm sure he has had many lawyers telling him that it was within his rights to do this. If you meet him, you'll like him."

"Erin, I take your portrayal to heart and I hope you're right."

As the months unfolded and the cult of Jason developed, I could sense that the DA's impression of him was taking a turn for the worst.

The DA argued that had one of the couples who wished to be legally married filed an Article 78 lawsuit against the New Paltz town clerk that, "this issue might have been resolved in a legal and timely fashion. Here we are eight months later and all the mayor has done is to create a media circus with no legitimate outcome except for the advancement of his own personal and political career." Like Justices Kavanagh and Bradley, the DA cautioned that the mayor's actions set a dangerous precedent. "He cannot substitute his judgment for that of the State legislature and the courts," said Williams. "They are the ones with the appropriate jurisdiction to decide this issue. But the mayor arrogantly chose to be a law unto himself."

I asked Williams if it bothered him that he may be perceived historically as someone on the wrong side of a civil rights fight. "Do you really want to go down in history, even local history, as someone who tried to prevent marriages between two people who love each other?" I asked.

"This office is not arguing whether or not same-sex couples should have the legal right to marry."

I kept trying to get him to go on the record that he did indeed support gay unions. He had told me as much off the record, but I wanted him to go on the record. I just felt this compulsion to portray the other side of him, as I did for Jason, to those who would otherwise demonize him. I questioned him from every angle and finally he relented.

"I want to preface my personal opinion with the statement that these opinions do not interfere with the operations of this office," he said. "I am a human being and I do have feelings and opinions on issues of the day. I believe that questions surrounding gay marriages must be addressed and addressed soon. There are significant constitutional and legal issues that impact many people. That said, I am a man of faith who believes strongly in the sanctity of the institution of traditional marriage as being between one man and one woman. I also recognize that regardless of one's sexual orientation, individuals must not have their basic rights refused. Same-sex couples should have their civil unions recognized legally." While it was a moderate view—one that would not win many points in the gay community or with civil rights advocates—it was something. And it appeared to have taken a lot for him to say that, and in fact, outside of our liberal bubble, his opinion was one that was shared by many people in this country.

The DA also told me about a gay man who worked in his office with whom he had a strong friendship. "He has shared with me the difficulties he and his partner have because they cannot share health benefits. It's terrible and it pains me to hear their struggle. His partner is very ill and the lack of recognition of their union has caused a great financial burden."

"This is not a crime I believe merits jail time," the DA relented. "And yes, I had a choice. But for me to ignore the actions of an elected public official who commits a criminal act, just because it might create political issues for me pursuing the career of my choice in the future, would constitute a conscious neglect of my duties. Judge Bradley said that the mayor's actions could cause 'irreparable harm.' Judge Kavanagh said that the mayor's actions 'set a dangerous precedent.' Attorney General Eliot Spitzer stated that the mayor had committed 'criminal acts.' How can I ignore that? There are people that may think very bad thoughts of me, but I believe they are for the wrong reasons. I did what was proper and appropriate."

There was something very appealing about the 5' 8" tough-on-crime, Giuliani-style prosecutor. Although he said repeatedly that he had a "face for radio," there was nothing homely about him. I think it was his confidence that was so appealing—his willingness to go against the tide, or with the tide, depending on your vantage point. But he exuded a clear sense of purpose, of duty, and of connection. That I could appreciate. He was working to defend his soil, protect it from perceived or real danger. So was I. His job was to eradicate the predators, the crop-eating insects, threats that eroded the sustainability and value of the larger flock. My job, at least as I imagined it, was to help offer the harvest to everyone, regardless of its successes or failures.

"I want to thank you for always treating me fairly," said Williams, in a moment of frankness that took me off guard.

"Of course," I said. "I try to treat everyone fairly."

"Erin, I know that you have a, well, let's say a left-leaning bent. But you have always quoted me accurately and fairly and gone out of your way to present my particular arguments."

"I'm just doing my job, Don," I said, blushing a little bit. "And you're just doing yours."

My cell phone rang and I knew it was Kazik, who had been kind enough to drive the kids around downtown Kingston while I conducted the interview. "I've got to learn to drive again," I thought. I thanked the DA for taking the time to speak with me and quickly wound my way out of the four-story building. As I waited for Kazik to pick me up outside the historic steps, I kept thinking that in his own way the DA was helping to advance the cause. This was not his motive, nor a by-product he would necessarily sanction, but without the DA's prosecution of Jason, the media hype would have never risen to the level that it did. "This story is only successful because of its adversaries," I said to Deb later that afternoon. "If there was no mayor-busting DA and lawsuit-happy Hebel, there would be no great media fanfare apart from the actual marriages themselves."

The other alternative, the one that did not come to pass, would have been for the DA to do nothing, for Bob Hebel to have done nothing, and for the marriages to have continued each week, with Jason holding more hands, making more proclamations, and solemnizing endless love. But had that track continued on, as it did in San Francisco, it might have ended the same way, with the State Supreme Court ruling that the marriages were invalid. But this was New York, and it was New Paltz, and nothing here was ever easy or simple. We had a way of complicating things, twisting them in such a way that their form took on a shape recognizable to us, but oddly incongruent to the rest of the world.

The tension was never more palpable than during the village board meetings, with veteran Trustee Bob Hebel, Jason's public enemy number one, sitting way off to the right of the conference table, his body turned away from the other trustees, and his voice completely silenced. Even after he decided to level the first lawsuit against Jason and after he made the public statements criticizing the mayor and demanding his removal from office, Bob had continued to weigh in on his pet passions like village water and sewers, the sidewalks, and Hasbrouck Park. But sometime towards the end of spring and beginning of summer, Bob stopped talking altogether.

I found his silence more intriguing than his habitual breakdown of the number of gallons of water used, lost, and processed.

No matter with whom I spoke or where I went, the questions, in relation to Jason and the same-sex marriages in New Paltz, were always: *Who is this Bob Hebel? What is he like? Does he just hate Jason? Does he have sights on becoming the mayor? Is he homophobic? A religious nut? What's his deal?*

I tried my best to answer. But truthfully, I knew little about the trustee. He was a wallflower of sorts, albeit an odd one, with its own color scheme and rangy stem, but I decided that I needed to find out more. So I scheduled an interview with him for an upcoming edition. He invited me to his home, a baby-blue ranch house in the heart of the village, just across the street from the Hasbrouck Park playground. On my way there, I realized I had to talk to Jason first. The village had some other issues to deal with, some of them pretty troubling.

Jason was not easy to contact these days. I found it much easier to track him down when he was still a housepainter by day and a mayor by night. I was pretty much the only press that hounded him back then and he seemed to look forward to an opportunity to get down off of his ladder and chat for a while. Now our media darling was completely overwhelmed, stretched too thin, staying out too late, and tracking him down was like swinging a flyswatter in the open air. If you caught him, you were lucky. So when I saw his rotting truck parked outside of Village Hall, on my way to interview Bob, I decided to stop and get a few quotes from him while I had the opportunity.

I found him in his tiny office, working at his new laptop computer. He was trying on a different look these days. It was half redneck, a quarter hip, and a quarter geek. The new attire consisted of a large straw cowboy hat, a beaded choker, his wrinkled, long-sleeve oxford shirts and a pair of army green cargo pants cut into shorts. He also wore dollar store flip-flops that made him look like a gigantic political cartoon balanced on two tiny feet.

"So, I'm going to interview Bob Hebel. Have any questions for him?"

"Ooh," he said, rubbing his hands together and turning off his computer. "Why does he continue to associate himself with Liberty

Counsel, a bigoted, homophobic organization that tries to prevent decent people from living happy normal lives?"

"That's obvious," I said. "What else?"

"Ask him if he plans to run against me for mayor. Do you know what his e-mail address is? NPmayor2@aol.com."

"That's interesting," I said, "So what about Christian billboards and neo-Nazis?"

The Christian Coalition of the Hudson Valley, based in Newburgh, which had continuously protested outside the marriages conducted every other weekend in New Paltz since late February of 2004, had announced a fundraising campaign to rent a billboard along Route 299 in New Paltz which would depict a man with his wife and two children. The caption would read, "I was a homosexual until Jesus saved me." Then underneath, there would be a second caption: "Devoted Husband, Loving Father."

If that weren't enough to rival the local press coverage of the ever-popular pig races at the Ulster County fairgrounds in New Paltz, there were claims from local downtown teens—the ones draped in shredded black clothes, with multiple piercings and blue and pink hair—that they were being threatened by neo-Nazis who wanted to recruit them into their new Hudson Valley National Alliance chapter, a well-established neo-Nazi organization.

Jason had immediately taken a stand, giving me quotes from a friend's cell phone while riding the Ferris wheel at the fair late one night. "The Village of New Paltz will not tolerate White Power members threatening our youth," he said. I could hear the swoop of the ride and imagine how close our mayor felt to the sky. "I believe these kids," he said. "And I'm proud as hell that they're taking power into their own hands and have formed an Anti-Racist Association. This is nothing new. We've had neo-Nazi activity in New Paltz for years. If you hang out in downtown or frequent bars like Snug Harbor, Cabaloosa's, or Oasis, you're aware of these people. I've had long arguments with them. They have a right to their opinion, but that does not mean that I will let it go unchallenged. And when it comes to threatening our youth, we have to take a stand."

"I had one of those fliers thrown on my front porch," said my mother after I told her about the threats. "It was terrible. It went on about how Hitler was right and we need to have white pride. Oh, god. I threw it right into the garbage."

In addition to the fliers, there were a handful of White Power symbols spray-painted around downtown, which the young members of the ARA quickly covered up with paint or messages that said, "Die Nazi Scum." There were unofficial reports of White Power enthusiasts verbally threatening a group of hippie-punk kids downtown—not a whole heap of evidence, but enough for our maverick mayor to make several scathing quotes in the local papers. He claimed that there was a "neo-Nazi problem" in New Paltz, that a local band had a known White Power member and attracted neo-Nazis for their shows. Before the week was out, the head of the band was threatening to sue the mayor for libel, the New Paltz police chief had to go public with a statement that said, "We *do not* have a neo-Nazi problem in New Paltz," and soon the whole issue began to explode before any of us knew what was real and what wasn't.

"The chief has said that there is not a neo-Nazi problem from a *law enforcement* point of view," argued Jason. "They're afraid to characterize the activity as a 'problem' because they have no reported criminal violations. That's fair. They're also concerned that by calling attention to the activity it creates a greater forum for White Power subscribers. But my only response to that concern is I can think of no time in history where silence was the appropriate or effective action against bigotry."

He was smooth.

"They had his fucking back," said Jonathon Wright, when he heard that Jason had made public statements about the neo-Nazi "problem" before speaking with Chief Zappone first. "I saw the police that first day and the weeks after Jason conducted the marriages and they had his back. They *protected* him. He's an idiot for going out on his own without contacting the guys who covered his ass during the most controversial days of his term. They work in the same building, for God's sake. But that's Jason."

I think we both knew that Jason's tendency to act before he had the time to think through how his actions would affect people around him was a quality we both respected and admonished. It was a sign of a leader, or at least a powerful force. It wasn't that he didn't know what he was saying or what he believed in, it was just that he didn't look at the larger ramifications before he took a stand.

I reflected on this as I interviewed him for the neo-Nazi story and thought that, in a sense, that tendency was refreshing—less calculating than most politicians and certainly honest. His critics could also say that it was selfish, impulsive, narrow-minded or immature. But sitting there in his triangular office with the sloped roof and skylights—a framed picture of a *New York Post* cover page with a jail cell superimposed onto the mayor's face with a caption that read, "Crime of Passion"—I had to smile.

"Is it the hat?" he asked self-consciously.

I'm not sure why I was smiling. A breath of fresh air maybe, a tinge of hope. The rain kept coming that summer in fits and bursts and wherever I went in our small town things seemed weighted by the fog. Everything was wet and clingy and it was hard to get a sense of the true forms of objects right in front of us. I really didn't know who Jason was, or what he would become, I only knew that in his presence, you could taste potential. Like a lick of mint or the hot steam of Irish tea, this young man, with all of his foibles and personal failings, was positioned on a trajectory that could only rise.

Bob Hebel's house was not remarkable in any way. Similar to the home Jason rented one block away with three friends, Bob's house was a raised ranch, situated in the village, across from Hasbrouck Park and dotted with ceramic lawn ornaments including frogs, rabbits and gnomes. Bob answered the door before I could ring the bell. The house, which sat in the shade, was unassuming on all levels except that it protected the anti-Jason, the man who was hell-bent on bringing the mayor down.

Bob was average size, all legs and a smallish potbelly born of age. He was a nervous person, an old Brooklynite who still seemed to be waiting for that baseball to fly over the stadium wall and land on his front stoop—only it had landed on Jason's instead.

He was welcoming and positioned me on a floral Lazy Boy chair. The interior of the house was how I imagined it, filled with lots of furniture, stale air, family photos and cat hair. Nothing too radically different from many of the homes in New Paltz or elsewhere in middle-class America. Two large cats rubbed against my calves then hopped up on my lap. Bob tried to kindly shoo them away. His dog, Sadie, lay loyally by his side. She was fifteen-years-old and suffered from hip dysplasia. He explained to me that he and his wife had to rig her into a harness to walk her, each of them holding on to one side to help take the weight off her legs that she otherwise could not bear. "My wife loves animals," he said. "She's always trying to bring home a cat or a dog from the shelter."

Once we were done swapping dog stories and the cats had repositioned themselves somewhere down the hall, I began asking him questions, trying to get a sense of who he was, what his motives were, what he believed in, if in fact he subscribed to any concrete belief system. I wanted to look at him more closely, reveal the secret Bob, pull him out of his lawsuit-leveling shell and see who he was in stark daylight, in the comfort of his own home. So my first question, innocent enough, proved to be the most revealing. I asked him what his day job was.

"I work at the Charles River Lab," he said. The lab sounded vaguely familiar but I couldn't place it exactly in my memory.

"What kind of lab is it?" I asked.

"We produce rodents for medical experiments," he said.

"And what is your job there exactly?" I asked, trying to hide how stunned I was.

"I'm in production," he said.

"Production?" I repeated.

"Yes, but I can't say more than that because they get a little touchy when it comes to press."

Already I could see throngs of New Paltz animal activists, gay rights activists and their county cohorts marching over the mountain to Charles River Laboratories holding up signs that said, "Free Jason West," with gruesome pictures of disemboweled rats and Jason wasting away behind bars.

I had to move on to another topic and quickly. He explained that he and his wife Bridget each had two children from a previous marriage. They met in New Paltz twenty-five years earlier when Bob, fresh from his divorce, met Bridget and hoped to start a new life. "So I decided to stay in New Paltz," he said.

He led me through his political career in New Paltz. It started, as many a local politician starts, with his frustration over rising taxes. "I was the vice president of the now defunct New Paltz Tax Base Association," he said. "I saw many residents upset that their taxes were too high, and they would go to the various boards and complain but few wanted to do anything about it. So I decided that rather than just complain, I would try and do something." Bob joined forces with local attorney Laura Zeisel to run for two available seats on the village board. The issue they championed was to put a referendum on the ballot that, if passed, would dissolve the village into the town.

"So you ran for a seat on the village board with your main platform being the dissolution of the village?" I asked.

"Yes, and thankfully it didn't pass. In fact it was defeated by a large margin. But back then I was just thinking about how it would affect me, not the entire village." Bob added that our current town supervisor, Don Wilen, was the "worst supervisor New Paltz has ever had" and that "Jason and the current village board are not far behind." He was angry about Jason's proposed salary increase, the overtime cost of the police during the gay marriages, and the fact that Jason tried to punish him by taking him off all of his favorite commissions and committees.

"That was the only way I could think of getting revenge—at least legally," Jason had said with a laugh a few weeks earlier. "I just rendered him politically ineffective. He is no longer assigned to water and sewer, parks and recreation, the fire department...none of it.

I'd assign him to a garbage committee if we had one, but unfortunately, we don't."

"I think that was childish," said Bob in reaction to being pulled off the committees he had supervised since he first took a seat on the board in 1993. "I guess he wanted to get back at me, but all he did was to get rid of someone with a lot of experience and expertise on those issues."

He attempted to regale me once again of his efforts to enlarge, improve upon, and keep a vigilant eye on the operations of the village's water and sewer systems. Halfway through his monologue on a digester system, I had to cut him off. That was not why I was there. As of late, it was not why he was there either.

"Let's go back to the beginning, Bob," I said. "Why did you decide to file a civil suit against Mayor West? And are you going to continue to move forward and try to have him removed from office?"

"My feelings haven't changed," he said. "The mayor put himself above the law and I believe that no elected official has the right to decide which laws they will follow and which ones they won't. If you don't like the law then try to change it."

"Are you opposed to same-sex marriages?"

"I'm not opposed to alternative lifestyles. But I also don't want to see New Paltz become the gay capital of the world. Those couples should get married where they live rather than all coming to New Paltz for their wedding. You know how Reno has become the divorce capital of the world? Well, I feel like New Paltz has become the gay capital. That's not right. That's not what we should be known for."

The cat was out of the bag. I felt wounded. All along I had believed him when he said he was not against same-sex marriages, just Jason's law-breaking attempts to move the issue forward. Like the DA, Bob believed that Jason was utilizing the issue to advance his own career. While Bob had once again stepped aside to allow his mentor Tom Nyquist to run for mayor instead of plunging into the campaign he desperately wanted to win, the now twenty-seven-year-old mayor, with no political experience, had become a media magnet, and Bob felt that the New Paltz taxpayers would have to pick up the bill. I could certainly understand his arguments against Jason, but I felt them to be ill-informed and small-minded. In fact, the New Paltz Equality Initiative was busy raising money to offset the police costs, and if there had been any way to tally up the amount of money CNN, Fox News, CBS, ABC, and the rest of the corporate lunches added to our local business tax-base, the few thousand dollars that the police had spent in overtime costs might not appear to be as large. That was my opinion, but I still had taken Bob at his word that his opposition was not about gay marriages themselves but about an elected official violating a state law.

Jason had consistently said publicly and privately that Bob was homophobic and a member of the Christian Right. "He can't have it both ways," argued Jason. "He can't say that he isn't opposed to gay marriage and then turn around and sign off on legal briefs compiled by Jerry Falwell's lawyers that refer to the Bible and 'traditional' definitions of marriage and how it is sinful for same-sex couples to lie down together. I'm sorry, but that doesn't fly with me. Read these legal briefs sometime. They're disgusting, and Bob has signed his name to them."

In Bob's defense, I would argue that while there was certainly a discrepancy between what he said and what his lawyers said, I truly believed that Bob just agreed to be represented by the first law firm that offered their pro bono services to him, regardless of their ultimate mission to reintegrate Church and State. I didn't think his intentions ran any deeper than that. Free lawyers, who cares about their message?

So when he said that his greatest fear was that New Paltz would become the gay capital of the world on his watch, I was floored. I called Deb immediately after the interview to share this revelation.

"He really is a homophobe!" I said. "This is not just about Jason breaking the law; this is really about gay marriages."

"Why does that statement mean he's homophobic?" she asked.

"Because he's saying that New Paltz being known as the 'gay capital' of the world is somehow shameful and denigrating to our community."

"I'm not homophobic but I don't want New Paltz to become the gay capital of the world either," she said. "I feel like everyone is laughing at us, like we've become a joke. We used to be known for the Shawangunks and our farms and SUNY and now we're known as gay headquarters."

"But why can't we be known for all of those things?" I pleaded. "Why can't we be known for our hiking, farming, *and* gay marriage? What's wrong with being known as a tolerant community?"

"But we're *not* a tolerant community," she said. "If you don't agree with the status quo, then you are labeled a racist or homophobe or stupid. We can't just disagree in this town without going at each other's throats." Deb was getting really heated, so I decided to just drop it.

I felt deflated after the interview with Bob. Part of me wanted to just throw in the towel and the other part of me wanted to run screaming madly through the streets. All I kept thinking was how two people could look at the same situation so differently. What some saw as privilege, others saw as an outrage. What some saw as a right of opinion, others saw as prejudice. I kept feeling that same twisting in my stomach that I had experienced when I was nine, and things were not as they first appeared to be.

It was 1979 and my family lived on Cherry Hill Road in New Paltz. Early that summer there was a tragic drowning during the town's summer recreation program, the one I was never allowed to attend because my mother thought there wasn't adequate supervision. She turned out to be right. The camp had taken a field trip to nearby Tillson Lake. When the camp counselors called for a "buddy check," a young girl started screaming because she couldn't find her buddy. An eight-year-old girl drowned that day.

A month later, a new family moved into the house on the corner of our street, just across the road from my best friend Maude Schwartz. Maude, whose family was Jewish, was the youngest of three girls and we played together nearly every day. My other best friend in the neighborhood, Fernando Schirripa, was Italian and my

183

family, the Quinns, were the token Irish on the block. The Clarkes, our new neighbors, were a black family with one seven-year-old son named Foluke.

We soon learned that this was the family whose eight-year-old daughter, Madupe, had drowned. The family, who had been renting a small apartment in town to save money for their eventual purchase of a home, had closed the deal on the Cherry Hill house only weeks before their daughter's death. A cloud of grief hung over their small, white house.

Because I was only nine, I was not privy to all of these details at the time. All I knew was that every morning I wandered down the street to meet with the Schwartz sisters and play basketball in their driveway. Shortly after his family had moved in, Foluke came over to ask if he could play with us.

"We can't right now," Maude's older sister Sarah said. Her cheeks flushed red. "We have to go inside."

"What do you mean you have to go inside? We haven't finished the game!" I said incredulously.

"Our parents don't want us playing outside today. It might rain," said Sarah as she and Maude began walking towards the house, shoulders slumped. I ran after them. So did Foluke.

"But it's sunny outside," I argued. "And if you can't play outside, well then, why don't we play board games inside?"

Maude couldn't even look me in the eye. Sarah made a feeble attempt. "No," she said. "We can't play inside. We have to do homework."

Since it was early August, I couldn't understand where homework came into the mix. I felt embarrassed and didn't even know why. Something was strange and that something had to do with the new boy coming over to play. That was all I could determine in my nine-year-old brain.

"Maybe tomorrow we can play?" I said to Foluke, with his tightly trimmed afro and wide, eager eyes.

"Okay," he said.

I ran home. I felt my stomach tighten inside and I began to cry. I knew something was terribly amiss but I couldn't name it.

"What's wrong, honey?" my mother asked as I flopped down on our plaid couch. "What happened?" I recounted the events as accurately as possible, looking at her for some sort of explanation as to why I felt so crappy. She caressed my brow and then marched quickly towards the phone.

"How dare you?" I heard her say. "After all your people have been through and suffered in this world. How dare you ostracize this little boy? We are all God's children." I could hear her voice escalating to a pitch that both frightened me and made me proud. "How can you possibly justify hurting this family who has already suffered so much? You ought to be ashamed of yourself."

The next day, after a bowl of cornflakes for breakfast, I went back to play basketball. Maude and Sarah were outside. We decided to play a game of Twenty-one. Halfway through the game, Foluke came over. We put him into the rotation. I breathed a sigh of relief. Whatever my mother had said had fixed things, at least for a while.

When the game ended I asked if we could go inside and play Risk, our board game obsession for the summer. "Not today," said Sarah. "We have more homework." Then she whispered to me, "Come back later, once he's gone home."

Again, I waved goodbye to Foluke and said, "Maybe we can play some more tomorrow," and then walked home. I didn't say anything to my mother this time. I wanted her to believe that she had been victorious, that we all had been victorious. The knot in my stomach and this new feeling of shame had to be something else entirely. When I snuck over to Maude's house a few minutes later, cutting through backyards and entering from the south side, I couldn't help but look at Foluke's house and wonder what he could have possibly done. He was not a great basketball player, but was certainly no worse than myself. He didn't smell or swear or hit anyone, and his parents, who both worked at IBM, seemed friendly. They had a cute Labrador puppy. What was the problem?

As we played Risk, strategizing about which countries to defend and which to invade, I posed the question to Maude, knowing that my best friend was incapable of lying. She was just too transparent and sweet. "Why didn't you want Foluke to come into your house?" I could smell the topical fluoride coming from their father's downstairs dental office. If we were really quiet we could hear the low humming of the drill. Maude looked quizzically over the fortress she had built around Madagascar. "I'm not supposed to say," she said, bringing her bony knees into her flat chest.

I decided to take her outside to divine the answer. She and I always liked interpreting the clouds. We would find shoes and alligators, lost cities and angels. We lay with our heads together just behind their woodpile and storage shed. "What do you see over there?" I asked, pointing to two clouds whose tips had merged as if holding hands.

"I see a young white girl and a young white boy who want to get married."

"What? How do you see all that? I just see two clouds rubbing noses or holding hands."

"White people are supposed to marry white people. That's what my parents say." She rolled on her belly, leaned on her elbows and looked at me with her Goldilocks hair and light blue eyes. "That's why they don't want us to play with the black boy. They think that one of us might marry him. But I told them that I don't want to marry anyone!"

It all came into focus. He was black, they were Jewish, I was some sort of Irish-Welsh mutt that never wore a winter coat and had fleas. Nando was Italian, always reeked of garlic and lived with his grandparents because his father, a shoe repairman in Poughkeepsie, had too many children to support. Somehow, we were acceptable. I realized that my mother had been only somewhat successful. She had shamed the Schwartzes into allowing their children to play with Foluke. But she could not control who they would or would not allow into their home.

When I finally understood that Foluke had been barred from their home, not because of something he did or did not do, but because of the color of his skin, I never entered their home again with the same innocent and childish enthusiasm. What had been fascinating to me—their extremely thin mother washing out all of their Ziploc bags and hanging them on a miniature clothesline in the kitchen; the rituals of Chanukah that they welcomed me into; the smell of latkes and gefilte fish and the hair pomade that their father wore—lost their rich flavor for me. Everything began to appear too clean, too stringent, too harsh. "That is what happens when we are judged," my mother said. "If we're not careful, then we begin to judge others."

I slowly weaned myself from the Schwartzes, spending more and more time with Foluke whom I grew to love. His family was from Trinidad and we would tease his father's accent. Their house smelled different, like hair products for afros and spicy meat dishes. His dead sister's artwork hung everywhere in the house. We would blast Michael Jackson's *Thriller* on the turntable and take turns lip-syncing the songs on their beige living room couch. We were both attempting to beat back the darkness.

Chapter 12
Free (for Now)

"It is time for justice to roll down like water. God loves us all the same-whether black or white, gay or straight, old or young. When two people marry, whether they be two women, two men or a woman and a man, their vows are just as sacred, just as holy," —Reverend Dawn Sangrey, outside the New Paltz Town Courthouse on March 6, 2004

By late spring everything had thawed out. The reservoirs had been replenished; tulips and daffodils tickled the landscape. Things felt easier, more hopeful, and as I walked down the street with a notebook in hand, I breathed in deeply the air being given off by leaves whose green growth was sponging up all of the harsh space carved out by winter.

Besides the run-of-the-mill village board questions, there wasn't much need to talk to Jason as frequently as I had during the thick of the marriages, arrests, and court appearances. We were all in a holding pattern and for a while it felt like life had returned to a pre-nuptial state.

The weddings continued, without Jason. The New Paltz Equality Initiative was marrying people in the home of Charles Clemens and Maurice Zinken, a gay couple from Holland (where they were married *legally*) who had kindly opened their doors for

189

the cause. They had bought one of the grand ancestral Victorian homes smack in the center of the village and turned it into a bed-and-breakfast. The wildly decorated rooms had names like "Purple Rain," "Green with Envy" and "Crimson Dreams." Bold pieces of modern art and an eclectic mix of furniture and throw pillows combined with walls that blended animal prints with toile patterns gave you the feeling that an upstanding Victorian family had been thrown into the wilds of Africa.

Spearheaded by the NPEI, dozens of Unitarian ministers, both male and female, filled the void left by West, Greenleaf, and Sangrey, and continued to marry the list of thousands of same-sex couples from around the country requesting to be married in New Paltz. A public notary was always present, and the affidavits of marriage, signed by the notary and the performing member of the clergy, looked official, although we knew they would not provide shared health insurance or benefits to the newlyweds or hospital visitation rights if one or the other should fall ill.

But it was always a festive occasion, whether we were huddled under a white tent in the rain, or sprawled out on their lawn lined with folding chairs in the sun. The marriages continued, the protestors across the street continued, the decisions of the courts came in, and their outcomes were celebrated or damned. It was as if a carnival came to New Paltz every weekend; the actors changed, the ringmasters switched off, but there was always a spectacle.

Spring fury must have gotten into the mind of one just-married man, who decided to flash his pasty white backside to the protestors across the street one Saturday. The protestors called the police, clutching their biblical quotes and "Marriage = One Man, One Woman" signs, regaling the detective with their account of how this particular man "just went and dropped his drawers at us." They pressed charges, of course, and enjoyed reporting to me this injustice that they had incurred at the hands of a now-married gay man. "There's no call for that," one protester told me, happy to have someone to complain to. "I have every right to be here standing up for the word of God and the honor of family. I don't make lewd gestures at them, or swear or drop my drawers! It just goes to show you...."

That one incident aside (which had my editors and me laughing for the rest of the week), the marriages went off without a hitch, and except for a few occasions-like when a straight couple decided to get married without an official marriage license to lend support to the civil rights of their gay friends, or when the gay grandmothers ended their cross-country bicycle trip in New Paltz to personally thank the members of the NPEI, the Unitarian ministers, and West for their heroism—the media had all but disappeared. I felt like one of those mangy humps of plowed snow that remained in some remote corner of a municipal parking lot after a heavy winter. I was still holding on, even though the season had, for all intents and purposes, passed us by.

I wasn't entirely alone. The Japanese TV crew held steady, and Jeremiah always made a showing for a particularly interesting news hook. Even my editor began to show signs of gay-marriage fatigue. "We can't cover this every week!" she would say. "I'm sick of gay marriages." I felt propelled to go anyway, even if I wasn't necessarily covering it for that week's edition. Some weekends I would stay only a few minutes, others a bit longer. Part of me was afraid of missing something. Ever since Jeremiah had scooped us on the mayor's impending marriages, I felt a need to be one step ahead-in a position where if news were to come, I'd see it coming down the interstate before it turned off onto New Paltz exit 18. Also, the weddings reminded me of why I cared about this story so much; they made me feel good and strangely proud and territorial. It wasn't everywhere that gay marriages were being conducted in public with applauding masses and municipal red carpet. We weren't San Francisco or Boston or Provincetown, we were tiny little New Paltz, where tie-dyes never went out of fashion and civil rights fights were part of our genetic makeup.

I would wander in and out of the weddings, but I never successfully attended one without crying. There was this one couple I dubbed the Gray Foxes. Both were in their sixties, with sharply cropped silver hair, spectacles, and finely tailored three-piece suits. It was hard to tell them apart. You could see in their faces that one was softer, the other more reserved, but still they looked like

191

Dominick Dunne at a murder trial, very serious, purposeful and without remorse. They had been together for thirty-two years, and like other couples I've known who had been married more than three decades, they had grown with each other and into each other so much so that their physical traits gave the impression of being genetically linked. I thought about family and what family means and looked at these two men, who had written their own vows, and then the more reserved one grabbed the hand of his beloved and began to openly weep. I couldn't believe it. The Japanese film crew zeroed in with their wide-angle lenses, and I stepped back, sensing that this moment was not only private, but a turning point.

Later, when the rest of the weddings had concluded I asked the Gray Foxes if we could talk, telling them that I was a local reporter and had a few questions to ask them. They agreed, the one Gray Fox having pulled back into himself, while the other negotiated the situation with ease. "The ironic thing is, I've never been political when it came to gay rights," said David. "John is always trying to get me interested, but I was too obstinate, too involved with my own work to really give it the attention it deserves. So when he told me that this young mayor from New Paltz, just across the river from us, was marrying same-sex couples, and asked if I wanted to get married legally, I said yes. It was time for me to take a stand, to publicly say that we have the right to marry just like anyone else. We've had our own, private ceremony and have been together for more than three decades. So I didn't imagine that coming here today would be that big of a deal. When I got up there, and looked into his eyes, and said, 'I do,' I was overwhelmed."

I walked away from that wedding, once again resigned to the inevitability of gay rights coming to pass. I didn't know how long it would take, or in what form it would take, but I knew it had to happen, if this country could ever call itself a democracy that provides all of its citizens the same rights and the same protection.

Later that afternoon, I was playing with my kids out on the front lawn. Kristen, nine months pregnant and swollen with anticipation and fatigue, had waddled across the street to say hello. She and her husband had recently purchased a home, only a stone's throw from ours. Seamus was up in a tree. Tadeusz was crying, pleading with me to put him up in the tree as well, and Zofia was lying on her back on a quilt, holding her rattle up towards the sun.

My cell phone rang. I had left it in my car, but I could hear its agitated rings seeping out from our battered minivan. I scooped up Tadeusz, told Seamus not to climb one inch higher, and went to find the phone. It was Jason. "What's going on?" I asked.

He said that he was tired, that he needed a few days off, and that he was hoping to get a grant the village had applied for to put photovoltaic cells on top of Village Hall. "We could turn back the meter," he said excitedly. "If you create more energy through these solar panels or windmills, then Central Hudson is required by law to pay you back."

"That's so cool," I said. "The village can make money using alternative energy sources. That's great publicity."

"But here's the thing. They're only required by law to do this for private homes, not commercial or municipal buildings. So if we get the grant then I have to convince them to extend that courtesy to the village."

I was talking with the phone pitched between my shoulder and ear while I held Tadeusz, who was still whimpering about not being allowed to climb the tree. "Anything else?" I asked, wondering why he had called, since this story, while an exciting one for a green-loving reporter like myself, was not ready to be written until the grant approval came through. "Oh yeah, we lost."

"Lost what?" I asked, confused.

"Kavanagh ruled against us. I'm now permanently barred from marrying gay couples. The Supreme Court judge ruled in favor of the Christian zealots."

I lowered Tadeusz onto the blanket next to Zofia, much to his chagrin.

"Jason, you could have started the conversation with that."

"I'm sorry. Once we started chatting I forgot why I had called," he said.

"Hold on. I need a pen and paper."

I asked Kristen if she could watch the kids for a minute. I felt bad asking her as she looked ripe enough to pop right there on my front lawn. For a moment I was envious of people who punched clocks and had weekends off; the delineations of their lives were much clearer; but then again, they didn't have the luxury of being with their kids as much as I did and avoiding day care bills.

"So, how do you feel?" I said, grabbing a credit card bill envelope and a leaky pen from my car.

"Justice will prevail," he said, and I knew what he meant.

"Well, it hasn't prevailed in this case," I said, disappointed in Kavanagh, though not surprised.

"My phone's going dead," he said.

"I'll call you tonight then."

"Great, call me tonight."

After my husband and I put the kids to bed, I had the chance to call Jason back, this time with an official steno pad and a new ballpoint, and without the fear that my kid would fall on his head while I took down quotes from our now injunctified mayor. Since it was late in the evening, I was lucky enough to be working in my pajamas, sipping wine, Kazik painting another still life in the kitchen. One of the helpful things about Jason being so young, from my perspective, was that he was a source I could contact at odd hours when necessary. Most of my regular sources were on their way to bed, just as the mayor was getting ready to start his night.

"Are you going to get drunk tonight to celebrate Kavanagh's decision that you are someone who, if allowed to roam free, could cause irreparable physical or mental harm on the innocent masses?" I asked, taking a sip from my glass.

He laughed. "I'm certainly going to get drunk, but I'm not going to celebrate."

"On the record now," I said. "Will you obey the court's order and will you seek an appeal of Judge Kavanagh's decision?"

He breathed deeply. I could almost hear the gears shifting in his brain. I could also hear him take a drag on his cigarette.

"I will obey this court's decision because I'm confident that a higher and more rational court will lift the injunction. My lawyers and I will meet this week to begin drafting our appeal. I'm very disappointed in Judge Kavanagh's decision. He chose to ignore our central argument, which was, while, yes, executive branches of government are required to obey the law, there have been four exceptions to this upheld by the courts. Since a ruling in 1870, there has been a one hundred and thirty-five-year precedent set that a mayor or another executive branch has the ability to violate a law, if they believe that the law is unconstitutional. Kavanagh had the power to decide in favor of the Constitution today, but instead, he chose to focus solely on a narrow interpretation of a New York marriage licensing provision, which is discriminatory. How's that?"

"That's great, but did you really want to say that you are confident a more 'rational' court would rule in your favor?"

"You're right, I don't want to go pissing off the judge."

"It's up to you," I said, heading toward the porch for a cigarette myself. "It's not like you'll be in front of him any time soon. At least, I don't think so, unless you decide to tie yourself to a tree to stop the Woodland Pond development."

"Go ahead," he said with bravado, "use 'a more rational court.' What the hell do I care at this point about pissing off a conservative judge?"

"He's a nice guy," I added.

"His ruling wasn't too nice now, was it?"

I began typing up the story, deciding to take out 'rational' and just use 'a higher court.' I knew Jason was emotional and had probably been drinking. I knew Kavanagh enough to know that he would not take kindly to such flagrant disrespect. It was one of those little editorial choices I had to make along the line to keep people focused on the issue and not on the personalities, but the personalities involved in this particular story were more like lightning rods standing in the middle of an open field during a thunderstorm.

An hour later he called me back. "You said you'd be up late writing."

"I am," I said, sitting at the computer.

"I've had a few shots of tequila now and so have more things to add. If Hebel goes through with that lawsuit to have me removed from office and he succeeds, I have the perfect solution." He sounded manic and filled with bravado.

"What?"

"Rebecca as deputy mayor will have to step up as mayor. That will create a vacancy on the board. Then she will appoint me to fill that vacancy. Once I'm back on the board, she will appoint me to be her deputy mayor. Then she'll step down and I'll step up."

"What makes you so sure she'll step down?" I asked, deciding that it was time for a second glass of wine. "C'est magnifique," I whispered to Kazik, who was just putting the finishing touches on a still life featuring a vase of wildflowers on a table with an apple leaning against the vase.

"She might not," he agreed. He obviously hadn't considered that option.

"She's also a marriage officer," I reminded him, walking back towards my computer, referring to the village board's recent 4-1 decision to name Rebecca a marriage officer, investing the same authority in her as the mayor has to solemnize matrimony. She argued that she had no intention of marrying gay couples, but that she had two dear friends who wanted to get married in the village of New Paltz and she would like the opportunity to marry them herself. She would, of course, go on to marry a gay couple as would Trustee Julia Walsh, but it would take another month for that to happen.

"What you could do is have her step up to the mayoral seat and begin marrying same-sex couples," I suggested, enjoying a break from work for a little conspiracy theorizing. I leaned back in my desk chair and sketched out an even more intriguing scenario: "Then Hebel will seek to have Rebecca removed from office, creating a vacancy, and you'd move up to the mayoral seat and begin marrying same-sex couples and appoint her as your deputy mayor, and it could be like a revolving door."

196

"You're brilliant," he said. "I have to tell Rebecca this. Really, I have nothing to lose," he mused. "The DA will never let himself go down in the history books as the man who put a mayor in jail for solemnizing same-sex marriages. Even if I incurred the maximum fines, what would they be? Twelve thousand dollars? I could raise that in a second. When I attended that gay fundraiser in Houston back in March, this one couple paid seven thousand dollars for a puppy! One of the men in that couple handed me his card—which I hope I didn't lose—but he told me that if I ever needed anything, any money whatsoever to fight these charges or pay the fines, that I shouldn't hesitate to call him."

"Really?" It was hard for me to believe.

"I'm serious. That Houston speech was my best ever. I have to show you the tape. I had a few drinks before so I wasn't that nervous at all and I just let it rip."

He went on to tell me about an idea that Michael Zierler had, which was to put a motion on the table during a board meeting to make Bob Hebel a "marriage officer" just to piss him off. "We have the votes," said Jason. "And I would just love to see his face when the press asked him if he was planning on marrying any gay couples."

The pissing match between Bob and Jason heated up during Bob's victory after Kavanagh ruled in his favor. "I anticipated this decision," said Bob when I called him the next morning. "Just because Jason doesn't like the law doesn't mean he can break it."

"Contrary to what Bob says to the press, the lawyers he has hired to speak for him speak of the 'natural law' and its insistence that a marriage should be between a man and a woman," countered Jason. "According to this logic, gay couples are 'unnatural.' Judge Kavanagh himself argued that same-sex couples already have the right and authority to raise children together, either biologically or adopted. So what's at stake here? Two people who love and are committed to each other? That's not part of the 'natural law'?"

"He better be careful what he says," cautioned Bob. "Or I'm going to bring a civil suit against him. I heard from another reporter that he called me a 'hypocrite' and a 'liar.' He's the hypocrite here, not me. He hides behind the Constitution when it suits him but doesn't want other people to have the same rights."

Jason only incited Hebel, the DA, and other more conservative constituents, when he told people at a campus "information session" on the same-sex civil rights movement that the twenty-four misdemeanor counts against him were "nothing more than speeding tickets. Don't worry," he told the crowd. "I just have a lot of speeding tickets."

"They were not 'speeding tickets,'" said Bob. "And as an elected official, he should not be saying things like that, especially to a group of young people."

Bob continued to tell the press that he was going to move forward, using the pro bono services of Liberty Counsel, to file a case in the Albany Appellate Court Division, whereby he would seek to have the mayor removed from office. Although the papers had not been filed, Hebel continued to threaten that he wanted to pursue the case, but was waiting for just the right time, based on the advice of his lawyers.

The difference two weeks can make between late May and early June is substantial. Spring had burst into summer and the heat was raw and welcoming like that first blast off an old radiator in the dead of winter. The skies were clear and the sun high and buoyant as I walked down the street to interview my friend and former high school classmate, Floyd Kniffen, who, along with his brother, was building an exhibition green-design house in a little pocket of village woodland. Floyd and I sat on a log in the shade and looked at what was at the time just a foundation and a lot of ideas yet to manifest.

"It doesn't look like much, I know," said Floyd, a very soft-spoken man, serious and focused. "But it will soon. At least we hope it will."

He took me slowly through the green design process, which required great pains and cost. Though it was a substantial undertaking to build an environmentally friendly and energy efficient home, the payoff was significant. Not only could you sleep better at night, knowing you were not burning up tons of fossil fuel, but when you totaled the savings on electric and heating bills, the extra cost of the green materials would pay for itself (and then some). Floyd continued to describe in great detail his passion for green design and what it entailed. I was riveted.

I was loving this story, sitting in the woods, half a block away from my house, talking to an old friend, who I believed was doing good work. I could almost smell the chlorine coming off the public pool only a third of a mile away from where we were sitting, and I had that balmy feeling that life would start to move a little more slowly. The way the smell of sunscreen can conjure up beach vacations years later, the smell of chlorine signals summer in New Paltz. Both can have a paralyzing effect on time.

As we walked around the foundation together and Floyd explained what the house would look like several months from now, my cell phone jolted the still air. "I'm sorry, Floyd, it's probably my husband." I looked at the number coming in and at first didn't recognize it. I hesitated until the numbers clicked into place in my head.

"Hi, Andy," I said. "What's up?"

"We won!" He was ecstatic.

"What did you win?" I thought maybe he won the lottery.

"Judge Katz's decision was just faxed to my office. He dismissed all of the charges against Jason on constitutional grounds."

"Yeah!" I screamed, having almost forgotten about the whole thing.

"Erin, it's brilliant, it's poetry. You've got to read this."

"Let me get some quotes from you."

"Now?"

"No, not now actually, later. I have to call the DA. It's Friday, and I don't have his home phone number. I have to get him at the office," I said, suddenly back in step with the story.

"Good luck," he said. "You can call me on my cell later or at home."

"Thanks, Andy. Congratulations."

Within a week, Judge Kavanagh had permanently barred Jason from performing same-sex marriages while Judge Katz had vindicated his actions, claiming that the DRL statute, as Jason and his attorneys argued, was unconstitutional as applied to gay couples. The big question now would be whether or not the DA would appeal Katz's decision, or let it rest. I knew that the DA had to be my next call.

"Wow!" I said to Floyd. We wrapped things up quickly and then I asked him if it was okay if I stayed on the log a little while longer to make some phone calls. "You can stay as long as you like," he said with a laugh, knowing how important this was. I called the DA's office, but he was at trial. His secretary promised she'd have him call me as soon as he got in.

I walked around the village streets, clutching my notebook, spreading the word to friends and family. I stopped by Jack's to get something to drink. Jason was there, buying the paper and his Red Bull Energy Drink.

"You're a free man!" I said and gave him a hug.

"The decision is incredible. Have you read it?"

"No, Andy just called me. I have to pick it up. Can I get your reaction?" I was all ready, pen in hand.

"Can I call you over the weekend? I'm late to catch a bus to the city. I'm a guest speaker at a gay fundraising event," he told me, guzzling his energy drink with one hand, trying to revive himself for the big night.

"Sure. But don't forget—and don't let your cell run out of juice, okay? You'll have some good news to impart at the event."

Just then my phone rang. It was the DA. "It's Don Williams; do you have anything to say to him?" I asked before I answered the phone.

"Tell him that 'justice *has* prevailed.'" With that, Jason headed out into the street, towards his newfound career as a public spokesperson for gay rights. I had to laugh.

"Hi, Don, thanks for calling me back. I just wanted to get your reaction to Judge Katz's decision and ask you whether or not your office plans to appeal."

I leaned against the meat freezer and scribbled furiously. Don was an articulate man, a deliberate orator and I never wanted to miss his exact phrasing of an argument.

"I've been prosecuting a murder trial for the last three days and haven't had time to give this as much thought as I'd like to. But I know you're on deadline so I will say this: Judge Katz's decision is unfortunate, but not unexpected. We respectfully disagree with the decision and we will file the appropriate notice of appeal. Unfortunately Judge Katz dismissed the charges based on what he considered to be constitutional impacts against the individuals who wanted to be legally married. But we did not charge any of the participants in the weddings; we charged the mayor who has not had his rights violated but who has knowingly and willfully committed criminal acts. Mayor West is trying to insulate himself from the consequences of those acts by arguing the constitutionality of a specific law. If it was an act of civil disobedience on the mayor's part then that should be for a jury of his peers to decide. There should be a trial."

Like Judge Kavanagh and Judge Bradley before him, the DA reiterated that Jason's decision to "knowingly and willfully" break the law set a "dangerous precedent for other elected officials who might then decide to break laws that they did not personally agree with." I thanked Don for taking the time to call me back. Then I walked down to Andy's office and sat in his air-conditioned conference room reading over Judge Katz's five-page decision.

"Cultural and political attitudes about homosexual rights and same-sex marriage are evolving rapidly. No recent act of the legislature suggests a policy favoring any form of discrimination against homosexuals or same-sex partnerships...I am unfamiliar with the arguments raised in the cases from other states addressing this issue and I understand the historical, cultural and religious opposition to same-sex marriage, but find that none of the reasons stated in opposition to same-sex marriage is paramount to the equal protection guarantees enshrined in the State and Federal Constitutions. In dismissing the information charging the mayor with violating the DRL 13, 17, I heed that admonishment by Justice Brandeis that 'We must be ever on our guard lest we erect our prejudices into legal principles'—*New York State Ice Company v. Liebmann*."

"What do you say, Andy?" I asked after I finished reading the decision. He was pacing up and down the conference room. Andy, like Don, measured his words carefully, particularly when talking to the press. Off the record, the two of them could dance a verbal tango, allowing their unedited thoughts to circle and explode and eventually rise like kites vying for position in a limited patch of sky. But on the record, they were careful, weighing each word with scrutiny.

"It's obvious from Judge Katz's decision that he researched the issues and gave great thought to his decision," he said. "It's also a wonderful affirmation that any laws which promote discrimination like the DRL 13 violate the Equal Protection clause in our New York and Federal Constitutions."

In uncharacteristic fashion, Andy began to say more. "I'd like to believe that the DA did not relish prosecuting the mayor. His decision to appeal Katz's decision begs the question as to why the DA would want to perpetuate more litigation, time, and expense on this case. The mayor has already said that he will abide by the permanent injunction Judge Kavanagh has placed on him. So he will not be performing any more same-sex marriages. Why not let it be?"

While I knew that Andy believed that the DA would be successful in appealing Judge Katz's decision, which would be returned to State Supreme Court Judge Michael Bruhn, a conservative judge who was probably the least likely to allow Katz's decision to stand, he had to jockey for position in the press. "I think that Judge Katz's decision is so formidably written that it would be incredibly difficult for any court to reverse, and we certainly expect it to prevail."

When Jason returned from his weekend sojourn to New York City he had little to say. "Let Andy say it," he told me. "He's more articulate than I am."

"But you're the one people want to hear from," I said.

"Okay. I feel completely vindicated by Judge Katz's decision. He is clearly someone with a deep respect for human rights and civil rights. This is the first time in New York State that a judge has ruled that it is unconstitutional to deny marriage licenses to same-sex couples. It is a landmark decision and one that I hope sets precedent in New York State."

He was a free man. At least for now. We all waited for what we knew was inevitable—a decision by Judge Bruhn on the DA's appeal of Katz's decision. It would take months, many months for Judge Bruhn to rule. In the meantime, we all moved back into our lives: Jason to his mayoral duties and speaking engagements; Andy to his practice; the DA to his murder trials and cases of sexual abuse; the New Paltz Equality Initiative to their "Purple Rain" weddings, and I to my brood, the weekly grind of sewer and water, provincial political disputes, book reviews and features on turkey vultures. While summer did move slowly, we were eventually caught by the early autumnal wind and suspended for a while, like that moment when a swift breeze picks up a falling leaf and gives it the impression of ascension.

Chapter 13
Red State, Blue State, Green Village

"I have come to believe over and over again, that what is most important to me must be spoken, made verbal and shared, even at the risk of having it bruised and misunderstood.... My silences have not protected me. Your silence will not protect you...and while we wait in silence for that final luxury of fearlessness, the weight of that silence chokes us. The fact is that we are here and that I speak these words in an attempt to break that silence and bridge some of those differences between us, for it is not difference which immobilizes us, but silence. And there are so many silences to be broken."—Audre Lorde, from her poem, "The Transformation of Silence and Action, Sister Outsider."

Although the profile in *People* would certainly be the apex of Jason's instant celebrity status, it was followed by less widely circulated, but arguably more noble, recognition. On October 6, 2004, he was chosen as the recipient of the prestigious Mario Savio Memorial Free Speech Award for Young Activists. Savio (1942–1996) led and mobilized Berkeley students in 1964 in support of racial justice and in opposition to the growing American involvement in the Vietnam War. Inspired by Savio, the students protested the severely limited political speech and activity on campus. The non-violent campaign culminated in the largest mass arrest in American history and helped change university rules on political speech and organization. Besides the prestige, the award would provide Jason with $4,000—half for himself and half for whatever not-for-profit organization or project he selected.

I knew Jason was in the running for the award, because Michael Zierler told me that he had nominated him. "What was really odd was their concern that he might talk about or encourage people to vote for Ralph Nader," Zierler said to me at a dinner party at the Lagodkas' house, only two months before the November 2004 presidential elections.

"I know a lot of people who don't want Jason to actively support and advocate for Nader," I said, as I noshed on Rachel's organic chips and tofu bean sauce. "People are so jumpy and cagey about this election that they want to censor fellow liberals rather than attacking the real beast."

"That's what I found so disconcerting," said Zierler, who was at this point already on the village board and enjoying working with Jason, even though the mayor constantly tried to get him to switch his voting registration from Democrat to Green. "It's a 'free speech' award and they were trying to censor him!" Even more ironic than that was the fact that Nader was listed as one of the members of the Mario Savio Memorial Advisory Board.

Jason and Rebecca, with their newfound leverage and Green currency, fought vehemently at the July Green Party National Convention to have Nader endorsed. Ultimately the Nader endorsers lost and a "safe state" advocate, David Cobb, was chosen as the party's official presidential candidate. The Cobb victory at the convention split the already marginalized Green Party. Jason, Rebecca and many of the core New Paltz Greens went on to publicly campaign for Nader's presidency, citing the need to "break up the duopoly" of the two-party system and let someone in who they saw as an icon of consumer rights, worker's rights, a committed environmentalist, champion of the poor, anti-corporate, pro-civil rights, and the only one, in their estimation, who said anything worth fighting for.

Jason did end up winning the award, regardless of any hesitation the Savio board may have expressed to Michael. I was sitting in the sun on our deck, basking in the Indian summer heat, while the kids looked for worms under rocks that bordered our garden, when my cell phone rang. It was Jason, returning my call several days late, just before he had to board a plane to Berkeley to accept the award.

"What are you going to say when you accept the award?" I asked curiously.

"I don't know what I'm going to do," he said, "Hold on, I have to down shift." He was driving somewhere. To the airport maybe?

"I'm very tempted to say something about their implied censorship, but I have great respect for Mario Savio. Can I tell you when I come back what I end up doing?"

I could hear him struggling. "Don't worry," I conceded. "Just tell me what you *know* you are going to say. If you end up throwing caution to the wind and highlighting their hypocrisy I can always write about it later."

"He doesn't have to think about it," said Rachel when I mentioned it to her later. "If they make any attempt to try and control what he says, then he'll just do the opposite. So, in a sense, it is really up to them."

I had heard tales of Jason giving Democrats hell at various fundraisers and parties and awards ceremonies he was invited to speak at over the last several months. According to Billiam, he had to be literally pulled off the stage after being handed an award by the Stonewall Democrats. No matter how much they booed and heckled him, he would not stop talking about what a poor choice Kerry was and asking how they, of all people, could support someone who would not support the right for gays to marry. It was one thing to criticize the Stonewall Democrats for their support of Kerry after accepting their award, and quite another thing to piss off the Mario Savio Advisory Board, who included Howard Zinn, Barbara Ehrenreich, and some of the hardest hitting liberals in the country. From what I understood there was no overt censorship, just some presidential anxiety on their part.

Jason would be introduced at the Mario Savio Award ceremony by none other than Molly Ivins, author of the best-selling books,

Who Let the Dogs In? and *Bushwhacked.* "You're so lucky!" I said. "Not only do you get a free trip to California but you get to hear Molly Ivins speak! I love her."

"I'm sure you'll be able to watch it live on the web," he offered.

For the upcoming edition of the *New Paltz Times*, which would come out the day Jason would accept the award, he gave me a summary of his standard speech that he gave when asked to speak at universities on the importance of young people getting out to vote or to become involved in politics. His angle was that young people who do not vote are often mischaracterized as being too apathetic or too ignorant to bother making it to the polls on Election Day. Jason liked to invert this theory and tell students that their lack of enthusiasm to get out and vote was a sign of intelligence, not apathy.

"They don't vote, because there is no one running for office that they believe is worth voting for," he said. "When you are given a choice of two candidates who say the same things, sign off on the same policies and do not offer the voter something they can believe in, I say stay home. You shouldn't just vote because the status quo tells you that you *should* vote. If you vote for what you don't want, then all you get is more of what you don't want. *But,* I also say, if there is no one running for a political position that you support, then get out there and run yourself or encourage someone you do have faith in to run for political office. That is our responsibility as citizens. If we don't like what we see, then we are obligated to do what we can to change it."

While this non-conventional approach towards motivating youth involvement in politics might have gone over big at various colleges where he delivered the lecture, it certainly raised some eyebrows at home. Not only did Jason say this to our paper during one of the most contentious presidential races in American history, one that rivaled an even more heated contest in 2000, where the Green vote, the Nader vote, was proclaimed by many to have "cost" the Democrats the election; but he was also saying, "stay home" if you don't like what you see at a moment in time when Democrats were virtually rabid in their defense of Kerry, even if many held their nose and voted for him anyway.

He didn't say this just once, he said it many times, in a local, democratically charged town, where he, as the symbolic leader of the liberal SUNY New Paltz campus, was chosen as one of the keynote speakers to congratulate the campus for winning the MTV-sponsored *Rock the Vote* contest. SUNY New Paltz had set the record number for newly registered student voters in New York State. At the MTV celebration, with the auditorium filled with eager voters, Jason said it again. He urged students to vote their conscience. I knew he wanted to tell them why he was voting for Nader, but the speakers, including Susan Zimet and Congressman Maurice Hinchey, were told by the organizers that their speeches could not reflect any partisan views. So instead, Jason just told them that if they couldn't find anyone to vote for they should get active themselves or "stay home."

"You can't say he's afraid of controversy," I said to Deb after the concert, where I could see organizers wringing their hands nervously when he spoke. "He's out on a limb now and should be wearing fireproof pants to protect him against the hot seat he's chosen to sit on."

"Why would I get off the hot seat?" he said to me shortly after his MTV speech. "I'm having too much fun."

"But what if it's not fun one day?" I asked him while we stood outside the Village Hall taking a cigarette break during a long and contentious board meeting, where the public came out en masse to support or oppose the wetlands law the board was trying to pass. "Will you sell out?"

He thought about this. "I'm as vulnerable as anyone to selling out," he said, as he waved goodbye to some of his environmentalist supporters who had come and commended the board for taking an action that would help preserve what remaining wetlands we had left in the village. "The political system we have now is corrupt and undemocratic. It's set up to make voters decide between the lesser of two evils." He cited the need for publicly funded elections and the end to corporate campaign contributions, corporate-funded lobbyists, and corporate control of the media.

I always enjoyed a good leftist rant, so I slid my notebook into my purse and listened, enjoying the break from the redundant public comment.

"The system is designed to make people sell short their ideals, to compromise on issues they should never compromise, to be dictated by corporate money and corporate power and political hypocrisy. I'll try not to sell out, but I'll try even harder to change the system," he said, taking another deep drag off his cigarette and looking nervously at his watch.

Jason and his fellow Greens advocated very strongly and convincingly for clean, publicly funded elections where everyone was on the same playing field. "What would you think if I tried to do that here? In the village," he whispered to me, crushing out his cigarette and making sure no one was within ear shot. Those in attendance at the meeting, who were adamantly opposed to the wetlands law, were more likely than not predisposed to shunning the idea of taxpayer-funded elections.

"We'd take a few thousand dollars out of the budget and put it aside for publicly funded elections so that everyone is given the same amount of money to run their campaign."

"I think it's a great idea," I said.

"Then we could incorporate instant run-off voting. If we had that, then what happened to me could never happen again."

"What do you mean?" I asked, confused now.

"If we had instant run-off voting, I probably would have never won. Look at that mayoral race. With IRV, the top two vote-getters would be subject, within twenty-four hours, for another vote. Feldman would have been out the first round, but more likely than not, all of those who voted for Feldman would have voted for Nyquist if the choice was between Nyquist and myself, and I would have lost. But IRV gets rid of the whole 'spoiler' notion."

Although I'd always been Green at heart, I was no political maven and knew little about IRV or how clean elections worked. But when Rachel or Jason or Jonathon broke these ideas down for me, they seemed so simple, so self-evident, that I couldn't understand why our government wouldn't support something that seemed so damn logical. I could feel their third-party frustration and would soon know what sort of flack they would get for pushing Kerry on his questionably shaky positions on gay rights, the war in Iraq and abortion.

As the presidential trail heated up, the political climate both nationally and locally would near a boiling point. It was only a week and a half before the elections that I was informed that the "greatest living threat to Kerry being elected" was on his way to New Paltz, to "Green Country," for one last rally before he headed to New York City.

"I just want to give you the heads up," said Rachel, whispering on the phone to me, as if we were being tapped. "*He's* coming."

"*Who's* coming?" I asked, although her tone gave the impression that the answer to this question should be quite obvious.

"You know *who*," she said, frustrated but sounding a little worried too.

"*No*, I don't," I retorted honestly, as Zofia was climbing up on my lap, her surprisingly strong little hand eagerly trying to pry the phone from my ear.

"*Nader*," she whispered. "He is coming. *On Halloween.* Don't say a word."

"You're kidding me?"

"No, I'm not."

There seemed to be some sort of underground current running through New Paltz that continued to bring attention and controversy to our small town. Just when things were slowing down, or we thought they were, something else unexpected would find its way in. This time, it was none other than Ralph Nader, probably the Democrats' most feared man, except for President George W. Bush himself.

"I can't believe he chose Halloween," I said to Jason during one of the planning sessions for the Nader visit. Only in New Paltz, I thought, would we have the Democrats' version of the Grim Reaper and the Republicans' version of The Savior, scheduled to give a pre-election rally on Halloween.

"I just want to convince him to stay for the Halloween Parade," said Jason, who I could tell was looking forward to the visit, regardless of the heat the Greens would take from their Democratic friends. "Then you'd hear people say, 'Hey, look, that guy is dressed up just like Ralph Nader!'"

One of the greatest New Paltz traditions was our annual Halloween Parade. It began at dusk, with thousands of young marchers and their parents dressed up as everything from superheroes to Sponge Bob. Because it was a politically inclined town, you could also see the entire cast of the current presidential cabinet, from Donald Rumsfeld to Condoleezza Rice. There was also the hippie element pushing through the fray with students marching down the street on stilts, clothed in giant puppet-heads with Medusa-like dreads and "Legalize Hemp" and "Peace" signs. The parade began at the middle school and moved down Main Street, into the heart of the village, like a midget version of Mardi Gras, then to the fire station, where the Lion's Club gave out candy and apples to the trick-or-treating tots. It was a chance to see if you could recognize, beneath their costumes, everyone that you had ever known from New Paltz that you hadn't seen since the last Halloween Parade or possibly the annual Elting Memorial Library's book fair. These two events brought out more New Paltzians than any other public or private events combined.

I kept the news quiet, so quiet that I didn't even tell my mother, one of those proud and recently edgy Democrats. She was busy traveling to Woodstock and Red Hook and Rhinebeck with her politically minded friends to conduct prayer circles, vigils, séances, whatever they could think of doing, to help charge the airwaves so that Kerry's televised debates with President Bush would be hailed as victorious and help move him into the White House, or more accurately, move "Dubya" back to Texas. To this day, my mother has never gotten over Texas death-row inmate Carla Faye Tucker's execution at the hands of then Governor George W. Bush. "He is a state-sanctioned murderer," my mother would say whenever his name was mentioned. Her typically beautiful face would clench up in anger and disgust.

While I understood people's fear and shared their animosity for Bush, I also knew that we were in a Democratic safe state. Already Nader's numbers had slipped greatly from 2000, where he garnished approximately three million votes. The 2004 pollsters were predicting his numbers would total slightly less than one percent, or one million votes. Many of my own friends who had voted for him in 2000 said that they just couldn't pull the lever for him this time around. "I wish I could," said my friend Amy. "You know I love my Ralph, but I can't justify it right now. We have to get that cowboy out of office."

Even Rachel, a die-hard third-party advocate and Nader supporter, was having her doubts. Not about Nader's role in the safe states, but what he may be able to do in the swing-states like Pennsylvania, Ohio, or Oregon. She was losing sleep, and at the last minute, on the eve of the elections, and running a fever, she decided to drive with a friend to Ohio in the pouring rain to bang on doors and encourage people to get out and vote for Kerry in the corn-belt swing-state.

But it was still late October. Students Against Empire, a radical campus organization, said they would gladly sponsor Nader's visit and secure one of the lecture centers on campus for his rally. They, too, kept the news very quiet. As the days clicked by and the deadline loomed, Steve Greenfield, the Green Party secretary, did everything he could to keep me informed and to time the release of the news so that the *New Paltz Times* could break the story. I had to admit that I was excited. Nader was being interviewed nightly on TV; he was the subject of all types of political shows and pre-election debates. I personally admired him for all he had done, from the seatbelts to organizing unions as well as more than a hundred civic organizations including NYPIRG that he had helped foster.

Although secrecy was paramount to the organizers, I did get permission to tell my editors, so that they had some warning as to what was coming down the pike. Deb was almost as excited as I was. Not because she was any self-declared Nader fan, not at all, but she loved when people shook things up and this, she knew, was going to shake things up.

Brian wasn't nearly as impressed. What he saw was a bunch of obstinate Green Party members, like Jason and Rebecca, publicly betraying their own party's choice of a candidate in favor of supporting Nader. "I think they deserve a political spanking by the Green Party," he said. "While you should certainly write about Nader coming, I think what would make it really interesting is to get an interview from him *before* he comes," he said flippantly, as if Nader, with a week left to go on the campaign trail, didn't have better things to do and greater readership to reach than our meager 15,000 circulation.

But in an attempt to please Brian, I said that I'd try, not having the foggiest idea of how to get in touch with Nader who, like Senator Kerry and President Bush, seemed to be moving around on a dizzying schedule, like invisible Concordes departing and landing and arriving within seconds from state to state. While I certainly didn't have Nader's private number in my address book, I did have Steve Greenfield's, and when it came to matters like this, Steve was the person you wanted in your court. His tenacity and assertiveness were character traits that made him indispensable to the local Greens and unbearable for more mild-mannered folks. He was great at courting the press, and within hours could have the national media knocking at your door, if that was what he believed the situation warranted.

"I need to interview Nader," I said.

"He'll be talking to the press before he gives his speech," said Greenfield, proudly, having helped to work out all of the details with Nader's people for this event, including security, timing, how he would enter and exit. After the spring visit from the Westboro Baptist Church and now with neo-Nazi activity brewing in New Paltz, the Greens felt that tight security was needed. Here we had not one, but two, very controversial figures, speaking in town, only days before the presidential election. "I'm not sure who the sharp-shooter will go for first," I said to Rachel, just days before Nader's visit. "Nader or Jason?"

I was only half joking. While the current that was running through New Paltz in 2004 gave us all a shot of adrenaline, or a panic attack, depending on how one viewed the current events, it also carried with it a modicum of fear. I still worried that the spot-light on our small town was a little too bright and that we could be vulnerable to some sort of darkness piercing through.

I explained to Steve that Brian wanted me to interview Nader prior to his visit, so that we could get his quotes for the upcoming edition. "By the time he comes on Sunday, it will be too late," I explained, listening to Steve preparing breakfast for his three small children in the background. If we waited until Nader came, then our story would run on Wednesday, or in the case of the Woodstock papers, Thursday, after the presidential elections had already been decided.

"If you need Nader, I'll get you Nader," he said confidently and then excused himself so that he could feed his kids.

I waited. Steve kept e-mailing me, letting me know that he was close to getting Nader, but not quite there yet. By Tuesday morning, knowing our paper went to the printers by nightfall, I began to lose hope. In fact, I think that I had lost hope, or was just too damn tired, daydreaming, and driving our kids around, hoping that the lull of movement and music would help to put some of them to sleep. We were playing the soundtrack to *Cats*, the Broadway musi-cal, a tape we played enough times that whole sections were warped. But the kids didn't seem to mind.

My cell phone rang. It was Steve. "Erin, Ralph is waiting for you. He's on his cell phone, in a car, driving toward Ithaca. They're giving you five minutes. Good luck. Here's the number."

I wanted to die. How could I interview this man without any preparation, without a pen or paper and with three screaming kids in the car? The cell phone had woken up Zofia who was now crying, very loudly. The two boys were fighting about who had crossed the invisible line in the back seat and I didn't know what to do or where to go. Kazik was working, my mother was working, my father was in Florida golfing, and I had five minutes, just five minutes to get this interview.

I pulled into our driveway and decided to plead with our oldest. "Listen, Seamus," I said to my five-year-old son. "Mommy has a very important phone call to make for work. It will only take five minutes. Can you sing to the babies and help them fall asleep?" He must have heard the anxious tone in my voice. It's not often that I have such pressing interviews that I have to stop our life, mid-drive, and run towards the phone. "Okay, Mom," he said. I went into the house, grabbed a notebook, leaned it on the front window sill so I could keep an eye on the kids and dialed the number. Ralph answered. I had no idea, what in the hell to ask him.

"Why did you decide to come to New Paltz this close to the elections?" I asked nervously, with one eye on my steno pad and the other on the minivan.

"Because I wanted to come to *Green Country*," he said, and immediately, I was put at ease. "New Paltz is a university town where members of the Green Party hold elected office and have made great strides both environmentally and for civil rights," he said. "I expect great voter turnout in New York for our campaign. Since New York will obviously go to the Democrats it is a state where people can truly vote their conscience, vote for a candidate who supports a living wage, universal health care, real environmental initiatives, and who pledges to fight this war—a war that the other two candidates support—and to bring our troops home."

I knew I had to get to the "spoiler" question, but I wanted to pay him more respect first and at least for four minutes talk about his platform. It was so odd to hear his voice on the other end of my phone, a voice so familiar to me from PBS or National Public Radio or Nightline. The voice was talking directly to me. It made me sweat a bit.

"What do you believe your campaign is doing to improve Democracy?" I asked.

"Everything has to start somewhere," he said, sounding tired, and I have to admit, a bit defeated, as if the road he had traveled was long and bumpy and full of disappointments. I had been reading daily about democratically funded law firms taking the Nader campaign to court, state after state, trying to get him kicked off the ballot, challenging his petitions, harassing petitioners themselves. I had also been reading numerous editorials on the Nader question, old lefty buddies of his criticizing his decision to run again, pleading with him not to, calling him arrogant, claiming he had lost touch. I had even witnessed comedian Bill Maher and documentary film maker Michael Moore begging him on national TV, literally, on their hands and knees, not to run this time around.

But there was no deterring Ralph Nader. His political convictions on democracy, or his arrogant stubbornness, or some mixture of the two, would not let him quit. Even if the majority of the Left was trying to convince him, or in some cases, strong-arm him out of running.

"One of our goals is to break this two-party system which makes a mockery out of true Democracy. We need more candidates, more parties, more young people willing to push for elaborate reform of our criminal justice system, our electoral system, and those who will stand up and move to reduce our bloated, wasteful military budget so that we can begin to reallocate those funds and repair America's public works programs, provide people with the skills that they need to secure good jobs and make sure that there is no way that those jobs continue to be exported to China!"

We talked about his platform in slightly more depth and I could feel my time running out. "What is your response to those people, mostly Democrats and self-proclaimed liberals, who say you played a 'spoiler' role in the last presidential election and might very well do so again in the upcoming election?"

I hated to do it, but I had to. And what I would learn about Nader is that he didn't mind this question at all. In fact, I think he welcomed it, because he was so skilled at turning it around and using it to advocate for his own platform.

"You can't spoil a system that is already spoiled to the core by electoral dictatorship and corporate-sponsored campaigns," he said defiantly. "In this race, Democrats have committed constitutional crimes to keep us off the ballot. They've used dirty, disgraceful, criminal tactics to silence us. In Oregon they've threatened our volunteers, stolen our petitions, harassed, intimidated our staff and slandered us all over the country with lies that we are being funded by Republican coffers. I do not believe that there is a better display of a fascist government than how my opponents have treated our third-party candidacy this year. It's a war of attrition."

"Thank you for taking the time to talk with me, Mr. Nader, and I look forward to meeting you when you visit New Paltz. Good luck with your campaign."

I hung up the phone, and quickly scribbled down some more notes, as Nader, a seasoned politician at this point, could talk much faster than I could write. I ran out to the car, anticipating the screams and tears of my children, only to discover that the two little ones were sound asleep, and Seamus was still singing, "We're off to see the Wizard, the wonderful Wizard of Oz." I was so proud of Seamus and so full of adrenaline from talking to Nader that I didn't know what to do with myself. I put Tadeusz and Zofia to sleep in their rooms and decided that sit-ups might be the only thing that could calm me down.

Only fifteen minutes later, my phone rang again. Seamus was lying next to me on our wooden floor, as I panted and tried to touch my elbows to me knees. He was watching a video of *Cats*, as it appeared that we needed a multi-media experience of the production.

"I heard you just got off the phone with Ralph Nader." It was Jason.

"Word travels fast around here," I said, very out of breath. I rolled over on to my side and asked Seamus to hand me my notepad. Might as well get it all done in one shot, I thought. "Do you want to give me some quotes for the article?"

"Sure. Fire away." I could tell that Jason was proud, certainly more proud than he was about the *People* magazine article or the

Conan appearance or even the Mario Savio award. His hero was coming to town and he would be the one to introduce him.

"I think it's great that we have a presidential candidate appearing in New Paltz during the final days of the campaign," he said. "I've been advocating all over the country for people to vote for Nader. He is the only presidential candidate who is anti-war, anti–Patriot Act, anti-corporate-funded elections, pro–marriage equality, pro-universal health care, pro-renewable energy resources. Those who would say he does not have a right to run for office and campaign as vigorously as the other two candidates are both un-democratic and un-American. In America, everyone has the right to run for political office."

I could tell he was getting on a roll now. "Why Nader is being scapegoated after all he has done for this country and for democracy is perplexing. Does anyone talk about why Gore lost his home state? Or that Kerry helped write the Patriot Act? Not only did he vote for it, he co-authored it. This is the document that has stripped us of our basic civil and constitutional rights. And now he wants to commit more troops to Iraq? And we're not supposed to have a choice in who we vote for?"

The article on Ralph's impending visit, entitled "Guess Who's Coming to Town?" was our front-page story. If people hadn't known he was on his way, they did now. Four days later I was running down the street, trying to make sure that I arrived at the pre-rally press conference with Nader on time. I stopped at the gas station on the corner, to get some breath mints in case I had to get up close and personal with the leftist demi-god. Outside, pumping gas, was Peter Savago, the chair of the county Republican Party and the former vice president of the state Republican Party. He was the figurehead for our community's now-Republican minority. I knew he had recently returned from the Republican National Convention in New York City. While he was there, proudly giving his endorsement for George W. Bush, there were sixty or so anti-Bush protestors staging a demonstration outside of his insurance building on Main Street.

219

Savago, a born and bred New Paltzian who played on New Paltz' first high school football team and was a veteran of the Korean War, had sued the previous village administration for requiring him to take down a banner he had stretched across the entire length of his building after the events of September 11, 2001. The banner had an enormous American flag and a caption printed on it that said, "Look Over Your Shoulder Terrorists, Because We're Coming After You! God Bless America." Several members of the public complained and wrote letters to the paper, claiming that the banner was offensive, violent, too big and gave a poor impression of New Paltz, since Savago's building was located right at the entrance to downtown. At the insistence of the village board, the building inspector, Alison Murray, told Savago he had to take it down citing the size limitations of the village sign ordinance, which Savago's banner far exceeded. His response was to sue the village board for violating what he believed to be his constitutional rights to freedom of speech. He won. I could only imagine what he would say about the protest planned outside of his building, while he went to cast his delegate vote for President Bush.

"Unbelievable," he said a few weeks earlier when I first informed him of the anti-Bush protest plans. "I went and fought for this country, risked my life, so that the same people that are protesting me now could have their free speech." he said. "I have earned my right to cast my vote for whoever I want to. You don't see me protesting their decision to vote for that dimwit Kerry do you?"

Although he privately, or not so privately, referred to our newspaper as "that leftist rag," he was always friendly with me and willing to talk about whatever the issue of the day was. That Halloween Day, while he pumped gas he talked to Dino Toscani, the owner of the Italian Deli and Piano Bar. Toscani, another born and bred New Paltzian talked like a Goodfella, but looked as warm and approachable as a teddy bear. He had disappeared to some tropical island for a while, but eventually he came back to New Paltz to help take over and expand his family's multigenerational business that provided a little slice of Italy to cannoli-crazy clients like myself.

"Pete," I exclaimed, looking at Savago with a sense of urgency. "What are you doing? You're not even dressed up and you're *late*. They're counting on you to give the introduction."

He looked baffled. "Where am I supposed to be?" he asked nervously.

"On campus, to introduce Nader. The Greens want you to give the welcome speech!"

He and Dino both started laughing.

"She got you," said Dino slapping Savago on the back. "She got ya good!"

"I ain't introducing that moron," he said. "Let him come. It will only steal more votes away from the Democrats and make sure the *right* man gets back in office."

Dino shook his head in agreement with Savago. "You can't change quarterbacks in the middle of the game," he mused.

"Yes you can, Dino," I said. "Especially if you're *losing* the game. But I'll try and save you both a seat," I joked, and ran off towards the campus.

Although it was late autumn, the day was sunny and unusually warm. Wind pushed the leaves around the brick walking paths outside of the lecture center. We had a post-parade Halloween party planned for all of our friends and their children. I wondered how I would cover the rally, write the story, clean my house, dress up the kids, and prepare food for seventy-five people—all within the span of hours. Thank God for pizza delivery, I thought.

"Am I late?" I asked, as I arrived outside the lecture center.

"He's on his way, but he's not here yet," said Rachel, dressed in green spandex pants and nervously trying to avoid certain of her SUNY colleagues who, after learning that Nader was coming to campus, had quickly organized a "New Paltz Progressives for John Kerry" ad hoc group that was frantically passing out leaflets, claiming that "a vote for Nader is a vote for a Bush-enabler." One professor, who Rachel could somehow recognize even in his costume, was dressed up in a suit, with a Dick Cheney rubber mask on and a sign that said, "Thanks Ralph, Love George and Dick."

Like the post-arraignment rally that the Greens and other supporters quickly organized back in March, the Nader rally was put together in a similarly fast and frenetic fashion. Steve Greenfield always seemed to dress like Jerry Seinfeld, with clean sneakers, tight blue jeans and his shirt tucked in (the only differences being that his shoes were Converse high-tops, not Nike, and, as a volunteer fireman, he always had a beeper clipped to his belt). He was busy checking the mikes, the sound system, giving the "One, two, three. Testing one, two, three" every few minutes into the rapidly filling lecture hall.

It was a five-hundred-seat auditorium that, by the time Nader arrived, was standing room only, with more people waiting in the wings, trying to get a peek at the seventy-year-old political agitator. I had Rachel save my seat in the front row of the auditorium while I went backstage to a smaller lecture room where Nader had agreed to meet with the press prior to his speech. I shifted in my seat nervously, realizing that my steno pad was out of paper. I found some extra fliers, the ones supporting marijuana reform laws that NORML had been passing out, and put them together so that I'd have some paper to write on when the big man arrived.

"Hi, folks," said Steve Greenfield. "Ralph Nader is in the house and he is ready to answer some of your questions. Let's try to limit this to ten minutes. There are a lot of people waiting for him out there," he said, pointing to the auditorium doors.

Camera flashes flickered like a strobe light as the tall, thin and very serious- looking presidential candidate walked in the backdoor and moved swiftly to the podium.

"Hi. I'm Ralph Nader," he said humbly. "I heard you might have some questions for me."

The other journalists were so quick that I just hung back and wrote Nader's responses to their questions. By the time I was able to formulate a question in my head, Steve signaled that mine would be the last question Nader would answer.

"Your campaign calls for an end to American involvement in the Iraq War," I said, my voice cracking a bit. "What exactly is your plan for pulling out the troops?"

Nader said that his plan called for a complete withdrawal from Iraq in six months. "I believe that we should have an internationally supervised election in Iraq so that we can give the country back to the Iraqi people and not allow them to be dominated by a puppet dictatorship whose main objective is to protect American oil interests," he said. "In the interim, we phase out our troops and bring in peacekeepers, particularly from neighboring countries who understand the culture and the language, and within six months, we're out."

It was so nice to ask a question and get an answer from a political candidate at his level. No sound bites, no personal anecdotes, no waffling, just "six months and we're out." Was it realistic? I didn't know, but then again, was it realistic that we had launched this war in the first place in an effort to "hunt down terrorists, smoke them out of their holes, and take down any government that harbors terrorists," as President Bush was so fond of saying?

Jason, who, along with Rebecca, was scheduled to make introductory speeches, arrived at the last minute, just when people were beginning to get anxious and resorting to dialing his cell phone compulsively. He was clean-shaven and dressed in his one and only suit. He looked happy and alert and strangely enough well-rested, an impression he rarely achieved anymore. I dashed back to my seat, made sure my cell phone was turned off and looked around the floor for more flicrs to write on. Rebecca and Jason took turns revving up the crowd before their icon took the stage.

"I'm a Native American," Rebecca told the crowd. "And you all know how much we have lost to the hands of injustice, are still losing, despite what the history books tell you. But one thing they can never take away from me is my right to vote. I will *never* vote for a pro-war candidate, a pro–Patriot Act candidate, a pro-corporate candidate, a pro–death penalty candidate. I will *never* vote for an anti–marriage rights candidate or anti–campaign reform candidate or anti-choice candidate. I will never vote for the least worst evil or the lesser evil because in the end, it is still evil."

Jason surveyed the crowd, placed his hands on the podium and bent his head down before he spoke. I couldn't tell if he had forgotten what he was going to say or if it was just a dramatic pause. Like Nader, Jason and Rebecca did not carry a copy of a pre-written speech or even crib notes on index cards. They knew what they believed, why they believed it, and even if it didn't come out perfect, you could feel their conviction.

"The man who won the election in 2000, the one who is *not* our president today, lost his own home state," said Jason. I could sense that he was about to launch an attack on the Democrats. "Despite this fact, Democrats, and most of my friends are Democrats, like to blame Nader for this. Why don't they blame the 250,000 Florida Democrats who voted for Bush? Or ask themselves why they sat back and allowed 90,000 black voters in Florida to be illegally thrown off the rolls? This is beyond my comprehension. What I tell my Democratic friends is that before they start scapegoating the man who put seatbelts in their cars, and who has fought for four decades for the underdog, and who has founded over a hundred civic organizations including our own NYPIRG, I say friends, you have to get your *own* house in order!"

Jason asked the crowd to give a loud, warm welcome for Ralph Nader who came out to the stage and gave our mayor a handshake and affectionate pat on the back before turning towards the audience. Nader opened up his speech by applauding New Paltz, particularly the New Paltz Greens and what they had accomplished the past year.

"The amount of publicity that this village of 6,500 people has received around the nation and the world this past year is astounding," he said. "You've gotten more publicity than cities twenty-five times your size. Obviously the national media recognizes that there is something big going on in New Paltz, something energizing. This is exactly what we have to do all over the country. Start at the local level and elect Green Party and other third-party members to our village boards, our town boards, our city councils and build from the ground up. The Democratic and Republican Parties are ossified—controlled by corporate greed—and have been unresponsive to the people of this great country. It is time we take our power back, and you have no idea how much power you have to change this country. Look what happened in New Paltz! Look at what you did! All of the social and environmental reforms going on right here, right now, are what we need to do everywhere."

The third-party candidate, always the underdog, and often overshadowed, but never deterred, spoke for almost forty-five minutes. The crowd cheered often, at times rising to their feet to applaud something he said, usually an attack on President Bush or Senator Kerry or various corporations that he claimed all but owned Washington, D.C. Like Rebecca and Jason, Nader cautioned the audience against voting for the "least worst."

"Never vote for the least worst!" he said. "I urge you to have higher expectation levels of those you elect to office. Have higher estimation for yourselves. Third-party candidates in the nineteenth century refused to vote for the least worst. They refused to back down on their belief in the abolition of slavery, women's right to vote, the rights of small farmers, issues that the Democrats and Whigs would not take on because they were 'too controversial.' They said it 'would never happen.' Well, thanks to these small, grassroots third-party challengers, we were able to end slavery, get women their right to vote and have farmers lead a populist revolt!"

It was sad to see him go. Not because he hadn't given us our fair share of information, encouragement and excitement, but because the presidential elections were only three days away, and I knew that this man would not be our president, and most likely would not, four years later at age seventy-four, take on the commitment, financial burden and political pressure of running another third-party campaign. As I walked out of the lecture center, I passed by Nader who had been quickly seated behind a folding table to sign copies of his various books. He was talking to Jason. "Hey there!" said Jason, giving me a hug and looking happier than I'd seen him in a long time. "Have you met Ralph?"

"Not formally," I said, shaking Nader's hand. "We spoke on the phone."

I handed him a copy of the paper, the one with his picture plastered on the front. Rebecca was the one who had encouraged me to give him a copy. She even asked her son, Lorin, to run to my car while I attended Nader's press conference, to get an extra copy I had on the passenger's seat. While I waited for him to arrive, I wrote in the margins of the newspaper, "Democracy is still alive and well and living in New Paltz."

"I look forward to reading this," he said, smiling as much as Nader smiles, and took the paper from me. After he finished signing his books, he was headed towards Indian Point nuclear plant where he told me he would "lend a hand to moth-balling that sitting death-duck." Then he was on his way to New York City to give his final rallying speech on Wall Street, in protest of the "corporate greed" he felt was poisoning our great Democracy.

Nader had a purifying effect. I suddenly felt like everything I believed in had been validated and that my upcoming vote for him could not be any cleaner, any closer to my conscience. Several friends of mine who came to see him agreed with everything he said. "You just sit there and nod your head," said my childhood friend Jen Alba. "It's so refreshing to finally hear a politician telling the truth, tackling the issues head on, and standing up for something." But she, like most other left-leaning friends that I knew, would not pull the third-party lever, no matter how much they liked what his campaign stood for; they were too frightened of what the country would look like after four more years of Bush.

Only a week before Nader's visit, Bobby Kennedy Jr., a leading environmental lawyer and part of the great American Democratic Dynasty, had come to this same campus, to read from his latest book, *Crimes Against Nature.* That night and the next day, our mostly progressive populace felt hopeful. Sure, after Kennedy's reading, we could better taste the toxins in the air and the mercury in the fish that the Bush administration was letting their corporate cohorts dump into our environment; but we were also emboldened by Kennedy's presence, as if his touching ground on our recently haloed soil meant something bigger than what it was, meant that the clean winds of change were about to sweep through and purify our American soul. Kennedy came and went, just as Nader came and went. And in the end, what most people in New Paltz were hoping for, save for Savago and his Republican allies, did *not* come to pass.

November 3 was a dark day. We were all sleepless, nursing CNN hangovers after having spent the night on the couch, watching TV, waiting for the results of those last swing-states to be counted. Before the final results from Ohio could even be tallied or contested or verified, my mother came to the playground on Huguenot Street to tell me the bad news.

"Kerry just conceded," she said. A few fellow moms and friends of mine let out a gasp. Until that moment, none of us had dared to believe it. When you looked around for some obvious sign that the world was not what we thought it was, or wanted it to be, or needed it to be for our kids and our future and our sense of justice and decency, the sun just kept on callously burning, and the leaves kept falling, as if nature didn't realize just how much this administration, this president, was willing to plunder it for the sake of profit and privilege.

That moment will stick out in my mind, almost like the way the bud of an about-to-bloom tulip looks, so full of promise and color, just before it is bitten off by a hungry deer or rabbit. Many of my friends were circling the drain and some pledged to wear black until Bush was impeached or ousted. Others stayed cocooned in their shock and disbelief. Rachel didn't leave the house for days. The death toll in Iraq continued to mount every day. The fusion of the administration with the religious Right had become so public and so proud that even the newscasters tended to forget that our Democracy was founded on the absolute separation of Church and State.

My favorite response came from Susan Zimet's seventy-one-year-old Jewish mother who was as lively as her daughter and as committed to the notion of democracy. "Why don't they just put a cross on the White House and get it over with!" she said, disgusted. "Why the charade?"

But eventually we had to move on. That was the nature of things, and I noticed that people, at least here in New Paltz, began to throw themselves into action in an effort to pull back the imbalance of some subconscious political scale that was leaning so far to the Right that it threatened to take us all with it—voluntarily or not. They became active in their various political parties. They become more interested in local politics. They joined various civic committees and boards, organized book clubs, planted sunflowers to represent their pledge to tolerance and peace and everything good and healthy that they felt slipping away from them on a national level after the elections of November 2004.

It was odd that during the post-election analysis, the major news organizations, particularly CNN, would show the clip of Jason presiding over the marriage of Billiam and Jeffrey. Although the gay marriages in New Paltz had happened eight months earlier, this was the clip that they ran every time they discussed what role the "gay marriage" issue and "family values" played in the outcome of the national elections. "Oh great," said Jason when I mentioned this to him. "Now they're going to blame me for Bush too."

It was ironic that gay marriage, which had become New Paltz's recent trademark, was also the issue that became so scrutinized in the presidential exit polling and in the eleven states that had resolutions supporting gay marriage on the ballot. Bush was re-elected at the same time that each of those resolutions failed. Living inside of our gay-friendly bubble, I hadn't realized what a knee-jerk quasi-moral and religious backlash was going on around the country against same-sex marriage. And how, at least on the nightly news, this issue came to be visually represented, not by Rosie O'Donnell marrying her lesbian partner on the steps of the San Francisco courthouse, but by the twenty-seven-year-old mayor of New Paltz, New York, who decided that his friends, Billiam and Jeffrey, had as much legal, civil, and moral right to be married as he, or any other heterosexual person.

Chapter 14
Out on a Limb

Adeep chill fell into the valley just after the presidential elections. Maybe it helped to numb us, or to force us to turn inward and focus on the interior landscape of our lives. Outside, pine-tree boughs were weighted down by wet snow. The sky shifted in shades of deep blue and gray. Most of the migratory birds had already fled south, and the ones that remained, like the Canadian geese and turkey vultures, looked both graceful and foreboding, their large-winged frames carved against the sky like dark ink prints from a woodcut.

Unpicked pumpkins and corn rotted in the fields. The Ferrante family farm, stretched out across the Wallkill River flats, dividing the small, urban village from the Shawangunk Ridge, closed its market doors each year on Christmas Eve, marking the commencement of winter for locals more than freezing temperatures or snowfalls ever could. They would open again in mid-March, and until then, we were, in a sense, cut off from our land, left to wander alone and survive on either the things that we had preserved, or the things we could purchase from tropical states and countries. We were not fed by our own soil anymore, at least for these three months; the freshness was removed, and in its place, a noble or not-so-noble determination to see ourselves through until those first yellow wildflower blossoms of winter aconite could pierce through the frozen ground.

We all enjoyed a good laugh and respite from the winter doldrums when Jason was coined in the January edition of *Mad* magazine as one of their "latest bunch of has-beens." Our gay marrying mayor was listed along with Amber Fry, Jason Alexander, and Smarty Jones. He claimed to be thrilled with the news. "I've been telling everyone for months that I'm a 'has-been,'" he said with a smile when I swung by Village Hall to get his reaction to his new title. "My novelty has worn off, thankfully. Now I can get back to real life and doing my job as mayor. But I have to say, they gave me a backhanded compliment. I love the epitaph."

One of the world's most notorious celebrity critics, Alfred E. Neuman, *Mad*'s gap-toothed zany icon, had this to say about our mayor: "Though marriage was banned / Many gays took the stand / That a wedding would make them feel gayer / Imagine their pride / When the Law was defied / By this gutsy small-town mayor."

While our mayor seemed to relish in his has-been status, the reality was that Jason had become, as Jeremiah would write in his column for the *Times Herald-Record*, "catnip to the country's star-making machinery." Regardless of Jason's "has-been" status, pop-culture could not stop working Westian sub-plots into their story lines. After an actor playing Jason turned up on *Law and Order* lecturing about First Amendment rights, the ever-popular *Simpsons* released a new 'gay-marrying' episode that bore great resemblance to the events in New Paltz.

Has-been or not, Jason was soon to become a criminal in the eyes of the DA once again. On February 2, twenty-five days before the first anniversary of the same-sex marriages in New Paltz, my answering machine and e-mail account were overflowing with all kinds of messages, protests, and woes, citing the decision that had finally come down from State Supreme Court Judge Michael Bruhn, on the DA's appeal of Judge Katz's ruling back in June that dismissed all charges against the mayor on constitutional grounds. As we had all predicted, Bruhn, though he took his time in doing so, ruled in favor of the DA and reinstated the twenty-four criminal counts against Jason. This thing was not going away.

After citing the decisions made previously on Hebel's civil suit against Jason, by both Justices Michael Kavanagh and Vincent Bradley, Judge Bruhn went on to say:

> This court takes judicial notice of the serious and legitimate debate now taking place in this state, the United States, and throughout much of the world regarding same-sex marriages and civil unions. The appropriate and proper vehicles to effect change in this area are legislative action and judicial proceedings in the nature of mandamus or declaratory judgment, not unilateral disobedience of the existing statutory scheme by a local official.... The decision and order of the Town Court of New Paltz dated June 10, 2004, are reversed and this matter is remanded to the Town Court for further proceeding not inconsistent herewith.

What I found so troubling about Judge Bruhn's decision, besides the amount of time it took him, was the inconsistency of the reasoning. In layman's terms, at least as I understood it, he was saying that Katz's decision was flawed because the mayor, as a third party and *not* one of the same-sex couples who had had a marriage license denied to them, did not have the legal standing to claim that the law was unconstitutional because his *own* civil rights had not been violated. The individuals that *did* have standing, in Bruhn's estimation, were the same-sex couples themselves. Yet, as his decision goes on, he references the Article 78 lawsuit brought on by Mayor John Shields of Nyack, the openly gay mayor and now a friend and ally of Jason's, who, instead of performing gay marriages himself, went on to pursue the courts in another, at least by Bruhn's reasoning, more legal approach. He and his partner, after requesting and being denied a marriage license, filed a civil suit against Rockland

County, claiming that their civil rights had been violated. Their suit was rejected by the courts.

So, the entire thrust of the DA's case, and Judges Kavanagh, Bradley, and Bruhn's decisions—that there were other, legal remedies for gay couples to pursue to ensure their civil rights, rather than have the mayor of a small village decide to "unilaterally" violate laws he felt were unconstitutional—was disingenuous. Because when those couples did pursue other remedies, as Mayor Shields decided to do, they were denied by the courts. It was like some Kafkaesque storyline where true justice would always remain elusive, or better yet, like one of those shell games they trap tourists into playing in the city where the prize promised is never revealed, because it is a trick, and the prize was never intended to be revealed.

Even more troubling to me was a recent conversation I had with a New York State judge at a private wedding reception near Albany. I told him how impressed I was when I had the opportunity to finally see him presiding in court a year before on another case. We got onto the topic of Jason and the charges that the Ulster County DA had brought against him. This judge told me that he, too, had a case before him where two gay couples had asked their city clerk for a marriage license and were denied, then filed an Article 78 claiming their constitutional rights had been violated.

"I was just saying to my wife on the way over here that when you read the Equal Rights Act, the denial of a marriage license based on gender is in clear violation of that statute."

"What are you going to do?" I asked, wide-eyed and curious. This was a very conservative judge, who had built his career on his Republican and right-leaning support. "I really don't know," he said to me, staring into his martini. "If I rule in favor of the gay couples I would certainly lose the support of my conservative base."

He also admitted to me that he had no immediate plans to run for higher office, that he was quite happy where he was. I had to believe that when the time came, he would make the most judicious decision and not one that would be swayed by any concrete or abstract political ambitions or allegiances. I had great respect for this man and we went on to talk about another high-profile case he was involved with years ago that he always believed would make a great book. I told him that I would love the opportunity to write about it for a feature-length article or possibly a non-fiction book. We went our separate ways that evening, but what he had said about the legality of gay marriages stayed with me.

There was another thing that bothered me about Judge Bruhn's decision. At least as he portrayed himself to me, he seemed to be not acting out of his best legal interpretation of the law, but was being influenced instead by the sort of potential political kudos or political retribution his decision would generate. On the other hand, although I had also disagreed with the DA, in my opinion, he had been operating from a true conviction that his interpretation of the law was correct. I was absolutely convinced that *his* actions stemmed from a deep sense of ethical and moral duties to his post.

The DA had said to me on several occasions that he knew very well that he was "committing political suicide" when he decided to bring criminal charges against Jason and then the two Unitarian ministers, Dawn Sangrey and Kay Greenleaf. He said that he was acutely aware of the way the county was changing politically. Within a year and a half he would have to run for office again, an office he had been easily elected to after being cross-endorsed by the Republicans and the Democrats, but one that he might now lose, because of this one issue, this one case. The murderers, child-molesters, and wife-abusers that he successfully put behind bars seemed to have been dismissed or forgotten by the increasingly liberal voters of Ulster County.

I was thinking about all of this when I called Jason to see if I could come in to Village Hall prior to their regularly scheduled board meeting to get his reactions to the decision. I had already spoken to the DA, and now felt it was Jason's turn to weigh in. I was also anxious to find out if they were going to forgo an appeal and return the case to Katz's court where there would then be a trial. I was dreaming of a big, flashy trial, one that would allow me to feel that same rush of adrenaline as I did during the weddings, and enable me to get out of covering some of the more run-of-the-mill stories I was responsible for.

"How does it feel to be a criminal once again in the eyes of the law?" I asked, settling into his small, cramped office.

"Would you like a drink?" he asked, uncorking a bottle of rosé and pointing it towards me. "No thanks, rosé makes me queasy. Are you having a drink in honor of Judge Bruhn?"

"No, I just finished my book!" he said. "What a weight off my chest."

"Congratulations," I said. "Now can we go to trial?"

He laughed. "I have a conference call scheduled with my lawyers on Monday. Can we wait until then to discuss my legal strategy? Since I have no idea what it's going to be yet?"

"You're the client," I teased. "Just tell them that you're sick and tired of being treated like a criminal, and that for the sake of God and Country and your fellow gay citizens that you are going to trial to be judged by a jury of your peers! I mean, come on Jason. Can you imagine Billiam taking the witness stand in his Versace suit, Kenneth Cole shoes and bow tie? Then Jeff would get up there in full military dress, with his medals hanging off him? You have to go to trial. You yourself said that there are wealthy gay people all over the country who would help you pay the fines if you lose, which I can't imagine happening in Katz's court."

Although he had, on many occasions, said that he would go to trial in Katz's court rather than appeal Bruhn's decision, when the time really came, he ended up deferring to his lawyers.

While the lawyers awaited their next conference call, I was busy trying to referee a verbal boxing match between the DA and the mayor. It was a "Clash of the Titans," and with this latest legal setback for Jason, one that could potentially put him behind bars and set the gay civil rights movement way back in New York State. Jason was holding nothing back.

The DA had responded as I imagined he would. "Obviously we agree with the court's decision," he said on the phone to me, shortly after Bruhn's decision was handed down. "The basis of his opinion is the crux of what our argument has been all along—that this is not the proper forum to litigate the constitutionality of same-sex marriage. Mayor West made a willful decision to put himself

234

above the law and to unilaterally decide which laws he would decide to uphold and which laws he would not. This is not just my interpretation, this is the interpretation of the New York State Attorney General, of State Supreme Court Justice Michael Kavanagh, and of two county judges, Vincent Bradley and now Michael Bruhn."

"What do you have to say for yourself?" I asked.

Jason had that boyish grin working while he polished off his glass of wine and poured himself another one. "I'll tell you my reaction," he said and then went on to reiterate what he had said to me many times: that Judge Bruhn, like the other two judges that ruled on the civil case against him, "chose to ignore 150 years of case law" and "rule against the Constitution."

"Can you give me a fresh quote? Maybe an anecdote or something?" I urged him.

"You're the writer, make it up for me."

"I wish I could, but you're more articulate than you think."

"Okay, let me put it this way. If a couple came to me and wanted to get married but didn't have a license, I would say, 'Sorry, according to the law you need to get a license before I can marry you.' *But* when a couple comes to me and says, 'We tried to obtain a license but because we are a same-sex couple we were not granted one,' then that's a different thing entirely. If I upheld the DRL in that case then I would be 'knowingly, consciously' violating the Constitutions of this state and of this country. And I take my oath of office too seriously to violate the greatest laws of the land which guarantee equality for every citizen regardless of race, creed or sex."

When I asked him why he felt that the DA had pressed on with an appeal of Katz's decision rather than just let sleeping dogs lie, he said, "If the DA really believed that the decision to uphold the Constitution and marry same-sex couples was such a 'terrible precedent' then why didn't he continue to prosecute Reverend Dawn Sangrey or Reverend Kay Greenleaf or the twenty-five other members of the clergy that married hundreds of same-sex couples in New Paltz? Why didn't he criminally prosecute my deputy mayor, or village trustee, Julia Walsh, who also solemnized same-sex marriages? Why is he only profiling and prosecuting me? *Because he has higher political ambitions*. He wants to ride my coattails and gain notoriety for himself. If he were truly interested in doing his job, according to his own principles, then I would be only one of thirty-five individuals to be prosecuted. But I help get him into the papers."

I knew I'd have to call the DA back to get further quotes, once Jason had finished his tirade. While it made for great print, Jason was now claiming that Don Williams, who had spent his entire career inside the Kingston Courthouse working as an assistant to the DA or as the DA himself, had "higher political ambitions" and wanted to "ride the coattails" of this twenty-seven-year-old.

I waited until the next morning to call the DA, when I could usually catch him at the office before he went to trial. When I got him on the phone, he said, "Are they still burning me in effigy down there?" He did have a good sense of humor. With the exception of Hebel, this was quite a witty crew of politicians and lawyers that I had the opportunity to interview. I read him Jason's comments from the night before. I could hear him sigh, as his phones rang in the background, and I could almost imagine his fingers moving up to his temples instinctively, trying to knead away the tension that Jason and the gay marriages had unintentionally caused him.

"Erin, I'm very tempted to respond to this," he said. "But I cannot dishonor this office by engaging in a debate of rhetoric in the print media with the mayor," he added. "Suffice to say, I think that if anyone examines who has made the most of the publicity surrounding this case and who has avoided the media spotlight, it speaks volumes. This is a very difficult task for my office and we have far more compelling cases before us which deserve our attention, including three murder cases since October, three cases of child abuse and, most recently, a high school athletic coach in New Paltz accused of raping a student. It would be relatively easy for me to ignore my responsibility in this case. But I took an oath of office and I knew at the time that it would not be easy, that I would have to make difficult decisions. And I still believe that I am up to that task and swayed not by public opinion or the inflammatory remarks by Mayor West, but by the duties of this office."

Something had unsettled the DA regarding this. He should have been happy to win the appeal, but instead, it brought the whole issue back to front and center. In just a few short weeks, a lone gunman would open fire at a Kingston mall, severely wounding two individuals—yet another high-profile case that the DA would have to lead the prosecution on, as he would later find out.

Only a few minutes after we got off the phone, he called me back to add more. So much of it was off the record that I began to feel like he just wanted to talk, wanted me to understand his sincerity on this issue, or perhaps make that sincerity known to Jason so he would back off. At one point, I had to call him back on his private line from my cell phone because I was late to pick up Tadeusz from nursery school. I continued to listen as I drove, and as I entered the nursery school basement where there were at least thirty toddlers riding plastic bikes around a cold cement floor. The acoustics made it sound like a Black Sabbath concert.

"I've never even met Jason West," he said exasperated. "From what you tell me, I might even like him. But I wish he would stop making these inflammatory remarks and accusations in the print media."

The last thing anyone wanted to do, I wanted to caution the DA, was to try and tell Jason what to do, unless they were keen on having him do just the exact opposite. When I eased him back on the record, as I pushed Tadeusz around on a Big Wheel, I could see some of the other mothers looking at me strangely. Not only was I trying to push the Big Wheel, talk on the phone and scribble down notes in my steno pad, but in the rush to get out the door on time, I had completely forgotten to take off my pajamas.

"Andy, I'm dying here," I said, calling him on his cell phone just after the Monday conference call was scheduled between Jason and his lawyers, who I learned, had staff in California as well as New York.

"You and Jeremiah both," he said. "I just hung up the phone with him. You guys have radar!" Andy said he was sorry to report that the conference call had been cancelled. "One of the lawyers on our team was stuck in L.A. traffic and her cell phone went dead," he said.

"You have to be kidding me," I said. This was too funny. What had Jason gotten himself into? Now he had conference calls and a "team" of lawyers on both coasts?

Like Jeremiah, Jason and me, Andy was also pushing for a trial. "Why get another black eye?" he said to me, while I sat in his office waiting for a copy of Bruhn's decision. "Why make more bad law? That's the point I'm trying to make. Why risk losing in the Court of Appeals when we can have a trial, right here in New Paltz, with a judge who has already ruled in our favor?"

"I couldn't agree more, Andy," I said.

But the problem was, Andy was only one of seven legal advisors and since he came onto the case after Rosenkranz agreed to represent Jason, he didn't feel that he was in the position to step on anyone's toes. "Josh believes that we win either way," he said. " Basically, he's arguing that we take a chance for the grand slam in the Court of Appeals. If they take our case, which they are not obligated to do, and they rule in our favor, then we *change* the law. If they don't, then we go back to trial."

In the end, we wouldn't get our trial, well, at least not that winter. Jason and his attorneys decided to appeal Judge Bruhn's decision with New York's highest court, the Court of Appeals. I ran into Jeremiah at P&G's and we commiserated on the appeal. "The least they could do for all of our hard work this past year was give us a trial," I said to him, while I poured ketchup onto my children's grease-saturated french fries. "I told Andy, for what it's worth, that *my* recommendation was to go to trial," said Jeremiah, who I often saw eating alone at P&G's, or with his wife, or being joined spontaneously by local political figures who wanted to work themselves into his good graces. "But an appeal?" he said, rolling his eyes. "Bo-ring!"

I was working on the "Clash of the Titans" story and four others over the weekend. Generally Kazik watched our kids so I could get my writing done by Monday morning deadline. But this particular weekend, he was busy painting, in our kitchen, two plaster Greek-style columns with a faux-marble finish for an anxious client.

"Why don't you just bring the kids and come to our house for the Super Bowl?" suggested Susan Zimet, when I explained my deadline dilemma. "We can help you watch the kids and everyone you need for the story will be here, well, almost everyone."

Except for Jason, the DA, and Bob Hebel, everyone who was involved with this particular story was at Susan's house. The Honorable Judge Katz was present, along with his wife Nancy and their two daughters; Andy and Vicki Kossover with their young daughter; Jeffrey McGowan, minus Billiam; and myself, with my three ratty children in tow.

The judge, the attorney, and the gay retired army major were all slumped on the two brown leather couches inside Susan's husband Steve's TV and exercise room. In fact, the space was more like a shrine to the cable gods than it was anything else, with an enormous, high-tech TV screen that seemed to stretch the entire length of the wall. My kids quickly dubbed it "the movie theatre." The TV seemed incongruent with the rest of their sprawling, historic house, located on Butterville Road, facing the Shawangunk Ridge with nothing to obscure the mountain view, just a sweeping vista of farmland and the mouth of the old carriage road that led to the fabled circa-1800s Mohonk Mountain House, founded by the Smiley family, a clan of politically progressive Quakers.

Just as I finished getting the kids settled at the kitchen table with their plates of food, and began to actually have a somewhat adult conversation with Susan, Nancy, and Vicki, my cell phone rang. It was Jason, but because the reception was poor, within a few seconds we were disconnected. "We should just invite Jason, the DA, and Bob over and get the trial done with right here and now," I said. Susan and I laughed. "It would save us all a lot of time and it would be sort of cozy, don't you think?"

During halftime, I figured it was the right moment to get Jeffrey to weigh in on the latest court decision. He was poised to release his memoirs, *Major Conflict: One Gay Man's Life in the Don't-Ask-Don't-Tell Military* (Broadway Books, 2005.) While many people were under the false assumption that Jeffrey's book was the result of his notoriety as part of the first and most photographed and quoted couples married by Jason, he had signed with his publisher months before he decided to come out to family, friends, his employer and the world to marry Billiam on national television.

"Where's Billiam?" I asked Susan. She whispered to me to follow her into the bathroom. "He and Jeffrey are having a fight. Billiam just called me in tears." I hated the idea of anyone fighting, particularly newlyweds on the eve of their one-year anniversary. In fact, Billiam was working day and night with Susan and the new gay periodical, *Inside Out Magazine*, planning a big same-sex wedding party to celebrate the anniversary, an event that was scheduled for the first weekend in March.

While Jeffrey showed no outward signs of distress, he did take an extra long time to provide me with quotes for my story on Judge Bruhn's decision. I loved this man. I didn't know why, I hadn't known him that long. He was just a class act. I kept imagining what courage it took for this career military man to leave the only life that he had known, in an effort to be true to himself, and then to announce that he was gay—not only gay, but getting married to another man, on national television. "Mostly, the men I served with were offended that I never told them," he said to me when I interviewed him about his book. "'That must have hurt to keep all of that inside of you,' said one of my soldiers. 'That whole time we were joking about women we never knew you were a butt pirate!'"

The Super Bowl revelers teased me for whipping out my notebook and taking quotes from Jeffrey. What they did not realize was that outside of caring for my husband and children and filing my five stories every week, there was no "off time." I had no room in my life to casually attend a Super Bowl party. If I was going to go, I had to get more bang for the buck and procure some quotes along the way. Predictably, Jeffrey staunchly defended Jason's actions and questioned the DA's motivation for prosecuting him.

"I think at this point the DA's motives can only be viewed as vindictive," he said, leaning his elbows on his knees as if in deep concentration. "There's no point in taking this any further. Mayor West was ordered by the court to stop performing same-sex marriages. He has honored the court's wishes, and has had a ruling by Justice Katz which affirms that the DRL does violate the New York State Constitution. So why did the DA appeal that decision? What does he stand to gain except for sticking it to the mayor?"

I shared my notes with him on what both Jason and the DA had said. Jeffrey shook his head. "Throughout history, we have relied on courageous leaders, like Jason West, to take a stand for those whose rights were being violated by the existing laws of the land. He knew the great risk he was taking, but he decided to accept that risk and act on his convictions which are soundly echoed in the New York State Constitution and the U.S. Constitution."

Billiam, a one-man PR machine, had set up various interviews for himself and Jefferey to take place during the week before their one-year anniversary, including two prime-time news spots on ABC and CBS. As a proud husband, Billiam worked around the clock to court the media in an effort to get more exposure for the gay civil rights movement as well as press for Jeffrey's book. "I don't know how he does it," said Susan, no stranger to media attention herself. "He's on NPR in the morning and ABC at night. I can't keep track of him."

Earlier that week, Susan and I had gone out to Billiam and Jeff's farmhouse for lunch and to show my children all of their goats, pigs, and roosters that roamed the grounds along with the couple's five black pugs. While I tried to keep my children from knocking the collection of blown-glass fish off their antique grand piano, Billiam announced that CBS had just called and wanted him and Jeffrey for a segment that night on the gay marriage issue. I corralled the kids upstairs to the TV room so that I could keep Billiam company while he ironed Jeffrey's shirt. The two bickered for a while on exactly which shirt Jeffrey should wear. Billiam eventually won, arguing that he needed to look as military-like as possible and not at all "fruity."

I played with the kids on the couch while Billiam talked. "I'm so exhausted," he said in a confessional tone. "I mean here I am, pushing forty, I haven't slept in days, and I have wrinkles all over my face!" He put the iron down and leaned over the board towards me and Zofia as if admitting something to us in great confidence. "Most people don't know this about me, but I'm really shy. These television appearances take so much out of me," he whispered dramatically, as if he were a child star like Judy Garland who was pushed beyond her limits.

I had to place Zofia in front of my face so that he would not see me laughing. Not only was Billiam *not* camera shy, but he actively sought out the press, almost always for good and noble reasons—for his sunflower planting project, trying to change the "Don't-Ask, Don't-Tell" policies in the military, and helping Susan in her efforts to shut down Indian Point nuclear plant, and to make sure that our war veterans were tested for depleted uranium when they came home from Iraq. He was a good man, and I adored him, but he was also a ham.

I left the Super Bowl party much earlier than the others. While I had been a relatively big sports fan in my past life-pre-children, have-plenty-of-time-to-kill years-I was now so oblivious to the sports scene that I didn't even know which teams were playing, let alone who won. Early the next morning I called Susan to ask her how Billiam and Jeffrey were doing. "Did they make up?" I asked nervously.

"Everything's fine," she said with a sleepy voice.

"Oh, thank God," I said relieved, thinking how bad it would look if our most celebrated married gay couple broke up before their one-year anniversary.

"It was just a typical marriage spat," said Susan.

Jason's criminal status notwithstanding, things did seem to get back to normal. Everything came together, as much as it could. Our local bookstore, Ariel, hosted a reading and signing for Jeffrey once his book came out. The place was packed and Jeffrey, dressed in a tweed jacket and pleated trousers, looked like a 1940s film star. Jason, on the other hand, looked exactly like himself, internally dignified yet outwardly like a schlep. He was there to introduce Jeffrey.

Of all the things Jeffrey said to the crowd that night, the statement that moved me most was when he talked about the past seven years he had lived in the New Paltz area. "Since living here, we have never, not once, experienced a moment of bigotry," he said. "Not one instance of homophobia, or any situation where we were made to feel ashamed. New Paltz should be very proud of itself. I'm proud to call it my home."

I, too, was proud of New Paltz and of the entire cast of characters that played their own personal role in our little drama, which had its opening night on a major stage. That cool night in early March tingled with victory, even though Jason still faced his day in court. At least he could rest easy at night, knowing that he had taken a stand for something and, whether or not the courts were ready to agree with him, that he had affected so many lives by helping to legitimize their love for one another.

After the book signing, almost everyone in attendance darted up to The Wave, a local disco and nightclub located on the outskirts of town just next to the Super 8 Motel and the thruway exit. The place catered to all kinds of clientele, with country music and line-dancing one night and hard rock the next. Because of its massive size and its weekly Wednesday and Saturday gay and lesbian disco nights, it was the logical choice for the same-sex anniversary party.

The part of the event that Susan and Billiam worked on was under the auspices of the New Paltz Social Society, an organization they had started to help launch a fundraising party at Susan's home for Congressman Hinchey. While advocating liberal policies and voting far left of the status quo in Washington, the Democratic representative had also managed to procure innumerable federal dollars for the Hudson Valley, so much so, that even in a predominantly Republican district, he had been elected and re-elected five times. Susan had hosted wildly successful fundraising parties for Hinchey in the past, but she felt that this one, in the midst of the upcoming presidential election climate, needed to be more dramatic and well attended. So she and Billiam came up with the New Paltz Social Society, which would be dedicated to raising awareness and funds

243

for good causes, but with a twist of fun and frivolity in the mix. The Hinchey fundraiser turned out like one of Truman Capote's masquerade balls, with Democrats of all shapes and sizes dressed in vintage garb or clever political costumes.

What could be more perfect for the Social Society, as a Hinchey fundraiser follow-up, than a gay anniversary gala? So they worked in conjunction with *Inside Out Magazine*, which, fortuitously, had launched its regional gay/lesbian/transgender magazine only days before Jason decided to solemnize gay marriages.

Billiam felt that besides reveling in their one-year newlywed status, that the gay couples had many people to thank and publicly recognize. I was flattered and a little taken off guard when Billiam called me to tell me that I was to be a recipient of an award that the New Paltz Social Society would be presenting at The Wave that night. My mother, who had been pining away for me to win anything, even last place, since the moment I was born, said that she wanted to come with me to the party to see me receive the accolade. I had to admit, I had some delusions of grandeur. Not grandeur necessarily—I knew well the small place I occupied in the making of the story—but I did envision a sort of Vanity Fair Goes to the Oscars–type celebration with white linen tablecloths, centerpieces designed by a gay florist, people delicately tapping their champagne glasses with forks, calling for someone to give a speech. I pictured slow-dancing with Kazik, my three kids dressed in white oxford-cloth shirts and khakis like some Ralph Lauren ad, and the smell of crêpes wafting through the ballroom air.

Imagine my surprise when I entered a packed, industrial-sized warehouse that was almost pitch black, with one spotlight on the center stage where transvestites were lip-syncing disco hits. They didn't want to let me and my mother in without proof that I was in fact a journalist there to cover the event for a story. I felt silly dressed in my new pink scoop-neck silk sweater and black capri pants. It was a real dirty jeans and tight tank-top crowd who were working hard to bring bandanas back into fashion. I felt like I was on the outskirts of L.A. rather than in my hometown.

244

My husband had declined the offer to accompany me. "I'll watch the kids," he said. "We could call a baby-sitter," I offered. "No. Go with your mom. You know I'm with you, always. But that's just not my scene. We'll have a champagne toast when you get home."

I couldn't force him to go, and when I surveyed the scene, I realized he would have been more lost here than I was.

My mother held on to my belt loop as I tried to navigate our way through the crowd, looking for Susan or Billiam or Jason—someone I recognized. Finally I saw a tall, thin man with a large white hand raised in the air, way above the heads of the masses. It was Billiam, but he had a cast on!

"What happened, Billiam?" I screamed into his ear, as the acoustics were so bad that you couldn't hear someone unless they were sticking their tongue into your ear, which I imagined was the type of atmosphere they were trying to achieve. "Just a little accident," he said. "We already gave out most of the awards. We just have yours and Jason's left. Where were you two?" he asked, while waving and welcoming dozens of other people through gregarious hand gestures and facial expressions, since you couldn't hear anything. I wanted to say that we were all at his husband's book signing while he was at The Wave ordering drinks for everyone, but didn't have the strength to shout anymore.

"Susan's up there," he screamed and gestured towards the stage. For a second I thought he meant that she was up there dancing with the transvestites. She had a wild side, so I didn't rule it out. When we finally found her she pulled my mother and me out a side door, where Jason and his latest girlfriend Lilah, who looked like a younger, softer version of Julia Roberts—and who I found absolutely endearing—were outside smoking. Susan explained to my mother and me that Billiam had cut himself with a chain saw while trying to saw off branches from the apple trees in his backyard for our "Out on a Limb" awards.

"It's a brilliant idea," said Susan, taking a drag off Jason's cigarette. Jason was busy being photographed with a very drunk gay couple. "He mounted these limbs onto wooden plaques with engraved name plates.... But what he didn't tell me was that he had used a *chain saw*. The doctor in the ER said that he nearly severed his thumb off!"

My mother, who was a very young and sexy grandmother, fit right in with the trendy smoking section folks, even though she had quit smoking and drinking twenty-five years earlier. Now she was worried for Billiam and was suggesting to Susan various essential oils that he could put on his wound to make it heal faster.

Soon Billiam returned, with a fresh drink in his good hand, and pulled Susan onto the stage. They had already presented their "Out on a Limb" awards to Andy Kossover, Joshua Rosenkranz, Robert Gottlieb, and a few others. Now it was Jason's and my turn. I was told to just sort of hover in the dark corner of the makeshift stage, next to the transvestites. Susan said some nice things about me and then she introduced Jason. While throngs of gay couples cheered Jason on, I gave a quick smile to my mom, took hold of my mounted tree limb and quickly shuffled back out of range of the spotlight. Jason gave his acceptance speech to the adoring crowd, pounding the Democrats once again for backing Senator Kerry in the presidential elections, a candidate who did not support gay marriages. "We must never give up, we must never stop fighting until we have equal rights for all Americans!" he bellowed.

Thankfully he kept it short. Within just a few minutes I was able to climb off the stage, pose for a few pictures and then go find my mom and Susan, who had procured a fresh drink for me.

Like me, Susan and Billiam felt the place was too claustrophobic and they suggested that we go out with all the award recipients for drinks at some quieter venue in the village. I told them to call me on my cell, because I had to go home and put the kids to bed. I had to pull my mother out of the bar; she was having a fine time chatting with Susan and Billiam and Rachel, but I was eager to leave and return to my small crowd. We bumped into Jason outside in the parking lot, while he was receiving dozens of congratulatory hugs and handshakes from the various couples whose marriages he had presided over a year ago. They had come from far and wide to celebrate the auspicious occasion. "What?" he called after me. "You don't want any quotes?"

246

"You have one ready?" I yelled back.

"Justice will prevail!" he said, and waved goodbye, quickly being sucked up into the embraces of the happy couples.

When I got home, the kids were so excited that I had won an award that they began fighting over who could hold it and exactly where it should be placed. Kazik and I sat together on the couch, laughing hysterically as they went over the various options to display my wooden accolade. Eventually, Zofia, frustrated with her brothers' choices, grabbed the award from Seamus and hit Tadeusz on the head with it. So, it remains, to this day, perched very high on a shelf, giving off a slight glimmer when the sun hits it just right, to remind me of the year that was.

Epilogue

After enduring more than a year and a half of litigation, New Paltz Village Mayor Jason West is finally a free man. As *Pride and Politics* was going to press on July 12, 2005, District Attorney Don Williams issued a press release announcing that his office would take no further action on the twenty-four criminal charges against West—charges Williams' office leveled against the mayor following West's decision to marry twenty-five same-sex couples on February 27, 2004.

"This office is declining any further action in the above entitled matter [People *v.* Jason West]," the statement read. The People *v.* Jason West was scheduled to go to trial in the town of New Paltz after New York's highest court, the Court of Appeals, refused to hear Mayor Jason West's appeal and instead remanded the case back to the New Paltz town court. But before a date could be scheduled for a jury trial, Williams decided to pull out.

"This is a complete victory," said West upon hearing the news. "We won. Obviously, the district attorney thought he would lose, so he backed down before we had a chance to argue the case before a jury of my peers."

The DA claims that his office is victorious because the mayor is still prohibited by the courts from marrying same-sex couples. West is pursuing an appeal to the two civil law suits filed by former New Paltz Village Trustee Bob Hebel, which enjoin the mayor and the entire village board from performing same-sex marriages. The appellate court in Albany is scheduled to hear oral arguments on September 12. Hebel also filed a suit to have all same-sex marriages performed in New Paltz invalidated.

"If we are successful—and we hope to be—then Mayor West will soon be able to continue to officiate the marriages of both straight and same-sex couples," said West's local attorney, Andrew Kossover, at a pro-West, pro–marriage equality rally held in the New Paltz Village Peace Park on July 13, 2005—one day after the DA made his announcement to stop any further action.

Joshua Rosenkranz, who continues to represent Mayor West, said that the defense in the civil cases will remain consistent. "It is our argument that Mayor West, by marrying same-sex couples, was only upholding the New York State Constitution which promises protection for all of its citizens, gay or straight."

Same-sex marriages are now legal in Holland, Canada, Spain and the State of Massachusetts.

Acknowledgements

This is the best part of the book, at least for me. As solitary as the writing of a book can be, the ultimate product, while driven by the author, is a team effort.

The first string on my team are small but formidable players. I want to thank my children, Seamus, Tadeusz and Zofia, who I adore and who put up with me when I have to pack myself away in the office to "travail." They are also kind enough to pretend to like my pancakes even though they taste like rubber.

My husband, Kazik Trzewik, is my constant companion and my greatest champion, and if it weren't for his steadfast love and pizza outings with the kids to give me an hour or two to write, this book would have taken much longer. My family and my home are my sanctuary and I love them more than words can say. I also want to thank my mother, my most enthusiastic reader and greatest fan, and my father, both of whose love and grandparenting I greatly appreciate. To my sister Kim Quinn Smith, my brother-in-law Tom Smith and my adorable nieces and nephews, thank you for all of your love and encouragement during the not-so-fun and not-so-glamorous day-to-day reporting and writing of this book. I also want to thank all of my husband's family in Poland and France.

My second string, of course, are my editors and colleagues at *The New Paltz Times*. Thank you Deb Alexsa for your sobering and steady guidance. Thank you Mala Hoffman for your copyediting of both my articles and the first round of this book. Thanks to Julie O'Connor, the editor of the Almanac, the arts and culture section of our paper, who I love dearly and who has taught me so much about journalism, about the history of New Paltz and pushed me to always be the best writer I could. I want to thank my publisher, Geddy Sveikauskas, who is a true pioneer in the world of local journalism and has held the reigns to our independent Ulster Publishing Company for decades, offering residents a true taste of homespun news. Thanks to Brian Hollander of the *The Woodstock Times* for his support on my same-sex marriage coverage, and I forgive you for chopping up my story on Toni Morrison.

Helen Zimmerman, a formidable agent and good friend, had faith in this project long before it found its rightful home. Thank you, Helen. You are a gem for all aspiring writers in the area and beyond. Thank you also to Professor Hal Jacobs for your interest and early support. I would also like to thank Danielle Chiotti of Adams Media, who first convinced me that my news articles on this subject were worthy of a book.

I can't thank the women, all power-houses, of Mix Multimedia Inc enough. Although I believe that Susan Zimet would make a damn good first woman president, I also think that she'd have a hell of a lot more fun making movies, publishing books and taking photographs, all of which she does with the ease and grace of someone who has been in the business for a long time. Susan's partner in crime, Beverly Spiri Halliday, thinks like a brilliant cinematographer and embraced this project wholeheartedly. Thanks for all your hard work and insight, Bev, and you were the only one, after twenty go-rounds, who noticed that I spelled "Farrah Fawcett" wrong! She also makes one hell of a coffee drink at the Bus Stop Café, which she owns with her husband Michael in downtown New Paltz. Caryn Carter is probably one of the brightest, most politically astute people I've encountered and I'm honored that she found this book worthwhile enough to invest her time and energy. Thank you, Caryn, and we're going to celebrate with Southern Comfort and hot chocolate beverages when it's all said and done.

Where would this book be without Bethany Saltman, editor extraordinaire? She is an excellent literary sculptor and helped make this book the best it could be. I also want to thank our scrupulous copyeditors, Schola Choi and Amy Nathanson. Both of your efforts are so seamless and professional. Great job. I also want to thank Mellissa Halvorson for her edits and continual support.

Thank you to my dear friends, Amy Raff and Kristen Masson, whose support I've enjoyed for a lifetime. I love you both. Thank you, Steve and Carole Ford, for your support since I was a little tot aspiring to be a comic actress. And to all my other gals, Rachel Silverman, Jen Barresi, Mary Marshall, Shari Osborne, Bonnie Schenker, Rebecca Stacy, Jen White, and all of the other mamas I spend the days with at the park, the pool, in toy-laden living rooms and buggy backyards—you are a great crew and I'm forever grateful for our informal mother's club.

Thank you to Ariel Booksellers, a real booklover's paradise, for your support of the project and of all of our local, national and international authors. I also want to thank all passionate and dedicated readers of books, ones I know, like Martha Watkins, and those I don't, but feel a kinship to anyway.

I want to express my gratitude and admiration of fellow writers who lent me their support on my first book-length project: Da Chen, Ron Nyswaner, Laura Shayne Cunningham, and Jeffrey McGowan, all excellent writers and wonderful people.

There are so many fantastic people in this book and I thank them all for taking the time to speak with me and share their insights. These include, among others, Andy Kossover and Joshua Rosenkranz, who both bring a bit of poetry to their lawyerly profession. Thanks to Rachel and Ryszard Lagodka, Rebecca Rotzler, Ralph Nader, and Ulster County District Attorney Don Williams, who always prioritizes my calls and shows a great openness and respect for local press. I also want to express my heartfelt thanks to Spencer McLaughlin, Jonathon Wright, Chief Ray Zappone and the entire NPPD.

Last, but certainly not least, I wouldn't have had such a great story to write if it wasn't for Mayor Jason West's decision to marry same-sex couples on February 27, 2004. I applaud his bravery, admire his bold Green Party initiatives, and thank him for making the Village of New Paltz such an interesting place to write about these days. I also want to acknowledge the courage and compassion of Unitarian Ministers Kay Greenleaf and Dawn Sangrey.

Thanks to Billiam van Roestenberg and Jeffrey for encouraging Jason to marry them and for their support of my book. They and the other twenty-four same-sex couples who were married that day are the real heroes of this book. I wish for them the right to legally marry as soon as possible and the opportunity to have happy and fruitful lives together.